EDEXCEL

AS AND A LEVEL MUSIC

Study Guide

HUGH BENHAM &
ALISTAIR WIGHTMAN

with a chapter on composing by Clive Osgood

RHINEGOLD
EDUCATION

First published 2017 in Great Britain by
Rhinegold Education
14-15 Berners Street
London W1T 3LJ, UK
www.rhinegoldeducation.co.uk

© 2017 Rhinegold Education
a division of Music Sales Limited

You should always check the current
requirements of your examination,
since these may change.

Consultant: Dr Nigel Springthorpe
Chapter on the Remix brief written by David Guinane
Editor: Thomas Lydon
Cover and book design: Fresh Lemon Australia

EDEXCEL AS and A Level Music Study Guide
Order no. RHG341
ISBN 978-1-78558-169-4

Exclusive Distributors:
Music Sales Ltd
Distribution Centre, Newmarket Road
Bury St Edmunds, Suffolk IP33 3YB, UK

Printed in the EU

**Available from Rhinegold Education
for your course:**

- **EDEXCEL AS and A Level Music
  Listening Tests**
- **EDEXCEL AS Level Music Revision Guide**
- **EDEXCEL A Level Music Revision Guide**

**You may find the following books
useful too:**

- **AS Music Harmony Workbook**
- **A2 Music Harmony Workbook**
- **AS Music Composition Workbook**
- **AS Music Literacy Workbook**
- **Writing About Music Workbook**
- **Understanding Popular Music**
- **Careers in Music**
- **Music Technology from Scratch**
- **Dictionary of Music in Sound**

Contents

(AS) set work for AS Level

(A) set work for A Level

The authors

Hugh Benham

read Music and English at Southampton University, where he was awarded a PhD for his study of the music of John Taverner. He is an organist and is active in the Guild of Church Musicians and the Royal School of Church Music, having formerly taught in a sixth-form college, and worked as a chair of examiners for GCE Music.

His publications include *Baroque Music in Focus* (Rhinegold, 2007); books on English church music: *Latin Church Music in England, c.1460–1575* (Barrie and Jenkins, 1977) and *John Taverner, his Life and Music* (Ashgate, 2003); contributions to *The New Grove Dictionary of Music and Musicians* (second edition, 2001), to *Die Musik in Geschichte und Gegenwart*, and to the *Ralph Vaughan Williams Society Journal*. He is the editor of Taverner's music for *Early English Church Music*. In 2011 Convivium Records released a CD of his choral and organ music (CR 011), some items from which have been published in the USA.

Alistair Wightman

has worked in primary, secondary and further education, and is now a freelance teacher and writer. For many years he was a principal examiner in history and analysis in A Level music.

His publications include *Writing about Music* (Rhinegold, 2008) and several books and articles on Polish music, including *Karlowicz, Young Poland and the Musical Fin-de-siècle* (Ashgate, 1996), *Karol Szymanowski: his Life and Music* (Ashgate, 1999), *Szymanowski on Music: Selected Writings of Karol Szymanowski* (Toccata Press, 1999), and *Szymanowski's King Roger, the opera and its origins* (Toccata Press, 2015).

Clive Osgood

studied music at Bangor University before completing a Master's degree in musicology at Cardiff University. He then did his teacher training in London and spent a year as an organ scholar at Salisbury Cathedral. More recently he completed a second Master's degree, in composition, at Surrey University. He has written a variety of music for choirs, orchestras and chamber groups and is currently the Director of Music and Organist at St Bartholomew's Church in Haslemere. He teaches music at Reed's School, Cobham.

This study guide will support your work for both the AS Level and A Level specifications available for teaching from September 2016. It is not a comprehensive textbook, but a study guide, supporting all components for both qualifications. It is designed to be used alongside the *Edexcel AS/A Level Anthology of Music* (Pearson ISBN 978-1-292-11836-9).

AS Level and A Level are separate qualifications. They have a similar structure, but some details are different, including (but not restricted to) the minimum length of the recital for Component 1, the composition brief requirements for Component 2, and the aural demands for Component 3. Make sure you check the correct specification for full details.

Outline of AS Level content		
Component 1: Performing	Live recital performance of one or more pieces. Performance can be solo and/or as part of an ensemble, with a minimum performance time of six minutes	■ 30% of the qualification ■ 60 marks
Component 2: Composing	Two compositions: one to a set brief and one either free composition or also to a set brief. Each composition must be at least two minutes in duration, and the total timing across both submissions must be a minimum of four minutes and 30 seconds	■ 30% of the qualification ■ 60 marks (30 for each composition)
Component 3: Appraising	A one-and-a-half-hour written paper based on: ■ The 12 set works ■ Application of knowledge to unfamiliar works ■ Aural skills: melody completion and identification of errors	■ 40% of the qualification ■ 80 marks

Outline of A Level content

Component 1: Performing	Live recital performance of one or more pieces. Performance can be solo and/or as part of an ensemble, with a minimum performance time of eight minutes	■ 30% of the qualification ■ 60 marks
Component 2: Composing	Two compositions: ■ one composition must be either from the set briefs relating to the Areas of Study or a free composition. This should be at least four minutes in duration ■ The other composition must be from a list of briefs assessing compositional technique. This should be at least one minute in duration, unless the brief specifies otherwise ■ The total timing across both submissions must be a minimum of six minutes	■ 30% of the qualification ■ 60 marks (40 for Area of Study brief or free composition; 20 for the 'compositional technique' brief)
Component 3: Appraising	A two-hour written paper based on: ■ The 18 set works ■ Application of knowledge to unfamiliar works ■ Aural skills: melody completion	■ 40% of the qualification ■ 100 marks

At the end of each 'Area of Study' chapter in this guide are five short questions on each set work. These are not 'exam questions' but are intended to help you get to know each work better. For each set work there are also two sample essay questions. These correspond to Question 6 in Pearson's Sample Assessment Materials for both AS and A Level.

You will find examples of the other types of questions (1–5) that appear in the Appraising papers for AS and A Level Music in the Rhinegold Education publication *Edexcel AS/A Level Music Listening Tests* (RHG342).

COMPONENT 1:
Performing

At AS and A Level, you are able to choose what you play. You can therefore – and should – choose whatever you can play best.

However, your choices should be made in consultation with your teacher(s), because:

- Your AS or A Level music teacher(s) will be overseeing your course generally, and will understand the AS or A Level assessment process
- Any specialist instrumental or vocal teacher(s) that you have will know your current capabilities well.

For both AS and A Level:

- Marks available: 60 (performances are marked out of 48, with a further 12 marks available for the difficulty of the piece – see 'Assessment and Difficulty Levels' below)
- Number of pieces to perform: minimum of one
- There is a minimum performance time (see pages 5 and 6), not including time taken to tune instrument and gaps between pieces
- Audience requirements for the final recorded performance recorded performance: at least two people.

To achieve the best result possible for you, keep firmly in mind the final assessment. This will take place between 1 March and 15 May in the year (or last year) of your course.

This final assessment is your opportunity to show what you can do as an AS or A Level performer. You will perform a short 'recital' of music that will be recorded, and then marked by one of Pearson's examiners (not by your teacher, as may have happened for GCSE).

If you play less well than you had hoped, it is possible, at your teacher's discretion, to re-perform and re-record the whole recital.

For ease of reference, 'play' generally means 'play or sing', and 'instrument' means 'instrument or voice'.

Four golden rules

1. **Play music that will not go wrong when the pressure is on.** Pressure *will* be on in the final assessment. It is unwise to play difficult music that you have not fully mastered.

2. **Take advice from others:**
   - This means mainly your AS or A Level music teacher and your specialist instrumental or vocal teacher (if that is someone different)
   - Also, listen to performances by other people who can play your pieces really well – using professional recordings, broadcasts, and high-quality online resources. If you use YouTube, be critical – much, but not everything, there is of a high standard.

3. **Practise as much as you can.**

4. **Perform as often as you can.** Performing repeatedly should help build confidence.

Solo performance, ensemble performance, improvisation

You can offer solo performance (as the great majority of students tend to do) or ensemble performance, or some of each – whatever enables you to do your best.

Details of a few 'minority' forms of performance (including improvisation) are given in the specification.

Solo performing

Solo performances can be without accompaniment, *but only* if the music was composed without an accompaniment. If there is an accompaniment, it must be used.

An accompaniment is often for a single keyboard instrument (e.g. piano accompanying clarinet), but if the music demands a fuller accompaniment or backing, that may be used.

Two important tips regarding accompaniments and accompanists:

■ Make sure (in consultation with your teacher) that the person or people involved are capable of doing a first-class job. If they are not, it will be much harder for you to play well

■ Make sure that you have worked with your accompanist (or your accompanying group) long enough for all concerned to feel comfortable and confident together.

You can perform with a backing track (which could be sequenced). But performing with a backing track can bring its own problems:

■ You have to keep with the pre-recorded track all the time

■ A backing track is 'fixed' and can restrict your opportunities for interpretation.

Ensemble performing

An ensemble (for the purposes of AS and A Level Music) consists of two or more people, who perform at the same time and have independent, undoubled parts. There may be, but need not be, additional accompaniment or backing with doublings.

The following are a few examples of ensembles for exam purposes:

■ Four solo voices (SATB)

■ Two solo voices (or two solo instruments) with keyboard accompaniment

■ A string quartet

■ Rock group with lead guitar, rhythm guitar, bass guitar and drums.

The following do not qualify, because some or all parts are doubled:

■ An SATB choir, with two more people on each part

■ An orchestra – except in a piece such as Bach's Double Violin Concerto in D minor (because here the string orchestra is in addition to the two solo violins)

■ A piece for 1940s-style big band.

> When a pianist accompanies a single instrument, such as flute or trumpet, this can count as an ensemble *for the pianist*. For the flautist or trumpeter it is a solo performance.

Ensemble performance is a good choice for those who regularly make music in that way. It can be particularly good for those who find solo performance nerve-wracking, but it is unwise if the other member(s) of the ensemble are unreliable.

If you offer ensemble performance, you will be assessed on accuracy and interpretation, as you would expect, but matters of balance will also be taken into consideration, as well as how you interact with the other player(s) or singer(s).

Improvisation

Improvisation requires much practice: it is not just 'making it up as you go along'!

> Improvisation can be solo, or might involve a small ensemble.

An improvisation must always have a starting point, often called the 'stimulus'. This could be devised by your teacher, by yourself in consultation with your teacher, or might be taken from an existing piece of music.

It can be, for example:

- A melody, or short melodic idea, without accompaniment
- A rhythmic pattern (especially if you are improvising on drums)
- A chord scheme
- A melody with chords (perhaps for use as a 'head' in a jazz improvisation).

For any of the above, the aim must be to:

- **extend** the stimulus material – that is, to add to it, bearing in mind the length requirements in the specifications
- **develop** it – that is, not just to make it longer by repeating it, but to 'do something with it'
- **balance** unity and variety – in other words, to provide an effective mix of repetition and contrast so as to create a satisfying form overall.

> You will need experience, guidance and teaching to be able to improvise effectively. Strictly in addition, it may be worth investigating one or two of the many available online resources that deal with improvisation. But, as always with online materials, be selective and if necessary sceptical.

Assessment and difficulty levels

For exams it is always wise to play music that you are at ease with. However, you need to be fully aware of the possible rewards available under the system of difficulty levels.

At AS there is a 'standard' level of difficulty, which is broadly equivalent to Grade 6 of the graded music exams system.

- If you perform music at this level, marks are added on to the 'raw' mark that you are awarded for the quality of your performing
- If you perform music above this standard level of difficulty, *more* marks are added on to your raw mark
- If you perform music at below the standard level, your raw mark is not increased, and even the most brilliant performance imaginable will get 'only' 48/60 marks.

> Example of scaling: a raw mark of 40/48 becomes 50/60 at Standard level and 60/60 at More Difficult level.

At A Level the system works in the same way, but the standard level is set at Grade 7, one grade up on AS.

For many people the deal makes sense. The harder the music performed, the higher the final mark. However, if you are safe only at Grade 5 for AS or Grade 6 for A Level, it is probably not worth taking the risk of playing more difficult music. If you play music that is too difficult for you, your raw mark may not be high, and the difficulty level increase may well not compensate for what you will have lost by over-reaching yourself.

What makes an excellent performance?

Here are ways in which performances can be excellent:

- You are technically confident – you know your instrument and can handle it well
- You keep going throughout at an appropriate tempo without stops and starts or hesitations
- You are 'engaged' with the music, which you clearly understand
- Through your playing, you are able to communicate your understanding of the music to your listeners
- Tone quality is appropriate to the music (with suitable variety and contrast)
- You present yourself appropriately for the occasion (e.g. in terms of posture and what you wear) (see box below).

> For AS and A Level Music, examiners listen to performances on audio recordings. But, although they cannot see your performance, it is worth giving thought to presentation – this can subtly influence the resulting sound.

Excellence when performing from a score in staff notation

In staff-notation scores, most composers indicate as clearly as they can as many aspects of the music as possible.

> Staff-notation scores are available for almost all 'classical' pieces and for much 'popular' music (including music-theatre songs).

To achieve an excellent performance from staff notation, you must play:

- The right notes and the right rhythms (although one or two small slips will not ruin an otherwise excellent performance)
- In tune (which means control over intonation, as with stringed instruments)
- At the correct tempo, and observing any prescribed changes
- Fluently – in other words, without unscheduled starts and stops, hesitation or stumbling
- With full control of the instrument
- With good tone quality (i.e. making a sound that is musically appropriate to the style of music you are playing)
- With attention to all the composer's performance directions, notably phrasing, marks of articulation and dynamics

- With awareness of the character and style of the music
- With good communication (i.e. engaging with the audience rather than playing to yourself).

Look again at the list above, and now work on the short task given in the box below. This can be done as a group task with other students, with or without input from your teacher.

- Look up the three Performance Assessment Grids for Component 1 in either the AS or the A Level specification.
- For each bullet in the list above, write down the number of the grid or grids dealing with that aspect of performance. For example, after the first bullet write '2' (because accuracy is addressed in the second Performance Grid).

Here are some points that are not explicit in the grids or the bullet points above:

- You must not fall short of the minimum length of performance required by the specification that you are taking. **This is vital – work that falls short of the minimum required duration will not receive any marks:**
  - The performance lengths given by the board refer to the time that you are actually playing. They do *not* include announcements before you start playing, gaps in between pieces, or any applause
- Each piece should be played in full. Do not, for example, play only up to a double bar in the middle of a piece or miss out a middle section
- With some Baroque music it is stylistically appropriate to add ornamentation that is not notated in the score:
  - Take advice from your teacher, and note the practice of established performers in professional recordings
  - You may want to consider adding ornamentation when a section is repeated (e.g. in the *da capo* from a Handel aria)
- In popular songs, and songs from musicals, singers sometimes take liberties with the notated rhythms, and even with pitch:
  - Again, take advice from your teacher, and note the practice of established performers in professional recordings
  - There is a difference between stylistic embellishment and inaccuracy – be cautious in particular about changing pitches or shortening long notes.

Types of score that do not use staff notation

Where a staff-notation score is not available, it is possible to submit one of the following:

- Lead sheet (for some forms of popular music)
- Chord chart
- Track sheets
- Tablature
- Stimulus (for an improvisation)
- Detailed written commentary (normally where no musical notation is possible)
- Tables or diagrams
- Reference recording.

The examiner must have a score or account, as listed above, for every performance submitted. Without a score, your work cannot be assessed.

With a lead sheet or chord chart, there should be as much detail as possible. Any lyrics should be provided. Make sure that the examiner can easily match up each part of the lead sheet or chord chart with the relevant part of the performance (e.g. make it clear where sections begin and end and indicate any repeats clearly).

With tablature, there must be rhythmic information. The specifications state that 'a guitar tab score with no indication of rhythm is unacceptable'.

For an improvisation, it usually helps to include something more than just the stimulus. This could be a few sentences and/or clearly labelled diagrams explaining what happens in broad terms – especially to show the structure.

A detailed written commentary and/or a professional reference recording (that is, a professional recording that the examiner can refer to when marking a student's own performance of the same piece) are appropriate for music from the oral tradition, which has never been notated. A written commentary must be 'detailed' (without being too long) and might describe the form of a piece, changes of speed or character, and note any other audible landmarks – so that the examiner can 'navigate' the music without difficulty.

Excellence when performing from a score that does not use staff notation

Look again at the list above headed 'Excellence when performing from a score in staff notation' list above. Most of these points apply to all types of performance, but some have limited relevance, chiefly as indicated below.

- Point 1 ('right notes and right rhythms') does not apply, for example, to an improvisation, where many details of pitch and rhythm have not been determined in advance of performance. Nevertheless, in an improvisation, notes and rhythms can be more or less *appropriate* in terms of (for example) harmonic suitability and melodic interest

- Point 3 ('correct tempo') likewise will not apply to an improvisation, but *suitability* and *stability* of tempo are nevertheless essential for success

- Point 7 ('attention to... the composer's performance directions') does not apply to non-notated music, for instance some folk and 'world' music. However, few performances without dynamic contrast, for instance, are likely to be musically satisfying.

COMPONENT 2:
Composing

Introduction

What do you need to compose?

For this unit, which is 30% of the qualification, you should create and submit the following:

AS Level	A Level
Two compositions ■ One to a set brief (30 marks). Minimum duration of 2 minutes ■ One to a different set brief or a free composition (30 marks). Minimum duration of 2 minutes The total duration of both works must be at least 4½ minutes. The maximum 'guided length' is 6½ minutes (submissions over this time will still be marked).	**Two compositions** ■ One 'Free choice' (40 marks): either following a set brief based on an Area of Study, or a 'free composition'. Minimum duration of 4 minutes ■ One to a brief assessing technique (20 marks). Minimum duration of 1 minute The total duration of both works must be at least 6 minutes. The maximum 'guided length' is 8 minutes (submissions over this time will still be marked).

The Briefs Relating to Areas of Study, which are released early within the academic year, are as follows:

- Vocal Music
- Instrumental Music
- Music for Film
- Popular Music and Jazz
- Fusions
- New Directions

The Briefs Assessing Technique, which are released in April in the year of certification, are as follows:

1. Bach chorale
2. Two-part counterpoint
3. Arrangement
4. Remix

Teacher supervision

Edexcel requires that you spend a certain amount of time working on your compositions in the classroom under teacher supervision, as follows:

AS Level	A Level
Set Brief - At least 2 hours in the centre under the teacher's supervision, to include development, final write-up and recording **Different Set Brief or Free Composition** - At least 2 hours in the centre under the teacher's supervision, to include development, final write-up and recording	**Free Choice** - At least 2 hours in the centre under the teacher's supervision, to include development, final write-up and recording **Briefs Assessing Technique** - The requirements here are rather different. The specification states: 'The student must complete their composition under controlled conditions, within 4-6 hours. This time includes the development of the composition, the final write-up and the recording of their composition in the centre under the teacher's supervision... Compositions can be completed over multiple sessions, but work must be collected and kept securely in the centre between sessions. Students must not have access to their work between sessions.'

If you are unsure about the rules regarding teacher supervision, it is always best to raise any queries with Edexcel directly.

What do you need to submit?

For every composition, at both AS and A Level, you will need to submit the following:

- A 'detailed notated score appropriate to the style of music' (except for the Remix brief, see below). Edexcel states that this can refer to any of the following: a full score in conventional staff notation, a lead sheet or chord chart, track sheets, tables or diagrams, a screenshot from music production software, or written account of the composition. Written accounts should not exceed 500 words.

For the Remix brief (Brief 4 of the Briefs Assessing Technique), you need to submit a recording (wav; 44.1kHz sample rate; and 16-bit bit depth), but no score should be submitted.

- A complete recording on an audio CD or USB stick. This can be made live or studio-produced. Students do not have to perform their compositions – the live performances for these recordings can be by anyone. The Remix brief has particular format requirements: see above
- Composition Authentication Form, completed by the teacher and signed by the student and teacher.

This guidance is not exhaustive; be sure to check the full requirements in Edexcel's AS Level or A Level Specification.

> This chapter will deal only with the briefs released by Edexcel. Note that there is also an option at both AS and A Level to write a free composition not related to a brief. Free compositions can be 'for any instrument or voice, or combination of instruments and/or voices, and in any style'.

In order to compose music it is absolutely vital to study examples of different types of music. Composers make choices about every aspect of the music they are writing. Listen to – and analyse – as much music as possible. Understanding the process of composition is the only way to write your own pieces.

Sketch ideas as you go. Remember that you do not necessarily need to start at the beginning. Your first idea may work well as a secondary musical theme later in your piece, or you may decide to add an introduction.

Set briefs relating to Areas of Study

OVERVIEW

- At A Level, one of your pieces must be either a free composition or a piece written in response to one of the 'Area of Study briefs'.

- At AS Level, one of your pieces must be in response to one of the 'Area of Study briefs'. The other piece can be either a free composition or a piece written in response to a different one of the 'Area of Study briefs'.

The minimum duration required for these compositions varies from AS to A Level (see the Introduction to this chapter).

Brief 1: Vocal music

Sample A Level brief from Edexcel:

> Compose a song using a poem of your choice for use as opening music for a conference about the protection of the environment. The setting of the song should reflect the meaning of the text. You may re-order the words.

Sample AS Level brief from Edexcel:

> Compose a song using a poem of your choice for use as opening music in a poetry slam competition. The setting of the song should reflect the meaning of the text. You may re-order the words.

For the Vocal Music brief, you will need to investigate different vocal pieces to understand the many different ways that words can be set to music and the structures that can be used. Music can often enhance the meaning of the words. The Norwegian composer Edvard Grieg, who wrote a large number of songs, explained his approach to word setting in a letter to a friend:

> *When I compose a song, my concern is not to make music but, first and foremost, to do justice to the poet's intentions. I have tried to let the poem reveal itself, and indeed to raise it to a higher power.*

Setting words to music

Words can be set to music in many different ways and in many styles, although it is always important to consider the natural stress of the text. Let us look at an example, *which has the stressed syllables underlined*. (It is an extract from a poem by the American poet Henry Wadsworth Longfellow):

> *The day is <u>done</u>, and the <u>darkness</u>*
> *<u>Falls</u> from the <u>wings</u> of <u>Night</u>,*

A first step is to think about the rhythm and the tempo. The sombre description of the end of the day suggests a slow tempo with a fairly relaxed rhythm. Emphasis can be given to the word 'darkness' by using a longer note on the first beat of the bar:

Adagio

The day is done, and the dark - ness Falls from the wings of Night,

Having considered the rhythmic elements, how else can you 'do justice to the poet's intentions'? The mood of these words could be easily conveyed by the use of a minor key with dark chromatic intervals. The word 'darkness' can be given even more weight by being placed as the highest point of the phrase, moving up and down a semitone. A falling scale can easily suggest the falling darkness:

Try to create vocal lines that use predominantly step-wise movement. The melody here, which moves entirely by step, is set in F minor and descends from C (the dominant) through an octave. Landing on the dominant also gives the phrase an open-ended feel, to carry on to the next line.

Finding the right song structure

Songs are structured in a number of different ways depending largely on the structure of the text itself. The most common type of song structures are as follows:

Strophic:

This basic structure uses the same music for all of the verses of a text, as found in a hymn, for example. With limited scope for developing ideas, it is probably best to modify the music to a basic theme and variations (so A, A, A becomes A^1, $A,^2$, A^3). This can be achieved in a number of ways: varying the harmony or figurations within the accompaniment, or decorating the melody itself.

A → A → A → etc.

Da capo:

This song structure, meaning 'from the head', was common in the Baroque period. It is a type of ternary form structure in which the first section (of two) is repeated at the end, with the same words and melodic decoration. This could be a useful way of structuring a text with only two verses.

A → B → A^1

Verse / Chorus:

In Verse / chorus form, which can be a modified version of strophic form, verses alternate with a fixed chorus. The verse / chorus structure is fairly common in popular music and will be discussed within that section.

V → C → V → C

Through-composed:

With through-composed music, there is no defining structure, because the music changes to follow the narrative. Do be careful though to have at least some unifying thread as the piece progresses.

A good example of a through-composed song – and one suggested by Edexcel for wider listening – is Schubert's *Erlkönig*. Written when the composer was eighteen, the song describes a man riding on horseback through the night. He comforts his desperately ill child, who imagines various ghostly images. The music follows the different characters of the dramatic story by moving between major and minor keys. It is given unity, and added drama, by the near constant right-hand triplets of the piano accompaniment (to symbolise the galloping horse), as well as the recurring pattern in the left-hand. If you are considering writing a through-composed song, do study this piece; the score and lyrics are easily accessible online.

Instrumental accompaniments

Another aspect of this brief is for you to include an instrumental accompaniment to your song. This can be for piano or other instrument(s). The accompaniment is there to support the voice but can set the mood even before the lyrics begin, and provide further characterisation. Schubert did not regard the piano as having a mere supporting role, but as being an equal partner, and his songs demonstrate many different ways in which an instrument can accompany the voice:

- *An die Musik* ('To Music') uses repeated quavers to provide continuous movement, and the bass line of the piano works in dialogue with the voice:

- In *Die Forelle* ('The Trout'), fast sextuplet patterns suggest the wriggling fish and the left hand of the piano part uses a common pattern to provide both the bass line and chords:

■ The whole of *Der Leiermann* ('The Hurdy-Gurdy Man') has a continuous tonic and dominant drone in the left hand to suggest the bagpipe-like drone of the hurdy-gurdy. The right hand of the piano works in dialogue with the voice:

The harmony for the accompaniment does not need to be complex; it is what you do with it that is important. In the last example above, *Der Leiermann*, the simple tonic and dominant drone perfectly conveys a sad, rustic mood. Harmonic interest is added by the simultaneous use of a dominant chord (E major) at points in the right hand.

EXERCISE

Explore a variety of accompaniment ideas using C major/A minor harmonies. These ideas could include repeated quavers, arpeggios, inversions or drones.

Composing to the brief

Step 1 – Find suitable lyrics

Find some lyrics that you feel would work well set to music, and would be appropriate for the brief. There are examples of songwriters who wrote the music first and then the lyrics (George and Ira Gershwin, for example), but they are rare, and it is not recommended. It is far easier to shape a melody around a text.

Step 2 – Create a melody to fit the words

Work out the natural flow of the words (for the first couple of lines) then find a suitable metre and rhythm. Use the mood of the text to point you towards an appropriate melodic idea. If a particular phrase is used more than once, use the same melody.

Step 3 – Create a suitable accompaniment

As seen with the Schubert examples above, the accompaniment not only supports the voice but also helps to establish the mood and engage in dialogue. Try to be as descriptive and imaginative as you can.

Over the page is a suggested accompaniment for the words set previously. It uses a slow series of minor chords spread between the two hands of the piano. A diminished chord is used to highlight the word 'darkness'. The passage is underpinned by a syncopated bass note – a dominant pedal that creates (unstable) second-inversion chords.

Step four – Structure

Think carefully about the structure on the melodic level by making use of balanced musical phrases, repetition and sequence. Think also about the structure of the whole piece. Ask yourself which structure will best suit the text and maintain a level of interest throughout the song. Will you be able to demonstrate that you have developed your musical ideas?

Brief 2: Instrumental music

Sample A Level brief from Edexcel:

> Compose a piece of music based on sonata form that would be suitable for background music at a formal occasion such as a wedding dinner.

Sample AS Level brief from Edexcel:

> Compose a theme and variations that would be suitable for a solo instrumentalist accompanied by piano. The composition would be played as part of a recital of Western classical music.

The Instrumental Music brief requires you to understand the characteristics of particular instruments and how to use musical form effectively.

Know your instruments

Make sure that you know the capabilities of your chosen instrument(s), such as the range and particular techniques. It is very easy, when using computer software such as Logic or Sibelius, to compose music that is unplayable on a real instrument. Try asking fellow students who play instruments that you don't play yourself to give you a demonstration of their instrument's capabilities. Be aware that the range of a midi keyboard often extends above or below the range of many instruments. It is also, of course, capable of playing more than one note at a time – unlike a flute.

You will also need to show that you can write idiomatically for your chosen instrument(s). This means showing off some of the subtle characteristics and qualities as well as understanding the technical limitations. Here are a few considerations for different families of instruments:

Stringed instruments:

- Each string has a different sound quality – explore these differences
- Double stopping on two notes should be played on two *adjacent* strings
- Use pizzicato ('plucking'), con sordino (with mute), and other techniques but be aware that time is needed to change from using the bow
- Explore using harmonics to create a flutey silvery sound but be careful how they are notated.

The double bass is a transposing instrument, playing an octave lower than written.

Woodwind and brass instruments:

- Be aware of transposing instruments (including piccolo, clarinet, cor anglais, trumpet, saxophone). Make sure you know their range at concert pitch
- Remember that the player needs to breathe!
- Not only do instruments have a characteristic sound, different parts of an instrument's range (or register) can also be very distinctive
- Moving between certain notes can be awkward due to fingering constraints (e.g. B to B♭ above middle C on a clarinet, and the same movement two octaves lower on a trombone)
- Explore effects such as mutes and double tonguing (for brass) and fluttertonguing on flutes, clarinets and saxophones.

Percussion and Keyboard:

- If writing for more than one percussion instrument, consider the amount of time needed for a player to switch between instruments
- Explore the variety of effects achieved by using different sticks/mallets
- The piano and organ have a huge range – don't be limited to the middle register. Make the most of the percussive quality of the piano and the sustaining power of the organ.

Know your musical structures

If you have studied music at GCSE level, you may be aware of a number of traditional structures that are used to sustain pieces of music. Here is a quick summary:

Binary form

This is a simple musical structure in two sections, in which each section may repeat. The first section nearly always ends in a related key, most often the dominant. The second section will begin in this related key and return to the home key by the end. It is usually restricted to smaller pieces.

Example:

- J.S. Bach: Minuet in G (No. 4 from 'A Little Notebook for Anna Magdalena').

Ternary form:

This is a three-part form, with the first section returning at the end. The scale of this structure can vary enormously, from a simple melody (such as *Twinkle, Twinkle, Little Star*, below) to a long 'da capo' aria or minuet and trio.

In ternary form, the 'B' section usually provides greater contrast than in binary form, and there is a sense of 'coming home' when the 'A' section returns. Ternary form can also be used in larger pieces with each section having its own structure (e.g. a minuet and trio).

Examples:

- Haydn: Symphony No. 6, III: 'Menuet and trio'
- Handel: *Messiah*, No. 23: 'He was despised'.

Sonata Form:

Sonata form was traditionally used to hold together the first, and longest movement of an instrumental piece. In some music from the 19th century, notably Bruckner's symphonies, sonata form could be used to create a piece lasting over twenty minutes!

Like ternary form, sonata form is in three sections; often called exposition, development, and recapitulation. The first section (exposition) is divided into two distinct groups. The first group is in the home key (tonic) while the second, contrasting group is in a closely related key, usually the dominant. The development usually sees the tonality move further away from the home key, develop ideas from the exposition, then prepare for the recapitulation. In this last section, the music from the exposition is repeated, but without moving away from the home key. A coda (or end section) is sometimes added.

Example:

■ Mozart: first movement from *Eine kleine Nachtmusik*.

Rondo:

Rondo is a musical form where the principal idea keeps returning between contrasting sections known as 'episodes'. It was sometimes used with a 'B' section in the dominant that later recurred in the tonic. This form of rondo is known as **Sonata Rondo**.

Exposition   Development   Recapitulation   coda

Examples:

■ Mozart: Horn concerto No. 4 (K.495), III

■ Mozart: Rondo in D for piano (K485).

Variations:

This is a musical form where an idea is repeated and varied. The melody can be changed, embellished or given a new harmony. Sometimes it is only the original harmonic framework that is maintained.

Mozart wrote a set of variations on the melody *Twinkle, Twinkle, Little Star* that demonstrates some techniques of melodic variation. In variations one and three, he keeps the general contour of the melody (marked by arrows) but hides it within a semiquaver turn figure and then triplets:

Mozart also groups certain variations together. The second and fourth variations, for example, use these same rhythmic figurations (above) as the accompaniment to the melody. In other variations, he uses an echo effect between upper and lower parts, moves to the minor key and even uses the melody in canon.

EXERCISE

Create your own melodic variation on the same theme.

Further examples:

- Paganini: *Caprice* Op. 1 No. 24
- Brahms: *Variations on a theme of Paganini* Op. 35
- Schubert: *String Quartet No. 14 in D minor* 'Death and the Maiden', Movement 2.

Ground bass:

This is a bass line that is constantly repeated, alongside varied melody or harmony.
A famous example is Pachelbel's canon, in which the bass pattern underpins three violins in canon.

Examples:

- Purcell: 'Dido's lament' from *Dido and Aeneas*
- Nyman: *Time lapse.*

Dance suite

This is a set of instrumental pieces to be played in one sitting. The traditional dances
in a Baroque suite often started with a prelude then continued as follows:

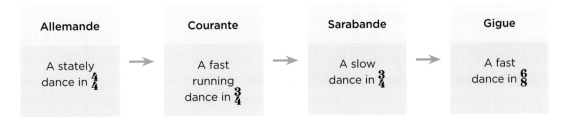

Allemande	Courante	Sarabande	Gigue
A stately dance in $\frac{4}{4}$	A fast running dance in $\frac{3}{4}$	A slow dance in $\frac{3}{4}$	A fast dance in $\frac{6}{8}$

Each dance within a suite would usually be constructed in binary form with a common
tonality throughout.

Example:

- Bach's French and English Suites.

Composing to the brief

You will probably need to compose to a brief along the following lines:

Compose a piece of music based on...	<ul><li>Sonata form</li><li>Variations</li><li>Rondo</li><li>Ground bass</li></ul>	... that would be suitable for...	<ul><li>A wedding</li><li>A gala concert</li><li>A service of remembrance</li></ul>

Step one – choosing instrumentation

Consider what instruments would work well for the particular brief. If you are writing
for an outdoor occasion, for example, you may decide to use brass or reed instruments
which are more durable, portable and audible than other instruments.

Step two – choosing musical elements appropriate for the brief.

Once you know what you are writing for, consider which musical elements – such as tempo, tonality and metre – will help you create the correct musical 'feel' for your composition. Put yourself into the situation described in the brief and imagine the sort of music that would be appropriate. If you were writing a wedding piece, for example, you would probably want to use major keys with a moderate to fast tempo. You also need to decide what metre would work best. Are you going to dance ($\frac{3}{4}$, $\frac{6}{8}$), march ($\frac{4}{4}$) or do a bit of both ($\frac{5}{4}$)?

Step three – working with your musical structure

Writing music to a particular structure will often dictate the sort of music you will write. A piece in sonata form will often begin with an attention-grabbing theme that will then contrast with a lyrical second theme. If the ideas in each section can be related in some way, this is even better. Variations or ground bass offer a different way of thinking through the piece. Try and think of your opening idea going on a journey, growing and changing. Remember always to think about the overall shape of your composition.

Step three – working with your performers

As this brief is designed for a live performance, you may find it very useful to arrange your own performance of your piece if at all possible. If other students or teachers are able to perform your piece, you will quickly discover what works well – and what does not. Even if it is in an early draft, find some people to play your piece. It is also a very good idea to submit a *live* recording.

Brief 3: Music for film

Sample A Level brief from Edexcel:

> Compose the title music for a science fiction action film. Choose instrumental timbres and textures to create a suitable atmosphere. Musical elements such as harmony, melody and rhythm should reflect the action.

Sample AS Level brief from Edexcel:

> Compose an overture for a 15-rated romantic comedy film. The overture should be based around leitmotives representing the two main characters.

To be able to write film music you will need to develop your skills in writing for a variety of instrumental forces and in a wide range of styles. Film music is often written for an orchestra. This can mean being familiar with different orchestral instruments and understanding effective ways to combine them. The wide range of musical styles often found in film music can embrace anything from 20th-century atonality, through sweeping romanticism, to jazz and pop styles.

Creating an atmosphere and mood

When writing for a particular moment within a film, it is vital to understand the particular emotion that needs to be conveyed. It is of course possible, within music, to suggest all manner of emotions.

Consider the following diagram:

If we needed a mood that is **dark**, we might consider using instruments with a low pitch, minor chords or small 'chromatic' intervals. Alternatively, we might need to provide **light** sounding music, with bright higher-pitched instruments, using major chords and wider intervals. If we then consider whether the music is **fast** or **slow**, we can explore an even wider range of moods, appropriate for different situations. Light-sounding music could portray a mood that is sad, peaceful, comic or energetic, all depending on the tempo.

Fast

Dark   Light

Slow

Layer the sounds / layer the emotions

A great feature of music is that you can represent more than one emotion at the same time. You could, for example, have fast and high music representing one thing, while simultaneously using low sustained music to suggest something else – some negative aspect of the story lurking beneath, for example.

Creating a character

Film composers use musical ideas to suggest particular characters. Any time we hear the musical idea, we are aware of the character's presence. This use of representative musical ideas, or 'leitmotifs', was common in 19th-century opera, and is applied brilliantly in many films, such as *Jaws* and *Superman* by John Williams and extensively in Howard Shore's music to *The Lord of the Rings* and the other two films in the trilogy.

Think carefully about how a theme suggests a character. For example, in the main *Superman* theme it is the wide leaps on the horn that make him sound heroic. In *Jaws*, it is the isolated double bass semitones that make the shark's theme all the more chilling.

There are many features of a theme that give it character. Look at the following two themes, which share the same melodic outline:

Theme **a**, a striding march, would sound quite heroic, especially played by brass instruments. Theme **b**, however, sounds far less confident, with a faltering skip and chromatic last bar that suggests an element of mystery. The harmony and instrumentation could exaggerate this characterisation yet further.

EXERCISE

Compose melodic ideas to suggests the following film characters:

- A wizard
- A superhero
- A supervillain
- A cartoon detective
- A princess
- A frog

Understanding musical conventions

In order to write film music it is important to have a good understanding of some of the musical conventions that have become commonplace in cinema. Certain musical styles can suggest a time and a place (e.g. a habanera rhythm could easily suggest Spain). Certain instruments are also used to express a particular place, emotion or situation.

It is important to study how these have been used and how some composers would sometimes go against such conventions. Here are a few musical conventions associated with particular instruments:

- **STRINGS** are often used to express emotion
- **TREMOLO** strings are often used for suspense
- **HORNS,** linked to military music and hunting, are often used to express heroism
- The unnatural sound of a **SYNTHESISER** (or earlier non-acoustic instruments such as **THEREMIN**) are often used in science fiction
- Old instruments such as the **HARPSICHORD** are used in period dramas
- Instruments are often associated with certain places, for example **BAGPIPES** with Scotland.

Instrumentation and tonality

Your choice of instrumentation is important when considering the type of film. An epic love story or an action film might call for a big orchestral sound, while a smaller ensemble may work well for a different genre such as a crime thriller.

Think about an appropriate harmonic language. You may want to write chromatic or even atonal music if the situation demands a particular sound. Similarly, film composers often use modal scales (such as the Dorian or Mixolydian scales for minor and major), particularly if they want to create a traditional folk sound. This can be seen in *Pirates of the Caribbean*, which liberally uses the Dorian mode.

Dorian mode   Mixolydian mode

Composing to the brief

Within the film music brief, you will be asked to write music for a given film genre. You will not be required to follow exact timings by synchronising with a particular film clip. As with all the briefs, the best way to compose is to study examples of existing music.

Here is a table of some film genres, with a number of musical features that may be appropriate, as well as some suggested listening.

Film genre	Possible musical features	Useful listening
Action/ Adventure	■ Repeated rhythms ■ Strong melodic ideas ■ Percussive elements ■ Brass fanfares	■ Zimmer: the *Pirates of the Caribbean* series ■ Shore: *The Lord of the Rings* trilogy ■ Steiner: *King Kong* (1933)
Crime/ Mystery/ Horror	■ Atonality / discords ■ Avoidance of melody ■ Electronic samples ■ Pitch slides ■ Pedals	■ Leonard Bernstein: *On the Waterfront* (1954) ■ Herrmann, *Psycho* (1960) ■ Carpenter: *The Fog* (1980) ■ Glass: *Candyman* (1992)
Comedy (Slapstick/ Romantic)	■ Major keys/jazz harmony ■ Disjointed melodies ■ 'Oom-pah' bass ■ Waltz tune	■ Elfman: *Pee-wee's Big Adventure* (1985) ■ Giacchino: *The Incredibles* (2004) ■ Mancini: *Breakfast at Tiffany's* (1961)
Historical drama	■ Traditional instruments ■ Expressive solos ■ Pastiche ■ Folk elements ■ Use of modal scales	■ Nyman: *The Piano* (1993) ■ Williams: *Schindler's List* (1993) ■ Barry: *Zulu* (1964) ■ Takemitsu: *Black Rain* (directed by Shohei Imamura, released in 1989)
Western	■ Guitar/whistling ■ Creating sense of space ■ Trad. American folksong ■ Simple harmonies	■ Moricone: *Once Upon a Time in the West* (1968) ■ Elmer Bernstein: *The Magnificent Seven* (1960)
Science fiction	■ Ambient synthesised background ■ Electronic samples	■ Goldsmith: *The Planet of the Apes* (1968) ■ Vangelis: *Blade Runner* (1982) ■ Davis: *The Matrix* (1999)

Brief 4: Fusions

Sample A Level brief from Edexcel:

> Compose a piece for string quartet that is based around an east European folk melody. The piece will be played alongside a programme of Western classical pieces.

Sample AS Level brief from Edexcel:

> Compose a piece of music for a performance at a world music festival. The music must contain stylistic features of African drumming fused with British pop style.

Musical fusion is the process of combining two different styles of music to create something completely new. In order to prepare for this brief, you will need to investigate examples of world music, such as Latin American or African music, then gain practice in handling some of the musical elements that characterise them.

Musical fusion: your tools

Different styles of music can be suggested by using the following:

- A particular instrument
- A characteristic rhythm
- A type of scale (melody and harmony).

Instruments

Using a particular instrument that is associated with a style is an easy way of evoking that type of music within a piece, especially if it also uses a characteristic rhythm or scale. The distinctive sound of a sitar, for example, can easily suggest Indian Classical music, while a rhythm on a djembe drum can evoke the culture of West Africa.

In one highly successful such venture, 'Parce mihi domine', a chant by the 16th-century composer Cristóbal de Morales, was recorded in 1994 by the Hilliard Ensemble and 'fused' with a freely improvised saxophone part by Jan Garbarek. The renaissance vocal music and jazz improvisation, although separated by centuries, combine well to create something quite new. The track appears on the ECM New Series album *Officium*.

Characteristic rhythms

Sometimes only a rhythm is needed to evoke a type of music, especially if it is one associated with dance, such as the characteristic rhythms of Latin American music.

In his opera *Carmen,* the composer Bizet creates an evocative Spanish dance, the habanera, by using its distinctive rhythm:

Types of scale

Some types of music can be suggested by the use of certain scales. For example, an obvious way of producing a 'blues' feel is to use the blues scale, while the use of the pentatonic scale could suggest the Javanese Gamelan.

Don't forget that a scale not only gives the characteristics of a melody but can also work vertically, providing the harmony for your piece.

Case studies

When you have worked out the ingredients of a style, consider how you could incorporate them into your piece. Do your ideas work in combination or could you set up a dialogue between two different styles? Here are five examples of traditional music from around the world that have been fused with other styles:

Latin American music

Latin American dance music from South and Central America, notably Brazil, Cuba and the Caribbean islands has been used extensively as an element of musical fusion. It is influenced by both European and African music and tends to use medium to fast tempos. There are numerous styles including Calypso, Bolero, Bossa Nova, Conga, Rumba, Samba and Tango.

Many Latin styles make use of a distinctive rhythmic pattern known as the son clave rhythm, which consists of either three notes followed by two (3:2)…

… or two notes followed by three (2:3):

There are often many layers of different rhythms happening at the same time in Latin American music.

INSTRUMENTS

- Percussion – including: claves, cowbells, timbales, cabasa, triangle, guiro, maracas, congas
- Double bass/electric bass
- Piano
- Electric and/or acoustic guitar
- One or two lead instruments (e.g. flute, trumpet, saxophone)

Fusion examples:

- Familia Valera Miranda: 'Para Ti Nengón' and 'Tú Eres mi Obsesión'
- Cubanismo: 'Descarga de Hoy'
- Jobim: 'The Girl from Ipanema'
- Bernstein: *West Side Story*
- Villa-Lobos: *Bachianas Brasileiras* No. 2 and No.5.

Classical Indian music

Indian classical music is an ancient type of music using complex patterns of melody known as ragas combined with particular rhythms known as talas. The single melody line is played over a fixed drone.

Ragas – These modal melodies have particular ascending and descending patterns and are associated with different times of the day or moods.

Talas – Repeated rhythmic patterns usually played by the tabla. They usually have between six and 16 beats grouped into small sections (eg. 4+4+4+4).

INSTRUMENTS

- Sitar (guitar-like instrument)
- Shenai (oboe-like instrument)
- Tanpura (provides drone)
- Tabla (small drums)

Fusion examples:

- Beatles: 'Within You Without You' from *Sgt. Pepper's Lonely Hearts Club Band*
- A. R. Rahman: 'Jai Ho' ('You are my destiny')
- Panjabi MC: 'Mundian To Bach Ke'.

British folk music

Common types of British folk music include jigs, reels, ballad folksongs and shanties.

A typical dance tune consists of two sections of eight bars, with repeats.

Drones or pedals are common, as is the use various modes, such as the dorian and mixolydian, which sound, respectively, minor and major. Here is the ballad folksong *Scarborough Fair*, which uses the dorian mode:

INSTRUMENTS

- Fiddle (colloquial term for a violin)
- Melodeon (a diatonic button accordion)
- Piano accordion
- Pipe and Tabor (primitive three-hole recorder and drum played by one player)
- Regional instruments including the Northumbrian pipes

Fusion examples:

- Holst: St. Paul's Suite
- Holst: Suite in F for military band
- Vaughan Williams: English Folk Song suite
- Vaughan Williams: *Norfolk Rhapsody.*

Gamelan

The Balinese gamelan and Javanese gamelan are the traditional instruments of Bali and Java in Indonesia, consisting primarily of metallophones (tuned metal percussion). The Javanese gamelan uses two tuning systems, one of which – sléndro – is similar to the pentatonic scale (the scale made by the black keys on a piano). The tuning is slightly different to Western classical tuning; On the example below, the notes marked (+) are slightly sharper than those notated.

Sléndro tuning

(+)   (+)

INSTRUMENTS

- Gong
- Kenong / Ketuk (small gong in wooden frame)
- Bonang (double row of small bronze gongs)
- Saron – like a glockenspiel

Fusion examples:

- Debussy: *Estampes* No. 1 'Pagodes'
- Poulenc: Concerto for Two Pianos and Orchestra, Movement 1.

African drumming

Many African traditions are highly regarded for their rhythmic complexity, containing such features as syncopation and cross-rhythms.

A great deal of African music incorporates standard rhythmic patterns of which the following two are important: the bell pattern and the tresillo, (which resembles the latin clave rhythm):

Bell pattern   **Tresillo**

INSTRUMENTS

- Djembe / Talking drums
- Balafon (xylophone)
- Mbira (thumb piano)
- Vocals

Examples:

- Robert Glasper: 'Afro Blue' from the album *Black Radio*
- Dee Dee Bridgewater: *Red Earth*
- Afro Celt Sound System – 'Éireann' and 'Riding the waves' from *Volume 2: Release.*

Composing to the brief

Step one: Research the given style

In all the other briefs you can compose your piece in whatever style you wish. For this brief, the style will be specified. You will need to study examples of the given style in its original context and work out the important characteristics.

Step two: Research examples of fusion (especially with the given style)

Find examples in which the given style has been fused with another type of music. Work out how the composer has incorporated the characteristics of a style within the new piece.

Step three: Plan your composition

Other aspects of your piece, such as the structure, need to be given just as much consideration as in the other composition briefs. Do refer to the sections of this study guide on writing instrumental and vocal music.

EXERCISE

Compose a piece for a string ensemble that is based around a British folk melody. The piece will be played alongside a programme of Western classical pieces.

Brief 5: Popular music and jazz

Sample A Level brief from Edexcel:

> Compose a piece of music for a jazz musician to play at a live concert as an encore. The solo part must be accompanied by at least three instruments.

Sample AS Level brief from Edexcel:

> Compose an electro pop song aiming for the top of the charts. There should be a catchy vocal hook integrated into a texture for synthesised instruments.

For this brief you will need to study the characteristics of instruments and instrumental combinations (acoustic, amplified and synthesised) that are associated with popular music and jazz. You will also need to study common song structures and structural devices and the role played by technology in the creation and production of popular music.

This is a very broad topic for which you should study a wide variety of different styles. The following gives an overview of the standard structures and devices found in pop songs, an introduction to jazz harmony and an overview of styles.

Song structures

12-bar blues

One of the most prominent chord progressions in popular music has three lines of four bars, using chords I, IV and V, often arranged as follows:

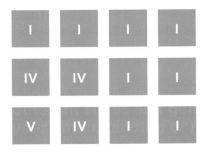

Examples:

- Louis Armstrong: 'West End Blues'
- Bill Haley & His Comets: 'Rock Around the Clock'
- Beatles: 'Can't Buy Me Love' and 'Day Tripper'.

32-bar song form

This was a standard way of writing the chorus of a song (with preceding verse) in the first half of the 20th century. A catchy eight-bar melody is presented, and then varied with different lyrics. It is then contrasted with eight bars of new material (the middle eight/bridge) before being presented again, giving the overall form AA^1BA^2. The song 'Somebody Loves Me' by George Gershwin uses this formula with some subtlety:

Extended song structures

The use of a contrasting middle section (middle eight) within a song creates a satisfying musical whole. This AABA structure was generally extended in the second half of the 20th century with a huge amount of variation:

Buddy Holly and the Crickets: 'Maybe baby' (1957)
Intro, A, A, B, A, A, B, A

The Kinks: 'Waterloo Sunset' (1967)
Intro, A, B, A, B, A, Coda

Public Enemy: 'Bring the noise' (1987)
Intro, A, B, A, A, B, A, B, Break, A

Britney Spears: 'Baby one more time' (1998)
Intro, A, Bridge, B, A, Bridge, B, Intro, A, B, B, B

Alternating between the 'A' and 'B' (verse-chorus form) is common in pop, rock, R&B and Country. When composing your own song, think carefully about the structure, using a balance of repetition and contrast.

Structural devices

Hook

This is a short idea that 'hooks' the listener's attention. It is often the song's title and is found in the chorus. In 'Somebody loves me' (above), Gershwin repeats the melody to these words in the first, second and fourth lines. The repetition of the words and the strong musical idea make it the most memorable part of the song.

Lick

This is a stock pattern or phrase used in one of the solo instrumental parts. Learning guitar, piano or bass licks by listening to songs will help you get a feel for a particular style. By way of example, here are a few bass licks in G:

Riff

This is a repeated ostinato pattern used in song accompaniments that can also form an important 'hook' to the song. It is distinguished from a basic lick by serving as the main musical idea in a song. A famous example is the guitar riff in the Beatles song 'Day Tripper'.

Creating Jazz

There are many musical elements that combine to create jazz. Rhythmic features such as swung quavers and syncopation are important. So is improvisation, which has been an integral part of jazz since its beginnings.

The performer's ability to compose 'on the spot' relies on a good harmonic understanding of the music through the knowledge of different scales and an understanding of voice-leading.

7th chords and extensions

In traditional classical music, harmonies are built upon the three notes of a triad. In jazz harmony, the building blocks tend to be 7th chords and other extensions of a triad:

The chords shown above (a minor seventh, a major seventh and two major sevenths with an added ninth and sharp eleventh) are all extensions of a C major triad. They are not normally played in a basic stacked version. The second version of each chord shows how it might be **'voiced'**, with a distinctive 7th above the bass and closer spacing towards the top of the chord.

AoS COMPOSITION BRIEFS: POPULAR MUSIC AND JAZZ

Voice-leading is very important in jazz, making sure that each note within a chord moves easily to the next, creating a smooth line.

Pentatonic and blues scales

Certain scales are common in jazz, including modes such as the Lydian and Mixolydian. The pentatonic and blues scales in particular are often used and have a certain similarity:

Blues Scale on C

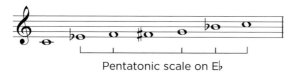

Pentatonic scale on E♭

Turnaround/II-V-I cadence

Harmonising the end of a phrase using chords II-V-I is common in jazz. It uses the circle of fifths and forms part of a 'turnaround' that can lead from one section to the next.

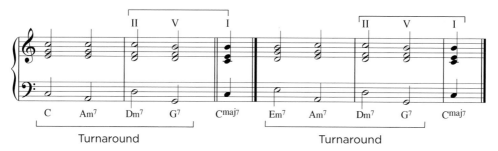

The sound of popular music

Jazz / pop style	Some musical features	Suggested listening
Traditional Jazz	Lively $\frac{4}{4}$, simpler than later jazz	Kid Ory: *Society Blues* (1922)
Big band	Large brass and reed sections. Swing rhythms, walking bass	Count Basie: *One O'Clock Jump* (1937)
Bebop	Fast with complex harmony	Charlie Parker: *Ornithology* (1946)
Cool Jazz	Spacious arrangements, slow tempos	Miles Davis: *Kind of Blue* (1959)
Jazz fusion	Jazz combined with elements of rock, funk and Latin jazz	Miles Davis: *Bitches Brew* (1970)
Blues	Call and response, elaboration of simple melodies	Bessie Smith: *St. Louis Blues* (1925)

Rhythm and Blues	Generally faster than blues, with a focus on vocals	Ray Charles: *Mess Around* (1957)
Rock 'n' roll	Energetic 12-bar blues patterns	Elvis Presley: *Hound Dog* (1956)
Soul	Emotional vocals with backing vocals, riffs	Aretha Franklin: *Respect* (1967)
Country music	Acoustic instruments	Hank Williams: *You Win Again* (1952)
1960s Rock and Pop	Many influences and huge advances. Use of new recording techniques (e.g. multi-tracking)	Beatles: *Revolver* (album, 1966) *Sgt. Pepper's Lonely Heart's Club Band* (album, 1967)
Psychedelic rock	Unusual timbres (for example, use of the mellotron)	The Doors: *The Doors* (album, 1967)
Progressive rock	Complex instrumentals	Pink Floyd: *Money* (1973)
Heavy rock	High-powered vocals	Metallica: *Enter Sandman* (1991)
Glam rock	Driving beats and distorted guitar	David Bowie: *The Rise and Fall of Ziggy Stardust and the Spiders From Mars* (album, 1972)
Disco	Dance music with a strict tempo	Bee Gees: *Stayin' Alive* (1977)
Funk	Energetic, syncopated	Stevie Wonder: *Superstition* (1972)
Reggae	Off-beat chords in guitar and piano	Bob Marley and the Wailers: *I Shot the Sheriff* (1973)
Punk	Fast and aggressive; anti-establishment	Sex Pistols: *Anarchy in the UK* (1976)
Hip hop	Use of repeated rhythmic patterns and riffs; rapping; sampling	Jay Z: *The Blueprint 3* (album, 2009)
Indie rock	Guitar and understated vocals	Blur: *Leisure* (album, 1991)
Electronic dance	(house, techno, trance) Up-beat dance music; use of synths and drum machines	The Prodigy: *Charly* (1991) Moby: *Play* (album, 1999)

Brief 6: New directions

Sample A Level brief from Edexcel:

> Compose a piece of electronic music to open an electroacoustic music concert. Your composition should explore the combination of human voice and natural sounds.

Sample AS Level brief from Edexcel:

> Compose a piece of music to open a chamber concert of 20th-century art music. The piece should be based around atonal ostinati.

The beginning of the 20th century saw a breakdown of the more traditional ways of ordering music. Traditional tonality, with its hierarchy of notes within a key, was often abandoned as composers branched out in new directions, searching for their own musical language. To compose for this brief you will need to study some of the many different ways in which this was achieved, which might include atonal music and the use of tone rows. You will also need to study how composers created new timbres by use of 'prepared' instruments or through electronic means.

New harmonic languages

Free atonality

Traditional tonal music has a reassuring sense of arriving back in the home key, and resolving the harmonic tension with a perfect cadence. This means that there is always the sense of being pulled forwards to one note. You may well wish to write music that feels as if it is floating free from such a directional pull.

Atonal music can therefore provide a different kind of musical experience, in which the listener can simply enjoy the moment. It concentrates the listener on the texture and the colours of the music. In order to write music that is free of any sense of tonality you must try and do the following:

- Avoid melodic or harmonic octaves
- Avoid major or minor triads
- Avoid using more than three notes in succession from a major or minor scale
- Avoid melodies that move by step.

EXERCISE

Write a short atonal piece for piano using the above criteria.

Various composers gave order to their harmonic language by devising musical systems. If you choose to write for this brief you would be well advised to use some sort of system to structure your piece.

Serialism

This is a method of composition, introduced by Arnold Schoenberg in the 1920s, in which all twelve notes of a chromatic scale are used within a fixed series. The idea is that every note sounds as often as every other, thus ensuring that there is no emphasis on one particular note.

The series of twelve notes is known as a tone-row (or a note-row, or just a series). Here is a quick guide to writing a piece using a tone-row.

Step one – create a tone-row

The first step is to decide on an order for the twelve chromatic notes. Give some thought as to which intervals you will use as this can give character to the piece. Berg's violin concerto, for example, uses the following row, which is largely made up of thirds which outline several triads, thereby giving the music an expressive, quasi-tonal quality:

Example 1: Tone-row from Berg's Violin Concerto

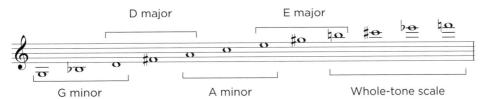

The next example uses increasingly large intervals as it progresses, starting with one semitone, then three semitones, and so on. To make the row easier to display on one stave, the notes following the intervals with brackets are shown in a lower octave.

Example 2

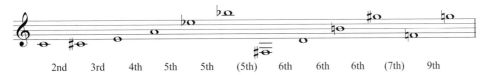

Step two – create a tone-row matrix

Once you have created your row, you need to explore different ways of changing it, for example using it backwards (retrograde) or upside down (inversion) or a combination of both. Start with a blank 12x12 grid and put your original row along the top (known as the Prime Order ('P⁰')).

Carefully work out the inversion (counting intervals on a keyboard) and put it in the first column, as in the following table, based on Example 2 above:

Prime Order 'P⁰'											
C	C♯	E	A	E♭	B♭	F♯	D	B	G♯	F	G
B											
G♯											
E♭											
A											
D											
F♯											
B♭											
C♯											
E											
G											
F											

(Inversion 'I' runs down the left column)

Now complete the table by adding transposed versions of your original row. Write them horizontally, taking a note from the 'Inversion' row (down the left column) as your first note each time. If you start one semitone higher than your original note (i.e C♯) the resulting row will be called **P¹**. It is well worth counting the semitones (ascending) in your original row (C – C♯ = 1, C♯ – E = 3 etc.) to work out the note names for the remaining transpositions. The inversions (**I**), retrogrades (**R**) and retrograde inversions (**Rᴵ**) are then miraculously worked out for you. Check that every row and column uses all twelve semitones. Here is the completed tone-row matrix for Example 2:

Tone row matrices tend to use note names from the relevant key with the fewest sharps or flats, so we say B♭ rather than A♯.

Tone-row matrix for Example 2

	I⁰	I¹	I⁴	I⁹	I³	I¹⁰	I⁶	I²	I¹¹	I⁸	I⁵	I⁷	
P⁰	C	C#	E	A	Eb	Bb	F#	D	B	G#	F	G	**R⁰**
P¹¹	B	C	Eb	G#	D	A	F	C#	Bb	G	E	F#	**R¹¹**
P⁸	G#	A	C	F	B	F#	D	Bb	G	E	C#	Eb	**R⁸**
P³	Eb	E	G	C	F#	C#	A	F	D	B	G#	Bb	**R³**
P⁹	A	Bb	C#	F#	C	G	Eb	B	G#	F	D	E	**R⁹**
P²	D	Eb	F#	B	F	C	G#	E	C#	Bb	G	A	**R²**
P⁶	F#	G	Bb	Eb	A	E	C	G#	F	D	B	C#	**R⁶**
P¹⁰	Bb	B	D	G	C#	G#	E	C	A	F#	Eb	F	**R¹⁰**
P¹	C#	D	F	Bb	E	B	G	Eb	C	A	F#	G#	**R¹**
P⁴	E	F	G#	C#	G	D	Bb	F#	Eb	C	A	B	**R⁴**
P⁷	G	G#	B	E	Bb	F	C#	A	F#	Eb	C	D	**R⁷**
P⁵	F	F#	A	D	G#	Eb	B	G	E	C#	Bb	C	**R⁵**
	RI⁰	**RI¹**	**RI⁴**	**RI⁹**	**RI³**	**RI¹⁰**	**RI⁶**	**RI²**	**RI¹¹**	**RI⁸**	**RI⁵**	**RI⁷**	

Step three – using the tone-row within a composition

You can now use all these versions of the tone-row in a composition. Study examples of how composers such as Schoenberg, Berg or Webern used a tone-row within a piece. Explore as many sound colours, registers and textures as you can. The following example, for wind quartet, uses the original tone-row from Example 2 in a melodic dialogue between the flute and the clarinet. The legato phrase is offset by a staccato oboe (playing the retrograde in its third transposition). A third part is added to the texture by a syncopated bassoon, playing the inversion, and descending to the lowest part of its register.

Notice that notes can be used in any octave – for example the A to Eb in the first complete bar could have been a descending augmented 4th rather than an ascending diminished 5th if the composer had wanted this.

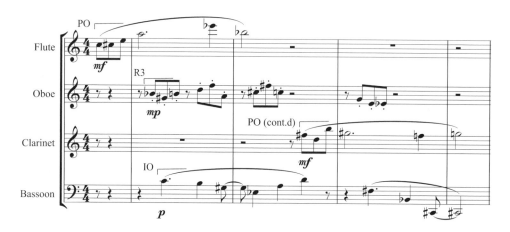

New sounds and textures

After seeking out new harmonic worlds, some composers wanted to go further and search for completely new sound worlds. Initially, this was achieved by finding new sounds from traditional instruments.

Later, electronic instruments opened up new opportunities. One of the first composers to explore these new sounds was the American composer John Cage, who created a number of pieces for 'prepared piano', initially as a way of creating a one-man percussion band where the performing space was limited.

Karlheinz Stockhausen in front of the mixer at the Hamburg Concert Hall in 2001

Writing for the 'prepared piano'

When writing for prepared piano, Cage added a meticulous set of instructions on how each string should be prepared; adding objects such as small nuts and bolts or fibre between the strings. Such instructions are essential in scoring any piece like this. His Sonatas and Interludes collection, which makes full use of the resulting sonic possibilities, are cast in a simple binary form. Do explore this interesting sound world yourself, but make sure that you have permission to alter the piano; it's certainly better to use an old one!

You can find out more about Cage's methods when you come to the chapter on the first of his Three Dances under Area of Study 6.

Writing aleatoric music

Aleatoric music uses elements of chance or unpredictability while maintaining elements of compositional control. When writing this type of music you need to decide which elements can be controlled, and to what degree. This is generally achieved in two different ways:

1. **Control the structure but leave the choice of material to the performer.**
   The composer defines which instrumental combinations to play, and for how long. The number of notes played at each point can also be specified.
2. **Control the material but leave the choice of structure to the performer.**
   The composer provides a number of musical fragments that can be played in any order or octave transposition, and at any dynamic level.

Writing electroacoustic music

In the early 1950s, pioneers of electroacoustic music, such as Pierre Schaeffer and Karlheinz Stockhausen, manipulated real and artificial sounds by cutting up tape recordings and using audio generators and oscillators. They combined these new sounds with voices, as in Stockhausen's *'Gesang der Jünglinge'* (1956), and created exciting new sound worlds.

It is certainly much easier to do something similar today. Digital audio workstations ('DAWs') such as Logic offer great opportunities for exploring different sound worlds, making it easy to mix and manipulate live recordings with other electronic sounds. As with all the composition briefs, however, you really need to immerse yourself in examples of the style.

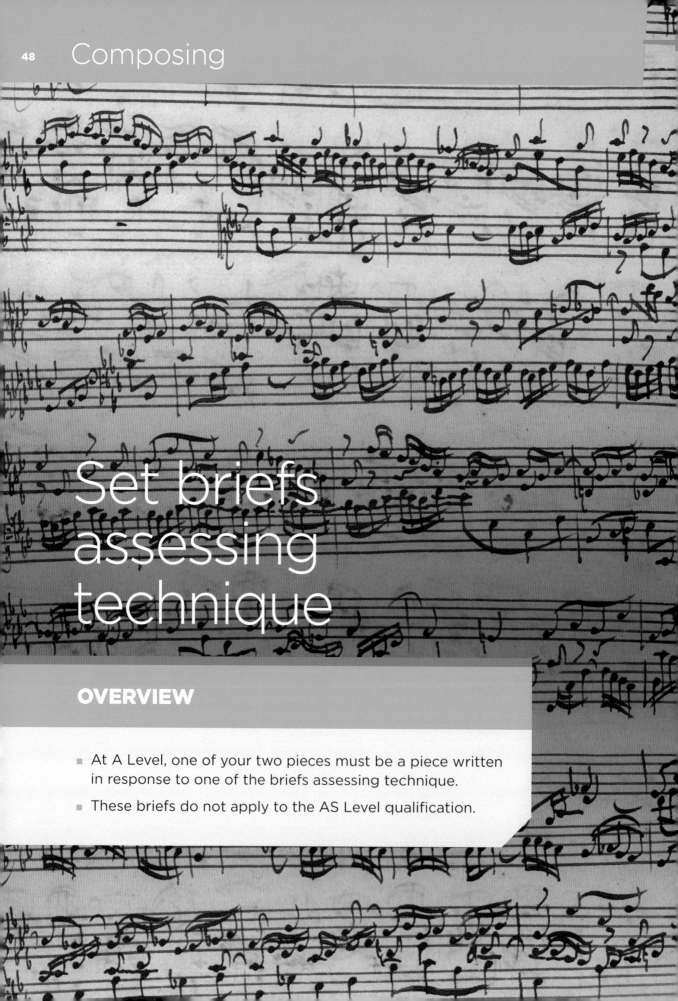

Set briefs assessing technique

OVERVIEW

- At A Level, one of your two pieces must be a piece written in response to one of the briefs assessing technique.

- These briefs do not apply to the AS Level qualification.

Bach chorale

Sample brief from Edexcel:

Add alto, tenor and bass parts to complete the following two chorales, in the style of J.S. Bach, for singing by the choir and congregation during the performance of a cantata.

A chorale is a type of congregational hymn from the Lutheran church in Germany. The harmonisations of these tunes by J.S. Bach (1685-1750) are excellent examples of four-part writing and usually concluded a larger work (such as a cantata or passion). Their direct style acted as a sort of summing-up of the religious text and mood that was being set.

To be able to harmonise a chorale in the manner of Bach, it is really important to get to know his chorale settings. Listen to as many as you can, in particular different harmonisations of the same chorale melody (Bach harmonised the famous Passion chorale 'Herzlich tut mich verlangen' 11 times). Have a go at singing them; they are beautifully expressive pieces of music.

There is not enough space in these pages to cover the skills required to fully master chorale harmonisation. Let's consider the following, however, in relation to Bach's harmonisation of the chorale *'O Ewigkeit, du Donnerwort'* (score over the page).

General points

- Firstly, notice that chorales are written in short score, with the sopranos and altos (S, A) on the top stave and tenor and bass (T, B) on the lower stave. Make sure that the stems go up for the soprano and tenor, but down for the alto and bass
- Take note of the vocal ranges within this chorale, which are fairly typical. The tenor line will often be quite high (i.e. at the end of the first full bar)
- There is no crossing or overlapping of neighbouring parts (e.g. a bass note written higher than a tenor or even moving higher than the previous tenor note)
- Notice that each phrase ends with either a perfect or imperfect cadence marked by a pause sign (boxes A-E). Most cadences are perfect
- Chords usually change on every beat until a cadence
- Some phrases modulate to closely related keys (see bar 8).

Opposite: Bach's fugue in A♭, from the second book of his
48 Preludes and Fugues, notated by the composer himself

'O Ewigkeit, du Donnerwort' (a typical Bach chorale harmonisation)

Cadence A
melody: 6-7-8

Cadence B
melody: 4-3-2

Cadence C
melody: 2-2-1

Cadence D
melody: 2-2-1

Cadence E
melody: 2-2-1

EXERCISE

Identify cadences A to E as perfect or imperfect. What key does the music reach in cadence D?

Chords

You will need to recognise chords and their inversions. Take a look at the first phrase (the first two bars) of 'O Ewigkeit'.

It uses chords I, IV and V, mostly in root position, with one instance of chord viib (marked with an asterisk). Chords I, IV and V, with occasional 1st inversions, should be your starting point in tackling chorale harmonisation. An important rule to remember is not to use any second inversion chord apart from Ic before the V in a perfect cadence.

EXERCISE

Identify the names of the chords in the first phrase of the chorale, using Roman numerals (for example: 'I', 'IVb').

Doubling

A triad of F major has only three notes. Clearly, when writing in four-parts, one note needs to be doubled, and it is usually the root of the chord. Other notes can be doubled depending on the context, but never double a note that feels it should rise or fall (such as a leading note) as this can, for example, result in 'consecutives' and therefore a weakening of the four-part texture. The third is only usually doubled within a 1st inversion chord (as in chord 3).

EXERCISE

Identify which notes have been doubled in the chords in the first phrase.

Spacing

Look at chords marked 1 to 6 in the score of 'O Ewigkeit'. They are all chords of F major, but each spaced differently; the high soprano and alto in chord 5 will give this chord far more prominence than chord 1, for example.

Notice also the space between the notes, especially in the very last chord of the chorale (6). The upper three voices are close together, while the bass part is further apart. Aim for this type of spacing as much as possible when writing chorales.

EXERCISE

The following chords contain missing alto and tenor parts.

Complete the chords so that they contain two roots, a 5th and a 3rd.

F major: I   F major: V   D major: I   D major: IV   E♭ major: Vb   E♭ major: iib

Voice-leading and the consecutive rule

Having considered notes within a chord we need to remember that a chorale is not just a series of chords, but four melodic lines moving together in harmony. Each note within a chord needs to move smoothly to the next. This is called voice-leading (or part-writing). Each line also needs to be independent to maintain a four-part texture. Read through each phrase of '*O Ewigkeit*' and notice the following:

- Melodic lines move mainly by step
- Any leap is usually followed by a step in the opposite direction
- Leading notes need to rise (except the alto at a perfect cadence, which often falls to the fifth of the tonic chord)
- Dissonant notes (for example 7ths) need to be prepared, then resolved downwards
- Parallel fifths, octaves and unisons between parts must be avoided!

Movement between the outer parts (soprano and bass) needs particularly careful handling. Avoid the soprano and bass leaping in the same direction, as they may create exposed octaves or fifths. You should even avoid consecutive fifths and octaves between S and B in contrary motion. Here is a summary:

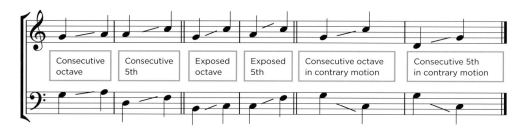

EXERCISE

The following passage contains a number of mistakes, including consecutives, overlapping and poor chord spacing. Find and label each mistake:

octaves by contrary motion

Cadences and their approach chords

Each phrase in a chorale ends with a cadence, which will almost always be either perfect (V–I) or imperfect (ending on V). When completing a chorale, the cadences are a good place to start as there are only a small number of melodic cadential patterns that come up regularly. Here are some of the common ones:

a. 3-2-1 can be harmonised by either Ic–V–I or Ib–V–I.

- Be careful with Ic! It contains a dissonant 4th above the bass (F above C) which needs to be prepared and resolved. Double the fifth of the chord (C).

b. 2-2-1 can be harmonised by either ii7b–V–I or using a 4-3 suspension on the two approach chords: V⁴–V–I.

- A soprano minim can be used for first two chords
- Alto leading note drops to fifth.

c. 8-7-8 can be harmonised by beginning on I, IV or vi, and continuing V–I.

d. 6-7-8 is usually harmonised with IV–V–I.

- Be careful when using the two adjacent chords (IV–V). It can easily lead to consecutive fifths or octaves. The example here shows how Bach gets out of this tricky situation.

The above patterns all normally use perfect cadences. Patterns e and f, which end on the supertonic, are harmonised with imperfect cadences.

e. 3-3-2 can be harmonised with I–Ib–V (see below).

f. 4-3-2 can be harmonised with viib–Ib–V or ii–Ib–V:

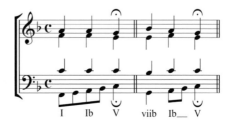

EXERCISE

Try harmonising these cadential patterns in different keys. Be careful not to take the lower parts too high or low.

Modulation

A chorale will usually depart from the home key within at least one of its phrases. If you see one of the standard end patterns finishing on a note other than the tonic, it could indicate a modulation. Any modulation within a chorale will be to a closely related key, but be aware that a phrase could end on an imperfect cadence – chord V – within that key.

The closely related keys (when you are in a major key, as in 'O Ewigkeit') are:

- The relative minor
- The subdominant, and its relative minor
- The dominant, and its relative minor.

Looking at the melody in bar 8 of 'O Ewigkeit', this could be thought of as scale degrees 3–3–2 in F, giving an imperfect cadence. However, a move away from the home key is welcome at this point, and sets up a pleasant sense of returning home when the music returns to F in the following final phrase.

Some phrases within a chorale will start in one key and then finish in another while other phrases can be seen to jump straight into a new key. The latter can be seen at the end of the fourth bar of 'O Ewigkeit', where the C♯ in the bass indicates a sudden move to D minor. At the end of the phrase (bar 6) the music has returned – via a perfect cadence – to F major. The move back to the home key is achieved by using a chord that fits both keys. The last chord of bar 5, a D minor chord, acts as chord I in D minor, but also chord VI in F major. This is known as a **pivot chord**.

Study examples to see the different ways in which Bach manages different modulations within a chorale.

Suspensions

Look at the last four alto notes of 'O Ewigkeit' (beginning at the end of bar 9). This shows the typical use of a suspension within a chorale. If you sing alto in a choir you will be aware how often suspensions turn up in your part.

A suspension must be made of three stages: preparation, suspension and resolution. 'Preparation' means that the note that will cause the dissonance of the suspension must be stated before it becomes dissonant. In the last bar of the chorale, the F in the alto part is prepared from an F major chord. While the altos continue to sing the F, the bass part moves to C. This creates a dissonant interval of a fourth above the bass (suspension), which must resolve down to the consonant interval of a third above the bass: E (resolution). This is an example of a 4–3 suspension.

Other suspensions that Bach uses are 7–6 and 9–8. For reference, the alto line gives a 7–6 suspension at the beginning of bar 4.

Other melodic decoration will be discussed within the following section.

Two pages from an early edition of Albert Riemenschneider's famous collection of Bach chorales.

Two-part counterpoint

Sample brief from Edexcel:

> Complete, in an appropriate style, the following dance movement intended for private performance in a domestic setting. Add the treble part in bars 5–7, 17–19 and 24–27, and the bass part in bars 8–11 and 20–22. [The score for this sample question is published in Edexcel's official Sample Assessment Materials booklet.]

For this brief you will be asked to complete a section of a Baroque sonata or dance suite for a melody instrument and bass. As with the chorale you will need to immerse yourself in the style by studying real examples. Performances and scores are freely available online for the following works.

Study these to get a feel for the style:

- Corelli – Violin Sonatas Op. 5
- Handel – 20 Sonatas Op. 1
- Marcello – Flute Sonatas Op. 2
- Vivaldi – Violin Sonatas Op. 2.

Key features

The following extract is taken from the Gigue finale of Marcello's Flute Sonata Op. 2 No.1:

As is typical of the Baroque style, this extract is crammed with patterns that are either repeated directly or used in sequence. The first bar, for example, uses a rhythm that is immediately repeated. This repeat also makes use of a melodic inversion of the first four notes of a..

We then see the following:

- The first three notes of the opening melody are used as part of a descending sequence at b. which itself is repeated sequentially a bar later
- At c. another sequence begins that makes use of the circle of fifths
- The note E in the box marked d. is an échappée. Instead of resolving smoothly down from D to B via the C, the melody 'escapes' first to the E
- The rhythmic interest swaps to the bass at e. in a pattern that is immediately repeated.
- At f. the melody and bass move together in thirds
- The bass line uses a typical pattern g. for a perfect cadence.

Baroque harmony

You will not be required to add, or work to, a figured bass. However, as a way of understanding Baroque harmony, you would be well advised to study the basics. The numbers under the stave in figured bass notation refer to the intervals above the bass made by the notes in the chord above.

Figured bass notation

	root position	first inversion	second inversion
notes counted above the bass	(5) (3)	6 (3)	6 4

The numbers shown in brackets in these examples are traditionally omitted. A performer will know by convention that, for example, a note with no figures signifies a root position chord, and that a single '6' signifies a first inversion.

Figured bass notation of 7th chords

	root position	first inversion	second inversion	third inversion
	7 (5) (3)	6 5 (3)	(6) 4 3	(6) 4 2

7th chords are used extensively in Baroque harmony, but the 7th is treated as a dissonant note. This means that, like a suspension, the seventh is usually prepared, before resolving downwards.

There are three types of suspension: 4-3, 7-6 and 9-8. They are all found extensively within Baroque harmony, providing wonderful moments of tension in the music. Each suspension must be prepared then resolved downwards. They are often used to approach a cadence and within a sequence.

Preparation – Suspension – Resolution

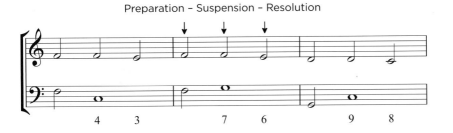

| | 4 | 3 | | 7 | 6 | | 9 | 8 |

Identifying patterns

When completing a two-part counterpoint exercise, you need to be on the lookout for repeated patterns. These could simply be moments within the music that are repeated exactly, or presented in a new key. It could even be the beginning of a sequence. Look at the following example, taken from a violin sonata by Vivaldi, in which the bass part needs to be completed:

The fact that the bass line begins with rests gives us a clue that there is some imitation between the parts. This is confirmed by the fact that the first given bass notes, descending semiquavers, are the same as the top line at the beginning.

If a pattern looks as if it could be used again, do try it, and check to see if it fits harmonically with the given line. Most of the time, the two parts should move in either thirds or sixths. In the solution below, notice that the resulting harmony moves through a circle of fifths. This sequence is then immediately followed by another ascending sequence in the last full bar:

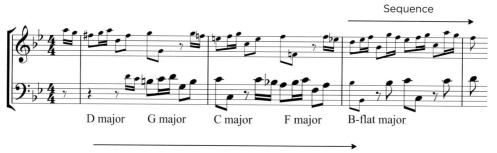

D major   G major   C major   F major   B-flat major

Sequence / circle of fifths

EXERCISE

Complete the following passage, taken from the same Vivaldi sonata:

Melodic decoration

Not all notes within a two-part texture are actual harmony notes. Melodic decoration is an important feature of Baroque music. Here are the main melodic patterns:

a. **Auxiliary note:** moving away from a harmony note by step then returning to it

b. **Passing note:** moving by step between two different harmony notes

c. **Accented passing note:** as before but on a strong beat

d. **Anticipation:** melody anticipates the harmony note on the next beat

e. **Échappée:** described in the Marcello example earlier in the chapter (bar 6).

Completing a two-part counterpoint exercise

It is important that you approach the two-part counterpoint exercise with an ordered working method. Be sure that you are confident with each of the following steps before progressing to the next:

Note which instrument is playing each part and be careful to stay within the range of that instrument. The top line will usually be for flute or violin. Remember that Baroque instruments generally used a smaller range than those today.

1. Identify the keys and cadences within the exercise. Remember that modulations within music of the Baroque period were generally restricted to closely related keys.

2. Complete an outline, using notes that fit harmonically with each part and notice any repeated patterns that could be used sequentially or at other points within the exercise.

3. Complete each line by adding rhythmic interest or appropriate elaboration. This is where studying examples of Baroque sonatas will help you gain stylistic awareness.

4. Check your work. This is absolutely vital. Many of the rules that apply to chorale writing (i.e the consecutive rule) also apply to the two-part counterpoint exercises.

Workable Baroque ranges

Flute

Violin

Arrangement

Sample brief from Edexcel:

> Extend the melody below to form an arrangement suitable for playing in the welcome area of an international arts festival. Your arrangement must be a minimum of three minutes long, and may be in any style. You may compose for vocal and/or acoustic and or amplified and/or synthesised forces.
> [The score for this sample question is published in Edexcel's official Sample Assessment Materials booklet.]

This brief requires a good understanding of structure, harmony and the instruments you will be using. You will be given a melody between 12 and 24 bars in length and the brief will specify an audience and an occasion.

Harmonising the melody

Let's assume that you have been asked to arrange the nursery rhyme *Twinkle, Twinkle, Little Star*. **This is a melody that is characterised by its major key and steady crotchet movement.**

The first step is to work out a harmonisation. As a simple nursery rhyme, this diatonic melody works well with the simplest of harmonies, using the primary triads (I, IV and V), which in the key of C are C, F and G.

This is not the only way to harmonise the melody, and at A Level you should be a little more ambitious and remember the value of inversions. You could also use other chords belonging to the scale (for example the secondary triad D minor instead of F) or find other chords outside of the scale. Try extending the triads to create jazzy major or minor 7ths and 9ths and explore different chord inversions. You could also change the harmonic rhythm. The harmony in the example above changes mainly every half bar, but could move faster or slower.

The following harmonisation makes heavy use of chromaticism. This is the result of using extended triads moving through the circle of fifths.

The harmonic rhythm is faster here, mostly changing on every crotchet beat:

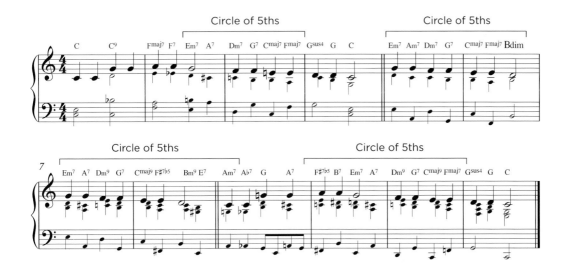

Making an arrangement

The structure of your piece needs careful planning. Here is one option:

- Introduction (based on the melody)
- Two to four variations of the melody (with changes in texture and key)
- Coda (possibly including a grand final version of the melody).

As the given example is a nursery rhyme, it would seem appropriate to make use of the child-like character. This could be achieved by starting the arrangement fairly high and by using only a thin texture. Here is a possible slow introduction, in an arrangement for string quartet. It starts quietly and slowly, allowing the arrangement to build later. It also focuses on the initial rising fifth, in imitation, starting on an up-beat, and with the emphasis on the higher note. The melody is then given to the viola:

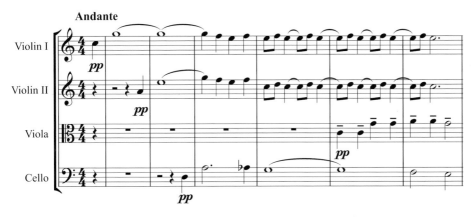

As you proceed with the arrangement you should explore a variety of textures, always keeping the overall structure in mind. At some point within the arrangement, you could also include a counter-melody, for example:

Remix

Sample brief from Edexcel:

Using the vocal *A Level Music SAMS Brief 4 Vocal* [from Edexcel's website] create an original electronic dance remix suitable to [be played] in a nightclub by a DJ. Your remix must be a minimum of three minutes long.

You must use the entire vocal recording. You may edit and re-order the vocal part.

Your remix must contain sequenced parts. Your remix may record audio parts that you have played yourself. Any recorded audio parts that you were not the performer [of] must be detailed on the Composing authentication sheet. If you use any pre-recorded loops and samples they must be manipulated, shaped, edited and/or processed.

You must:

• Use original sound design such as synthesis, sample manipulation or creative effects

• Produce a high quality stereo recording of your composition that pays attention to EQ, dynamics, effects, stereo field and balance.

The content of the stimulus audio file:

• The audio file is aligned with the beginning of a bar to ensure that it plays in time

• The tempo is 131bpm

• The vocal was recorded in E minor

• This recording is dry with no EQ, compression or any other effects.

The remix brief will allow you to take full advantage of your skills using a digital audio workstation (DAW).

What you need to know

■ You will receive an instrumental or vocal sample:

   ■ The **key** and **tempo** will be given to you

   ■ The sample will be free from effects, manipulation or processing

■ You will need to create a piece of music that is suitable for a particular setting or occasion

■ You will usually need to produce a piece that is at least 3 minutes long

■ You **must** use sequenced parts, and *can* use recorded parts should you wish to

■ Read the brief for your assessment year carefully. The above example brief specifies that you **must** use the whole sample you are given, but you *can* edit and re-order the sample if you want to.

How to approach this brief

Listen to music that manipulates samples.

Find pieces of electronic music that use a vocal or instrumental sample throughout. Make a list of the ways the sample is changed or edited in the piece. How often is the sample played? What does the music around the sample sound like?

Here are a few pieces that use vocal or instrumental samples:

- 'Get a Move on!' by Mr. Scruff (uses a saxophone sample from 'Bird's Lament' by Moondog)
- 'Levels' by Avicii (uses a vocal sample from 'Something's Got a Hold on Me' by Etta James)
- 'Stronger' by Kanye West (uses a vocal/instrumental sample from 'Harder, Better, Faster, Stronger' by Daft Punk). In fact, Kanye West is a prolific user of samples in his music – many videos online explore in detail how he uses samples.

Start with the pieces above and then find your own. Here are a couple of places that you might want to visit:

- The website www.whosampled.com: a huge catalogue of songs that use samples
- The TED talk 'How Sampling Transformed Music' by music producer Mark Ronson: a fascinating exploration of how several artists have exploited samples. Ronson is full of good ideas for this task.

Listen to the sample you are given over and over again. If you are tackling the sample brief opposite, ask yourself how it would fit in a piece of music that could be performed in a nightclub. Then listen to some club dance music. Make a list of the key musical features you hear and get ready to use and exploit these in your own piece.

To begin with, here are some key musical features of nightclub music:

- A $\frac{4}{4}$ time signature and a steady tempo
- Use of electronic, synthesised sounds
- A strong sense of pulse, with every crotchet beat of the bar emphasised
- Complex drum patterns, containing several layers of sound
- A bass line with a limited range
- Short riffs or melodic ideas.

Get the basics right

The music that accompanies your sample needs to work well with the sample itself, in order to create a successful piece of music. Be sure to match the tempo and key of your piece with the sample you are given. Ensure your composition has a strong sense of structure and that it contains enough melodic and harmonic ideas to keep the piece interesting.

Exploit the sample

Ensure that you show knowledge of a range of techniques by manipulating and editing the sample in a number of different ways.

Ideas for this brief

Ideas for the sample

Listed below are some of the ways in which you might edit or manipulate your sample, as part of this composition task:

- Add effects, such as reverb, delay or distortion. Edit the parameters of each effect to achieve the greatest musical impact
- Use compression, EQ, panning or noise gates to ensure your sample 'blends' with the music around it
- Use EQ filters. Interesting effects can be had by filtering out some frequencies, then changing this over time using automation
- Speed up or slow down the sample. This can be powerful, but be careful: you may change the key of the sample, meaning that it may not fit with the rest of the music. Depending on how you edit the sample on different pieces of software, you may be able to keep it at the same pitch, or change it, depending on the effect you are looking for
- Use a sampling keyboard. By using the sample as the input for a sampling keyboard (a built-in 'instrument' on many DAWs), you will be able to trigger the sample at a variety of speeds and pitches throughout the piece
- Break up the sample. Try to isolate certain notes, words or patterns from your sample, and use these to add interest to your piece. Combine this with the sampling keyboard, and you could create melodic or harmonic ideas with the sample itself
- Use the stereo field. Having the sample appear in the left or right channels, centre of the field, or move from right to left (or vice versa) will create a powerful effect in your remix.

Ideas for the music

As well as manipulating the sample, you need appropriate music to accompany it. Here are some ideas:

- Chord progressions: chord progressions in club dance music often use three or four chords, lots of repetition, and long sustained sounds
- Bass lines: stylistic bass lines will be repetitive, have a strong sense of pulse, and make use of 'sub-bass' frequencies, to enhance the experience for listeners in a nightclub
- Melodies: again, repetition is stylistic for club dance music. Short melodies, or riffs, are usually heard, with some development as the piece progresses
- Drum parts. Complex drum parts with a strong pulse are important. The changes in your drum part can help shape the structure of the piece. You may choose to begin without drums, have them drop out in the middle, or have them enter suddenly, depending on the effect you want.

Sequencing/recording/loops

The majority of your musical ideas will be sequenced, and use electronic sounds. Remember to apply the appropriate effects, and to play with the settings on each synthesiser/drum machine to get the right musical effect.

You may choose to record additional sounds using live instruments. You could record an alternative version of a vocal/instrumental sample to complement the sample you are given by Edexcel, since you are allowed to combine live and electronic drum sounds in your piece. Remember – you are being assessed on how well you manipulate the sample, so don't make live sounds too prominent in your final submission.

If you are going to use loops, you must edit them, or use an effect or process. Don't just use them on their own.

Mastering

Mastering is a key stage in preparing this submission. Check for distortion, clipping and other unwanted sounds. Ensure your automation of effects is how you want it throughout the piece. Check your mixing; check your levels for each track; and your panning. Ensure that you are making full use of the stereo field. Listen on several stereos, monitors and headphones, in several locations. Don't neglect the mastering process before deciding that your piece is finished.

Submission

Unlike the free composition option and the compositions in response to an 'Area of Study' brief, no score is required for this task.

You only need submit a recording, on an audio CD or USB stick. It must be a **.wav** file, have a sample rate of **44.1kHz**, and a bit depth of **16 bit**. These requirements are pretty standard, but make sure they are selected when you finally export your mixdown for submission.

COMPONENT 3:
Appraising

For the Appraising components of AS and A Level Music, you have to:

- Study set works from six Areas of Study
- Listen to music other than set works
- Develop your aural perception skills.

All six Areas of Study are compulsory at AS and A Level. Areas of Study 1 and 2 (Vocal Music and Instrumental Music), represent the Western classical tradition, which is deemed for examination purposes to extend from 1650 to 1900 (with allowance for the occasional work that is a little earlier or later). Put together with the other four Areas of Study, there is a wide range of music covered.

You investigate each Area of Study chiefly through:

■ Set works. There are two for each Area of Study at AS Level. The same two works
  and an additional one are prescribed for each area at A Level

■ Wider listening, consisting of:

  ■ Works suggested in Appendix 4 of each Specification

  ■ Other music related to the Areas of Study and set works.

Practice tests, including on unfamiliar repertoire, are provided in the Rhinegold
Education publication *Edexcel AS/A Level Music Listening Tests* (RHG342).

The written paper

The structure of the written paper that comprises the assessment for Component 3 is similar for both qualifications, but there are important differences, as shown below.

Each student will have a CD containing the extracts of music relating to the exam, and will be in control of listening to the extracts relating to each question.

	Q	AS Level ■ One-and-a-half-hour exam ■ Marked out of 80 marks	A Level ■ Two-hour exam ■ Marked out of 100 marks
Section A	1	Listening question based on audio extract from the set works (skeleton score provided)	Listening question based on audio extract from the set works (skeleton score provided)
	2	Listening question based on audio extract from the set works (skeleton score provided)	Listening question based on audio extract from the set works (skeleton score provided)
	3	Listening question based on audio extract from the set works (skeleton score provided)	Listening question based on audio extract from the set works (skeleton score provided)
	4	4(a) Melody completion question, phrased in the form: 'Listen to track [-]. Complete the melody in bars [-] to [-]'. 4(b) Error identification question, phrased in the form: 'Listen to track [-]. The written music given below contains [-] errors. Identify the errors and write a correct version of the melody on the stave below'	Melody completion question, phrased in the form: 'Listen to track [-]. Complete the melody in bars [-] to [-]'.

The terms [-], indicates that there will be a number at that point on your question paper.

Q	AS Level ■ One-and-a-half-hour exam ■ Marked out of 80 marks	A Level ■ Two-hour exam ■ Marked out of 100 marks
Section B 5	Essay question based on an unfamiliar work related to one of the set works (but not actually one of the set works or wider listening works recommended by Edexcel). Audio will be provided, but there will be **no score provided**.	Essay question based on an unfamiliar work related to one of the set works (but not actually one of the set works or wider listening works recommended by Edexcel). Audio will be provided, but there will be **no score provided**.
6	Essay question on a set work. Students will be able to choose which question to answer from a choice of three, each from a different Area of Study. **No audio will be provided**, and there will only be an 'illustrative excerpt' of the score. Students are expected to use their 'knowledge of the set work as a whole' (and other works) in their answer.	Essay question on a set work. Students will be able to choose which question to answer from a choice of three, each from a different Area of Study. **No audio will be provided**, and there will only be an 'illustrative excerpt' of the score. Students are expected to use their 'knowledge of the set work as a whole' (and other works) in their answer.

Pearson's Sample Assessment Materials (available online) show the different nature of the Question 6 essay titles in the Appraising component for AS and for A Level:

- Essays for AS generally refer to two elements (for example, structure and texture), while those for A Level generally refer to three
- Essays for A Level have additional wording to apply the question to some particular aspect of the music's context.

Essays at the two levels are marked from different assessment grids, as may again be seen from the Sample Assessment Materials. The allocation of marks is different, with fewer marks at AS implying the need for less information. At A Level there is greater emphasis on saying *how* and *why* particular things happen in the music, and relatively less on just saying *what* happens.

General introduction to the study of set works

The set works were chosen as important examples of different styles and genres to help you widen and deepen your understanding of music.

They are to be studied largely in terms of what the Specifications call musical contexts, elements and language. Study of each element of a piece in turn is somewhat artificial, but it is appropriate preparation for some of the essay topics to be expected in the examinations.

Musical contexts

Understanding the context of a set work is a good place to start. It involves being aware of the work's original purpose and intention and the historical, social and cultural circumstances of its composition.

Each work has:

- A composer – and sometimes a 'commissioner' (perhaps a wealthy individual, or an organisation such as the BBC) who pays the composer and may even arrange for a performance
- One or more performers who turn the composer's ideas into sound
- An audience (either present together at a live performance or listening separately to broadcasts or recordings). The audience's reception of a work will determine its 'success' over time.

Musical elements

The Specifications list these musical elements:

AS Specification, pages 41–43; A Level Specification, pages 55–58.

- **O**rganisation of pitch (melody and harmony)
- **T**onality (often synonymous with key, but embracing other methods of tonal organisation, e.g. in modal or atonal music)
- **S**tructure (form)
- **S**onority (to some extent synonymous with 'timbre')
- **T**exture
- **T**empo, metre and rhythm
- **D**ynamics.

Why not memorise this list? There is no obvious mnemonic or acrostic, but you might like to invent one.

Musical language

The 'musical language' most frequently used by composers is staff notation. You need to be able to read it (notably when studying the scores of set works). You also need to write it in dictation exercises, and in many styles of composition.

The expression 'musical language' also covers knowledge of chords and chord symbols, as well as standard musical vocabulary and technical terms.

Standard terms are not always explained in this book. There is a vocabulary list in each Specification (Appendix 3), and for any other terms, use a good-quality musical dictionary, such as the *Rhinegold Dictionary of Music in Sound* by David Bowman (ISBN 0-946890-87-0)

You must understand commonly used musical terms partly because:

- It is easier to use a technical term than to write many non-technical words to describe the same thing – for example, the term 'melodic sequence' is preferable to the expression 'where a few notes in one part are repeated at a higher or lower pitch'
- Musical vocabulary appears in exam papers, and must be understood if questions are to be answered correctly
- The assessment criteria for essays make it clear that good use of musical vocabulary will be rewarded.

For example, in Question 6(a) from the Edexcel A Level sample Appraising paper, 'some basic musical vocabulary used with errors/inconsistency' is part of the description of an answer worth 1–6 marks out of 30, whereas an 'excellent use of musical vocabulary' is required for a mark of 25–30. (The Sample Assessment Materials are available online from the Pearson Edexcel AS and A Level Music page.)

Wider listening

Listen to as much music as you can (in addition to getting to know the set works really well).

Some of this additional listening should be connected with the Areas of Study and set works, because essay questions in the exams will require you to refer to such music.

As stated above, there are suggestions for wider listening in Appendix 4 of each Specification. There are also concise references to other works in the following pages.

Aural perception

'Aural perception' means 'perceiving (i.e. being aware and understanding) with the ears' – something vital for every musician.

In the exam you are expected to demonstrate aural perception principally by answering questions on recorded passages from set works and from 'unfamiliar' music.

There is practice material for such questions (and advice) in Rhinegold Education's *Edexcel AS and A Level Listening Tests* (RHG342), which also includes dictation exercises and tests in the correction of errors.

'Unfamiliar' music is music that examiners think it highly unlikely that you will have heard previously – but music that you should be able to relate to other pieces that you *have* encountered (notably the set works and suggested wider listening).

Dictation

Dictation involves listening to a short passage of unfamiliar music, and writing it down in staff notation.

In practical terms it is one way that a composer (yourself, perhaps?) might 'capture' a musical idea that suddenly comes to mind.

Here are some suggestions on how to tackle dictation exercises if (as many people do) you find them difficult:

- The first time that you hear the test, find out how many notes you have to capture, perhaps by writing down a dot for each note
- Then concentrate on rhythm by deciding where the barlines come in relation to your row of dots, before working out the length of each note
- Then work on pitch by plotting the *shape* of the melody showing how it rises and falls, before working out the exact pitch of each note.

You can, if you wish, tackle pitch *before* rhythm when completing dictation exercises.

Correction of errors (AS Level only)

Part of Question 4 in the AS Level Appraising paper involves detecting differences between written and recorded versions of the same short melodic passage. This test, like dictation, requires a good understanding of staff notation, and the ability to compare what you see with what you hear.

Study of set works

Starting from page 74, there are notes on each set work. You do not need to study them in the order in which they appear in this book.

Some set works must be studied both at AS and at A Level. Others belong only to A Level.

In the A Level course, the greater number of set works provides greater *breadth* of study.

The greater *depth* of study expected at A Level can be seen by comparing the AS and A Level Specifications and the Sample Assessment Materials for each level.

For example, at A Level:

- Questions and essay mark schemes are often more demanding. Compare the top descriptors in the A Level essay mark schemes with those for AS
- The examples accompanying the list of musical elements (Specification, pages 55–57) are more extensive than those provided for AS (pages 41–42).

For each set work, we consider the following:

- Musical context
- Musical elements
- Musical language.

Some general advice

Where a work is set both for AS and A Level, information is presented once only. You won't find minutely detailed bar-by-bar analyses of each piece in this guide. This level of study is not required for AS or A Level, and the first aim must be to grasp broad principles and broad outlines, and then to supplement these with examples. You may, for instance, draw on some or all of the examples that are provided, but sometimes (with your teacher's help) you may also be able to find your own. Repeated attentive listening to set works will help you retain important information.

If you are preparing for AS (either on its own, or before moving on to A Level), the advice is to absorb as much as you can about each work. Naturally, the more that you know, the greater will be your chances of good results. In previous specifications, it was noticeable that a fairly large number of high-scoring students 'over-shot the mark' and approached or reached A Level standards in their AS year.

There is some advice on how to write about music in the appropriately named *Writing about Music Workbook* (Rhinegold Education, RHG 429) by Alistair Wightman.

Vocal music

OVERVIEW

The Vocal Music set works introduce you to three important categories: church music, opera and song.

AS **A** **Cantata 'Ein feste Burg ist unser Gott' BWV 80, Movements 1, 2 and 8 (Bach)**

AS **A** *The Magic Flute*, **excerpts from Act 1 (Mozart)**

A *On Wenlock Edge*, **Nos. 1, 3 and 5 (Vaughan Williams)**

Set work:
Cantata 'Ein feste Burg ist unser Gott' BWV 80, Movements 1, 2 and 8
Johann Sebastian Bach

The letters 'BWV' stand for 'Bach-Werke-Verzeichnis' ('Bach Works Catalogue').

Musical context

Composer

Johann Sebastian Bach (1685–1750) is one of the most important of all composers. His work, together with Handel's, represents the culmination of the Baroque era in music.

Bach is most widely known for his instrumental and keyboard works. But he was first and foremost a composer of choral works for the (Lutheran) church in Germany.

The cantata genre

A cantata in Bach's day:

- Was a work for voice(s) and instruments in several movements
- Was of medium length, rather than the extended length of oratorios such as Handel's *Messiah*
- Was either sacred (for church use) or secular (for non-church use)
- Most commonly had some movements for soloist(s), and others for chorus.

The Bach monument at St. Thomas Church, Leipzig, where Bach worked from 1723 until his death

- About 200 church cantatas by Bach survive; about 100 more have been lost.
- Bach's *Christmas Oratorio* is really six separate cantatas, each for a different day in the post-Christmas season.

In Bach's church cantatas, movements for soloists were generally

- Arias (extended and often elaborate pieces with much repetition of text and associated melodic motifs), or
- Recitatives with clear projection of a text as priority.

It is perhaps surprising that church works include arias and recitatives – types of movement characteristic of opera. This was part of a modernising tendency in the Lutheran Church that had begun in the late 17th century.

Handel's *Messiah* (some items from which are among the suggested wider listening works) was not intended for performance in church, despite the sacred text. It too has recitatives and arias (Handel was first and foremost an opera composer), but no chorales (which were peculiar to the German Lutheran tradition).

In Bach's church cantatas many movements (chiefly those for chorus) were based on chorales.

The term **CHORALE** refers to the congregational hymns sung in German Protestant services. They were simple, singable tunes that the congregations would have been familiar with, and Bach often used them as the basis for his instrumental and vocal compositions, including many of his cantatas.

Cantata 'Ein feste Burg ist unser Gott': original purpose

Many of Bach's church cantatas were composed for performance at Sunday morning services in Leipzig, where Bach was musical director at St Thomas Church from 1723 until his death. The cantata followed the Gospel reading, and preceded the Creed (a statement of Christian belief) and the sermon. The whole service was very long, so the singing of a cantata was not out of proportion.

Cantata 'Ein feste Burg' was composed c. 1727–1731, during Bach's years at Leipzig, for Reformation Day (31 October), a major festival in the Lutheran Church (which in the 18th century was *the* church in Bach's part of Germany).

In fact, some of the music had been composed much earlier. On the other hand, the **oboe d'amore** and **taille** parts (see 'Sonority and Dynamics') were added in (probably) the mid-1740s. Bach's son Wilhelm Friedemann (1710–1784) added parts for trumpets and timpani, but these are not included in the Anthology score.

The cantata was performed by the singers and instrumentalists of St Thomas Church, but the congregation would have joined in with the chorale melody in the final movement.

> The reference here to 'singers' rather than to '**choir**' is deliberate: there are strong grounds for supposing that Bach habitually used only one singer per part, rather than a 'choir' with several or many singers to a part.

Cantata 'Ein feste Burg ist unser Gott': the text

Movements 1, 2, 5 and 8 set four verses of a hymn by Martin Luther (1483–1546), which was almost the 'signature tune' of the Reformation in Germany. (Its opening is based on Psalm 46, verse 1.) All of Movements 1, 2, 5 and 8 employ the chorale melody traditionally associated with this hymn.

There is a listing of all the movements, with full text, at www.bach-cantatas.com. The original German is given, along with a very literal English translation.

The texts of Movements 3, 4, 6 and 7 were by Salomo Franck (1659–1725), who provided the words for some of Bach's other cantatas.

In Movement 2 Bach sets to music the second verse of Luther's hymn (for soprano) and a poetic text by Franck (for bass) *simultaneously* **– an apt combination:**

- Soprano (in free translation): Nothing was achieved with our own strength. Straightaway we are lost. A righteous man [i.e. Jesus Christ] fights for us, whom God himself has chosen
- Bass: Everyone who has been born of God [i.e. through baptism] is chosen for victory.

It would not have worried Bach that the congregation could not follow two sets of words at once. The whole complex movement was above all (like his sacred music as a whole) an offering of his labour to God in worship.

Musical elements

Organisation of pitch: melody

Treatment of the chorale melody

The chorale melody is heard in its fundamental form (which the congregation would have known) only in Movement 8 as shown in the music example below. It is a rhythmically simpler version of a 16th-century original, probably by Luther himself.

This melody is mainly conjunct (stepwise), with some repeated notes and occasional leaps, chiefly between phrases. The phrases are of unequal lengths in order to match the different syllable counts of different lines of the text: 8.7. (both repeated) 6.5.5.6.7.

In Movement 1 each phrase of the melody is heard in turn.

The voices share each phrase in imitation (see 'Texture'), often ornamenting the melody, especially in phrase 1 (the music example below shows the tenor's opening entry) and in phrase 3, which is melodically identical to phrase 1.

Notes from basic form of chorale melody are marked 'x'

The three oboes (in unison) and the violone (with organ) conclude the vocal presentation of each phrase by presenting a melodically plain version of the same phrase in canon (see 'Texture') – although, to make the canon work, Bach sometimes has to modify the rhythm.

In Movement 2 ornamentation of the chorale melody is more intense (as in the following example).

Notes from basic form of chorale melody are marked 'x'

The soloist is doubled by the solo oboe, which has additional ornamental detail.

> The oboe is presumably intended to support the soprano soloist, but is allowed a little scope for independence when this is considered safe!

The bass solo part (not related to the chorale melody) is even more ornate than the soprano, with some extended melismas. The opening bass melisma may be a response to the word 'all-(es)' (i.e. with many notes symbolising 'every'one'), but elsewhere melismas are principally a means of melodic extension and development.

The writing on 'alles' is chiefly stepwise (up and down a scale with one or two momentary changes of direction). Elsewhere, especially in some non-melismatic passages, there are bold leaps, which help to give an almost instrumental character to the vocal writing.

This quasi-instrumental style of vocal writing is quite common in Bach.

The two elaborate vocal parts are plotted against a bold part for unison upper strings, based largely on triadic shapes and repeated notes. As quite often in Bach, it almost gives the effect of two melodic lines combined – one with relatively high notes, the other with relatively low ones.

Violin I, II and
Viola in unison

In Movement 8 the chorale melody appears plainly in a 'congregational' form in the soprano. Every other part (especially the bass) has considerable melodic interest and character, with several adventurous moments (as in bar 2, middle parts).

Contrast the lower lines here with the relatively inactive lower parts in some traditional English hymn tunes.

Some other aspects of melodic writing

In Movements 1 and 2 Bach often uses sequence to build a melodic line. Look, for example, in Movement 1 at the cello part in bar 1 and at the sopranos, doubled by first violins in bars 10–11.

There is some striking chromatic melodic writing in Movement 1, with

- Rising and falling chromatic phrases (bars 97–99)
- The notes A♯–B–A♮–G♯ (alto, bars 85–86, 'groß Macht und viel…') – adapted and transposed from line 7 (counting repeats) of the chorale melody – C♯–D–C♯–B. See also soprano, bars 86–87.

In Bach's day chromaticism sometimes highlighted sinister or painful text. 'Groß macht und viel List sein grausam Rüstung ist' means, in a rough translation from www.bach-cantatas.com, 'Great might and much guile are his [the devil's] horrible war equipment'.

Organisation of pitch: harmony

Bach employs functional harmony to establish major and minor keys, first and foremost through tonic and dominant triads (chords I and V), especially when these form perfect (V–I) cadences.

Triads (not just I and V) in root position or first inversion are fundamental to Bach's harmonic vocabulary.

The harmony is often enhanced by the addition of non-triadic notes.

Many of these are passing notes: for example, the C♯ and E in bass and tenor on the word 'Das' at the start of Movement 8. Passing notes chiefly produce additional rhythmic movement and melodic flow rather than harmonic tension or dissonance.

In suspensions, however, there is real dissonance. For two examples, see the first phrase of Movement 8. There is a 7–6 suspension in the alto at the start of bar 1, and a 4–(♯)3 suspension, again in the alto, in bar 2.

> Suspensions are numbered according to the intervals heard between the suspended part and the bass. For more on suspensions, see Rhinegold Education's *AS/A Level Harmony Workbook*, by Hugh Benham.

Structure and tonality

> As with many set works, explanation of structure is impossible without reference to tonality, even though tonality and structure are listed as separate elements in the specification.

Overall, the eight movements of the cantata have an almost symmetrical arrangement: chorus, duet, recitative, aria, chorus, recitative, duet, chorus.

The structure of Movement 1 depends chiefly on the structure of the chorale melody. Counting those that are repeated, there are nine phrases (corresponding to the nine lines of the text).

Phrase	Text	First vocal entry	Entry in oboes
1	'Ein feste Burg'	bar 1, tenor	bar 12
2	'ein gute Wehr'	bar 3, tenor	bar 24
3 (= 1)	'er hilft uns frei'	bar 30, tenor	bar 41
4 (= 2)	'die uns itzt hat'	bar 33, tenor	bar 54
5	'Der alte böse Feind'	bar 60, bass	bar 69
6	'mit Ernst'	bar 72, alto	bar 79

7	'groβ Macht'	bar 82, tenor	bar 88
8	'sein grausam Rüstung'	bar 90, soprano	bar 96
9 (= 2)	'auf Erd ist nicht'	bar 100, tenor	bar 108

In Movement 1 the tonality is linked to the tonality of the chorale melody: in particular, the movement begins and ends in D major as the chorale melody does. But some melodic phrases are capable of interpretation in more than one key.

The following table outlines what happens. Modulations from and to D major are structurally important; those involving minor keys are very brief, but are important in helping to colour the text.

Bars	Key(s)	Chorale phrase numbers and implied key
1–30	D major With hints of A (e.g. parts of bars 1–3) and G (21–24)	1 and 2: D major (although phrase 1 can be harmonised to end in A, as in Movement 8)
30–60	as above. The hints of A fall in bars 31 and 32, G in bars 51–53	3 and 4 (= 1 and 2)
60–72	*Minor* keys – used to set text about the 'old, evil enemy' ■ E minor in 63–64 ■ B minor in 65–66 ■ F♯ minor in 67–68 All these keys are closely related to the tonic, D major Hints of D minor near end	5: A major at end
72–82	*Minor* keys (F♯ minor, E minor, B minor again) as suggested by text Final D major chord I already sounds more like G major V (see below)	6: D major
82–90	Begins major: G, D, A in rapid succession Then the same three minor keys as above are touched on Ends in A major	7: A major

| 90-100 | C♯ minor (mediant minor of preceding A major), F♯ minor, B minor

Ends with a long dominant pedal (F♯) in B minor | 8: D major (but capable of ending with B minor V or even E minor V) |
| 100-end | Chiefly D major | 9: D major (= 2 and 4) |

In the section based on chorale phrase 7, Bach alters the chorale's C♯–D–C♯–B (as at 83–84, bass) to become A♯–B–A♮–G♯ (85–86) and D♯–E–D♮–C♯ (86–87), thus providing additional short-term tonal contrast.

The chorale is also altered in the section based on chorale phrase 8, with the second note sharpened.

Movement 2 begins and ends with a **ritornello** for unison upper strings and continuo. Material from this ritornello (which is independent of the chorale melody) is heard for most of the piece, in various keys.

After the opening ritornello, the soprano soloist sings an embellished version of the chorale melody, using verse 2 of the text.

The bass soloist has a busy florid melody with an independent text, to provide a 'commentary' on verse 2.

The following table outlines structure and tonality.

Section	Bars	Key(s)
Ritornello	1-9	D major
Phrase 1 (and Phrase 3)	10-13, 24-27	D major to A major
Phrase 2 (and Phrase 4)	15-18, 29-32	D major
Phrase 5	37-39	D major to A major
Phrase 6	44-46	D major to B minor
Phrase 7	48-50	A major
Phrase 8	54-56	B minor (touching on F♯ minor)
Phrase 9 and Ritornello	63-69, 69-77	D major

In Movement 8 the chorale melody is harmonised in homophonic style. Phrases 3 and 4 are repeats of phrases 1 and 2.

Phr.	Key	Comment
1, 3	D major–A major	Could have ended in D, but then phrases 1–4 might all have been (rather monotonously) in D
2, 4	D major	Solitary G♯ (tenor) soon neutralised by alto G♮
5	A major	
6	D major	Alto C♮ (soon neutralised by soprano C♯) is chromatic. This is not a sign of G major
7	A major	
8	E minor	The phrase could have been harmonised in D major, but a touch of minor provides effective contrast
9	D major	

Why is there so little minor tonality, given that, from line 5, the text speaks of the possible devastating loss of goods, reputation and family? (After all, references to the Devil's activities in Movement 1 are matched by minor-key music.) The overall theme of Movement 8 is overwhelmingly confidence in God, and Bach presumably wishes to avoid any musical underlining of contrary ideas that would have compromised this.

Sonority and dynamics

In Movement 1 soprano, alto and tenor voices are doubled by first and second violins and violas. The vocal bass part is frequently doubled by the cellos (or presented in a more ornate version as in bars 20–22).

String parts may sometimes have been taken by single players.

The violone plays only in the canonic sections, answering the oboes at a lower octave. There are *three* oboes in unison (rather than just one or two) to help bring out the chorale melody against all the remaining forces. Presumably W.F. Bach (see above) considered that even three oboes were not sufficient for the task: he added trumpets an octave higher.

> The **VIOLONE** was a stringed instrument, probably with a similar range to the modern double bass.

When the violone plays, it is the lowest instrument – and is completely independent of the violoncello (cello) part, not an octave doubling. Here the organ provides harmonic support, based on given figuring.

> Bach required a harpsichord (labelled 'cemb[alo].') to provide chordal support for the cello, which provides the instrumental bass when the violone is silent. No figuring is provided, however.

No instrument was identical to its 21st-century counterpart. In particular, oboes had much simpler keywork.

Movement 2 provides a strong contrast in sonority with Movement 1. Such contrasts were usual between adjacent movements in Bach's cantatas.

There are soprano and bass soloists, the former doubled by oboe. First and second violins and violas play in unison, and there is an instrumental bass line labelled 'continuo' for cellos (probably doubled at the lower octave by violone) and no doubt with the organ providing harmonic support.

In Movement 8 instruments (other than trumpets) would have doubled the vocal parts. The oboe d'amore was a mezzo-soprano or alto oboe in A with a gentler sound than the ordinary oboe. The word 'taille' refers to a tenor oboe in F.

As in most Baroque music, no dynamics are indicated.

Texture

Movement 1 is contrapuntal throughout – indeed it is one of the finest examples of the phenomenal contrapuntal skill for which Bach has always been admired.

The voices, doubled by instruments, work the first phrase of the chorale in imitation. After this, the same phrase (in a simpler form) is worked in canon at the octave by oboes and violone, with the former always half a bar ahead. Each phrase is treated in broadly similar fashion – imitative entries first (voices doubled by instruments), then (instrumental) canon between oboes and violone.

The treatment of phrases 1 and 3 is special in that the four vocal parts do not merely engage in imitation, but create complete fugal expositions, with entries on D, A, D and A. The first appearances of phrases 2 and 4 (see tenor part, bars 3 and 33) are as countersubject to the second fugal entry (alto, bars 3 and 33).

The simultaneous presentation of two versions of a melody (a plain version sung by the basses and a more ornate version in the cellos, as in bars 20–22) is an example of heterophony. Compare the ornamented doubling of the soprano part by the oboe in Movement 2.

Movement 2 is also contrapuntal throughout, with its combination of the instrumental ritornello idea, the embellished chorale in the soprano, and the florid melodic line of the bass soloist – a remarkable compositional feat.

Movement 8 is homophonic – the unembellished chorale melody in the soprano being accompanied by alto, tenor and bass parts. Bach's skill lies in creating an elegant bass line and inner parts with considerable melodic interest of their own.

Tempo, metre and rhythm

As was often the case in Bach's day, there are no tempo directions for Cantata 'Ein feste Burg ist unser Gott'. Performers were expected to judge tempo from the character of the music and the note values used. In Movement 2, for example, the semiquavers must be rapid and the occasional demisemiquavers very quick but still capable of clear articulation.

Movement 1 has the time signature $\mathbf{\complement}$. This normally signifies simple duple time with two minims per bar ($\frac{2}{2}$ or 'cut common' time), but here, as sometimes in early music, it indicates *four* minims per bar. Movements 2 and 8 are both in simple quadruple time (with signatures $\frac{4}{4}$ and $\mathbf{C}$ respectively).

In Movements 1 and 2 Bach often has different rhythmic patterns or note values in different parts, as a way of achieving textural clarity. For example, in Movement 1 the canon stands out so well partly because of the relatively long notes used.

In Movement 8 the chorale moves mostly in crotchets, but with some elaboration in quavers. As in most chorale harmonisations of this type, there is much quaver movement in the lower parts, except on the last chords of phrases. There is just one pair of semiquavers in the final phrase. Most chorale harmonisations have few semiquavers or none at all.

> Pause signs mark out final chords of phrases. In Bach's day, such pauses were probably just punctuation, rather than directions to make notes significantly longer.

Musical language

In Movement 1 the **violone** part has figuring to indicate to the keyboard player what chords should be played.

Each numeral refers to an interval above the bass (for instance, the 4 and 3 in bar 13 indicate that G and F♯ must be played above the bass Ds). Because most figured bass indications are abbreviations rather than full chord specifications, the player has to understand that 4-3 implies a suspension over a root position triad.

> For more on figuring, see Rhinegold Education's *AS/A Level Harmony Workbook*, by Hugh Benham.

Set work:
The Magic Flute, Act 1 Nos. 4 and 5
Wolfgang Amadeus Mozart

Musical context

Composer

The work of Wolfgang Amadeus Mozart (1756–1791), together with the music of Haydn and with Beethoven's earlier compositions, represents the flowering of the Classical style.

Mozart's musical gifts were phenomenal. He began composing at a very early age, and produced more than 600 works in his short life. Most important of all are his operas, piano concertos, symphonies and chamber music.

Opera

In the great majority of operas all the text is sung, but some operatic traditions include spoken dialogue.

Mozart's *Die Zauberflöte* (usually referred to in English-speaking countries as *The Magic Flute*) belongs to one such tradition of German comic opera – the Singspiel ('sung play'), but it is a highly sophisticated example of the genre.

Mozart, painted in 1819 (after his death) by Barbara Krafft

In most contemporary operas, including Mozart's own *The Marriage of Figaro*, it was recitative that separated the solo songs (arias) and ensembles, whereas in singspiel it was generally spoken dialogue. The solos and ensembles in singspiel tended to be lighter, and sometimes strophic or folk-like – listen, for example, to Papageno's song 'Der Vogelfänger' (Act 1, No. 2)

The Magic Flute

Composed in 1791, *The Magic Flute* was first staged in September of that year at the Theater auf der Wieden in Vienna. The librettist (writer of the libretto or text), Emanuel Schikaneder, was connected with this theatre, and he himself sang the role of Papageno.

Although *The Magic Flute*, with its German libretto and spoken dialogue, is often referred to as a singspiel, Mozart called it 'eine grosse Oper' ('a grand opera'), or 'Deutsches Oper' ('German opera') to distinguish it from the then dominant Italian operatic tradition. *The Magic Flute* is 'grand' in the sense that the music, although sometimes as light as that of other singspiels, is more substantial and ambitious than usual.

The plot

The plot is a curious and difficult mixture of fairy tale, rituals and ideas derived from freemasonry, and the ideals of the Enlightenment.

The Enlightenment was a European intellectual movement, powerful in the 18th century. It promoted ideas of personal freedom, equality, and the exercise of human reason, as opposed to the traditional and accepted world view supported by the Church and the absolute monarchies. The 18th-century European freemasons shared broadly similar ideas, but its members, who included Mozart, also engaged in various secret ceremonies and initiations, some of which underlie the 'ordeals' in Act 2 of *The Magic Flute*. For further information, see *1791: Mozart's Last Year* (Thames and Hudson, 1988) by H.C. Robbins Landon.

In outline, the hero Tamino (a prince) is accompanied by Papageno (a bird-catcher) on a quest to rescue Pamina, daughter of the Queen of the Night, from the supposedly wicked (but actually good) priest Sarastro. Eventually Tamino and Pamina are united in marriage, after Tamino has undergone ritual ordeals, and the (actually wicked) Queen of the Night and her accomplices are defeated.

There is no need to remember the whole plot. Concentrate on what happens in the set work.

In the dialogue preceding No. 4, the Queen's three ladies-in-waiting show Tamino a picture of the Queen's daughter, the beautiful Pamina. They hint that he must be bold if he wishes to win her, as she is imprisoned by an evil tyrant.

In No. 4: 'O zittre nicht' (a recitative – even though this is a singspiel – and aria):

- The Queen, apparently grief-stricken, addresses Tamino, explaining that a villain ('ein Bösewicht') has captured the terrified Pamina
- Tamino is told that he must rescue Pamina. If he is successful, Pamina will be his for ever.

In No. 5: 'Hm! hm! hm!' (a light ensemble much more characteristic of a singspiel than no. 4):

- Tamino is unable to free Papageno from a padlock that the Three Ladies had earlier placed on his mouth as a penalty for lying

- The Three Ladies appear, at the Queen's command, to release Papageno
- The First Lady then gives Tamino a magic flute whose sound will guard him from harm and transform sorrow to joy
- The Three Ladies tell Papageno that he must accompany Tamino on his mission. They give him a casket containing silver bells to protect him
- Tamino and Papageno ask the Ladies how to find the way to Pamina's place of imprisonment. The Ladies reply that three boys will guide them on their journey.

Musical elements

Structure and tonality

No. 4: 'O zittre nicht'

'O zittre nicht' (sung by the Queen of the Night, a soprano) consists, as we have seen, of a recitative and an aria.

> Mozart avoids the type of **secco recitative** used so widely in, for example, *The Marriage of Figaro* (with accompaniment for cello and keyboard).

The recitative has orchestral accompaniment. It is made up of:

- A 10-bar orchestral introduction, in B♭ major
- A balancing 10-bar section with voice, which moves from B♭ (via F major) to G minor (see box below):
  - The accompaniment twice refers back to the style of the introduction
  - Elsewhere detached chords support the voice
  - The vocal ending G–D (tonic to dominant), followed by a V–I cadence, is the typical conclusion of a recitative.

> Recitatives, unlike other types of piece, often begin in one key and end in another. The aria in No. 4 is unusual in beginning in G minor and ending in B♭ major.

The aria is in two main parts, in different tempi. Arias with this type of structure were fairly common in the late 18th century, particularly as showpieces. The Queen of the Night's aria is certainly a showpiece, of a type sometimes termed *aria di bravura*, in which the singer had to show considerable bravery, courage and spirit!

> The Queen has another aria in Act 2, with an even more striking vocal display – 'Die hölle Rache'.

Part 1: Larghetto

This part is in $\frac{3}{4}$ time. It is chiefly in G minor, and has a binary structure.

Bar	Key(s)	Comment
21	G minor–B♭ major	'A' section, with change of key and character, as the subject changes from the Queen's sorrow and loss to more vigorous representation of the evil one who captured Pamina
36	moves into C minor, ending on G minor chord V	'B' section – tense music as the Queen refers to Pamina's distress
44	G minor	Continuation of 'B' section, with, at bars 45–46, a repetition of bars 28–29 to provide additional unity

Part 2: Allegro moderato

This part has the time signature **C** and goes straight into B♭ major at 61^3–64^1 with V–I , V–I. It is in two sections, but without the characteristic key scheme of a binary structure.

Bar	Key(s)	Comment
61	B♭	First section: The Queen assigns the task of rescuing Pamina to Tamino in bold, confident-sounding music
74	B♭, apart from brief suggestions of E♭ in 80–83	Second section: The Queen asserts Tamino's right to Pamina if he returns victorious

No. 5: Hm! hm! hm!

No. 5 is an ensemble – which in operatic terms means a piece for more than two soloists (with or without chorus). It enables the drama to advance through the interaction of different characters.

The five singers are, in order of appearance: Papageno, Tamino, and the Three Ladies (who mostly sing together, although there are separate parts for the First and Second Ladies).

There is no overall form (such as binary or ternary). Instead, the piece is through-composed with five main sections – but unified by beginning and ending in B♭ major.

Section	Bar	Key(s)	Comment
1: Allegro	1	B♭ major	*Papageno and Tamino. Papageno's mouth is still padlocked (he can sing only 'Hm! hm! hm!').* ■ At first Tamino and Papageno sing alternate four-bar phrases, before: 　■ Bar 19: briefer exchanges 　■ Bar 28: singing their separate ideas and texts together (if 'Hm!' counts as text!). Further, see first box on facing page) ■ Papageno's first four-bar phrase returns at 27, and is extended by a partial repetition (see second box on facing page)
2	33	F	*All. The First Lady frees Papageno, then all sing in praise of brotherhood on earth.* ■ Dialogue between Papageno and one or all Ladies, much of it based on 34–38 ■ From 54 all voices are in homophony or unison to signify universal agreement
3	77	chiefly B♭ (briefly in F at 96–101)	*All. Tamino receives the magic flute.* ■ Brief solo for First Lady as she presents Tamino with the flute, then all Ladies together ■ Then all join in praise of the flute's powers – brief antiphony, but mostly homophony to emphasise agreement. Bars 121–123 recall 74–77 from section 2
4	132	G minor, D minor (142), G minor (164), E♭ (172). Chiefly B♭ from 179	*All (but chiefly Papageno and the Three Ladies). Papageno must accompany Tamino: he is given the magic bells. At the end the Ladies bid farewell, but Tamino and Papageno delay with a question – where do they go next?* ■ Chiefly dialogue between Papageno and the Three Ladies 　■ much is based on the phrase first heard at 141–143 　■ note also the 5-note triadic accompaniment figure first heard at 143 (perhaps representing the bells) ■ At 184 all sing in praise of the bells and the magic flute, before bidding farewell ■ At 203 Tamino and Papageno begin in dialogue (similar phrases), before singing together with increasing urgency, even impatience (the rapidly alternating chords are not, in spite of all the E♮s, V–I in F major, but V⁷-of-V (a secondary dominant) and V in B♭

| 5: Tempo changes to Andante | 214 | B♭ | *All. Largely dialogue between the Three Ladies on the one hand and Tamino and Papageno on the other. Tamino and Papageno learn that three Boys will direct their journey.* |

■ The Three Ladies' homophonic phrase beginning in bar 217 is repeated (in a different octave, and adapted for two parts rather than three) by Tamino and Papageno. The rest of the section is based on 217–225, with, from 237, extension and development of 224–225

In other operatic ensembles (as in parts of the two final ensembles of *The Magic Flute*) Mozart sets different texts simultaneously more widely than in 'Hm! hm! hm!', in the interests of lively interaction. Generally in No. 5 he emphasises *agreement*, not confrontation or development of character.

N.B. Use of two texts together in Movement 2 of Bach's Cantata 'Ein feste Burg ist unser Gott' is quite different in effect from simultaneous text in opera.

Mozart frequently ends a section by repeating a phrase in a modified or extended form (to supply weight and finality). See also, for example, bars 61–69 and 69–77.

Organisation of pitch: melody

In No. 5, vocal melodic lines are simple and mostly diatonic, with fairly limited ranges and stepwise movement, repeated notes or small leaps. However, see Papageno's mock-solemn chromatic passage (rising in semitones) in bars 158–159, when he pretends to be afraid of Tamino, and the touching descending chromatic passing notes (expressing 'Farewell, until...') in bars 242 and 244. There is mostly periodic phrasing (balanced phrases in multiples of two or four bars).

Papageno is the chief centre of interest in this comic ensemble, and the melodic simplicity of his part suits his character as a humble bird-catcher. The other characters, even the princely Tamino, broadly match Papageno's style.

Often the singer's part is doubled by the orchestra (see the music example on page 93). At the start, Papageno's melody is doubled by the bassoons – whereas Tamino's part (for a stronger singer, no doubt) is left undoubled.

In No. 4, the Queen of the Night's part is *much* more adventurous in range and in general melodic style and rhythmic diversity (despite a relatively gentle start to the aria).

In particular, notice:

■ A greater number of leaps, including a few wide or 'difficult' ones – notably the plunge down an 11th from top F to the cadential long C (with trill) in bars 92–93, and the rising diminished 5th on 'Ach helft!' (Oh help!) in bars 46–47

- A striking descending chromatic passage (bars 41–43) when the Queen refers to Pamina's terror, and inability to resist, when abducted
- The 'sighing' cadence at bar 27 (the G can be heard as part of chord Ic, but is really more of an appoggiatura over chord V)
- The triadic shape at bars 64–65 (assertive, and a clear confirmation of the change of key to B♭ major
- The repeated-note accompaniment at bar 68 – providing rhythmic motion and reinforcing the harmony without taking attention away from the vocal melody.

Organisation of pitch: harmony

Harmony is functional, with much emphasis on chords I and V$^{(7)}$ and their inversions, frequent perfect cadences (V$^{(7)}$–I) and some imperfect cadences (ending V).

There is, for example, the conventional end-of-recitative perfect cadence in No. 4 (bars 20–21). An 'inverted' (see box below) imperfect cadence is heard soon afterwards (bar 24), with G minor chords IV–Vb (not V); this is followed by an ordinary uninverted imperfect cadence at bars 26–27 with chords II–Ic–V.

> **INVERTED IMPERFECT CADENCES** are so called because the final chord (V) is in (first) inversion.

Interrupted cadences are exceptional. At bars 55–56 in No. 4, Mozart could have written a perfect cadence in G minor and ended the Largo section at that point. The V^7–VI interrupted cadence actually used is a delaying tactic: the section *must* be extended to provide greater weight and finality and to end 'properly' with a perfect cadence (at bars 60–61). See the music example opposite.

Compare the use of more than one cadence at the end of the aria. At bars 93–94 there is a strong perfect cadence, complete with a conventional long cadential trill on the supertonic (C). But after so much momentum, the weighty progression of bars 94–98 is needed as well – and then there is much more exposure to chords V and I in the instrumental postlude. (How many V–I progressions are there altogether in these bars? How many of these are actually *cadences*?)

Other harmonic highlights include:

- The Neapolitan 6th chord in bar 19 of No. 4 (♭IIb in G minor), underlining the word 'tiefbetrübte' (= 'deeply troubled').
- The following diminished 7th chord (bar 20^1) – one of a considerable number of diminished 7th chords in the piece where special harmonic tension is required (often because of strongly emotive text).

> Note the Queen's descending diminished 7th melodic interval (E♭ to F♯) at bar 201, reinforcing the effect of the diminished 7th *chord*.

Finally, look at the following music example, which is annotated to show various aspects of harmony and dissonance treatment. Suspensions and especially appoggiaturas are vital in achieving the necessary harmonic tension.

There is no need to memorise everything that is annotated. But do try to develop your own ability to identify different types of chords and dissonances.

Sonority

Nos. 4 and 5 feature only some of the cast (e.g. there is nothing for Pamina or the chorus).

The Queen of the Night's part has to be sung by a soprano with an astonishing upper range, which is revealed very gradually. The Queen sings only up to F (an 11th above middle C) in the recitative, then up to A♭ in the Largo, and to B♭ early in the Allegro moderato. In the coloratura section (with extended melismatic display), after reaching these notes several times in bars 80–84, she goes higher still (with several top Cs and Ds) before reaching a single top F (almost an octave above normal choral range) in bar 92.

At the first performance, the Queen of the Night was played by Josepha Hofer, one of Mozart's sisters-in-law, who is known to have had a very high (but apparently not very attractive) voice.

Tamino is the hero of the opera, and according to convention his role was for a tenor. Papageno (baritone) was sung at first performance by the librettist Emanuel Schikaneder, whose vocal talents were probably comparatively modest, but whose theatrical skills would have brought the role alive.

No. 4 is scored for two oboes, two bassoons, two horns in B♭, and strings (first and second violins, violas, cellos and double basses). Flutes, clarinets, trumpets, trombones and timpani are all silent.

> It may well have been expected that a harpsichordist or pianist would provide a continuo-style accompaniment in No. 4, but no figuring appears to exist.

The scoring for No. 5 is as for No. 4, until the Andante, at which point the clarinets enter. Despite the giving of the magic flute to Tamino, the flutes do not play in No. 5. There is no glockenspiel to represent the bells (although this instrument is optional in the trio for Pamina, Papageno and Monostatos in Act 2).

Texture

The texture is homophonic, usually being 'melody-dominated', with a melody standing apart from a more or less unified accompaniment, as at the end of the Largo in No. 4. Occasionally the texture can be described as homorhythmic, with all parts, including the vocal part, sharing the same rhythm (e.g. at the beginning of the Larghetto in No. 4, presumably for simplicity and clarity).

In ensemble passages all singers often have the same rhythm against an independent orchestral part. This unanimity underlines the singers' agreement and aids clear projection of text: see for example 'O so eine Flöte ist mehr als Gold' (No. 5, bars 111–115).

Occasionally there is monophonic writing, as in the linking passages that begin at bars 64, 72 and 103 of No. 5. Such passages contribute to the lightness and elegance of the orchestral writing, whereas octave passages (e.g. at bars 77 and 105) are more assertive.

Contrapuntal textures are almost entirely avoided as unsuitable for the light, comic nature of most of the music (see box opposite). An exceptional passage comes in the Larghetto of No. 4 (from bar 36; part of this is shown in the music example below). There is a chromatic countermelody in violas and bassoons under the Queen's tortured solo line. First violins double the vocal melody but always with groups of semiquavers beginning off the beat to provide additional movement in this slowish tempo – a form of heterophony.

Mozart was prepared to write contrapuntally when appropriate, as in parts of his Symphony No. 41 and his Requiem.

Dynamics

By Mozart's time, dynamics were commonly added to musical scores.

In Nos. 4 and 5 most markings are *f* or *p* or *cresc.* We find also *fp* (*forte piano*, loud followed immediately by soft – effectively a type of accent) and *sf* (*sforzando*) accents. 'Extreme' dynamics such as *ff* and *pp* are not indicated, and *mf* is exceptional.

As now, *f* and *p* were not absolute indications of volume, and probably changes from one to the other did not always involve strong contrasts. Dynamic changes were sometimes reinforced by additions or reductions in orchestral forces.

Dynamics are used regularly in the orchestral parts, but very rarely in the vocal parts. Singers were on stage and were no doubt considered capable of choosing appropriate dynamics in response to the text and in accordance with what they heard from the orchestra.

Nevertheless, there are dynamics in some ensemble passages. At 184 of No. 5 the marking *sotto voce* (literally 'under the voice') is used – presumably as a kind of equivalent of *pp*, to indicate an almost whispered delivery.

Tempo, metre and rhythm

No. 4 begins with a short orchestral introduction marked 'Allegro maestoso', the word 'maestoso' indicating a majestic or stately manner appropriate for the Queen's first appearance. The recitative is marked in German ('Rezitativ'), to indicate a free tempo set by the singer.

The aria has slower and faster sections ('Larghetto' and 'Allegro moderato') as explained above.

No. 5 is quick ('Allegro'), as suits the comic nature of the text, until the change to the slower 'Andante' near the end. The more relaxed tempo at that point establishes a slightly calmer atmosphere at the reference to the three Boys who will be 'hovering' over Tamino and Papageno.

In No. 4, the simple triple metre ($\frac{3}{4}$) of the Larghetto contrasts effectively with the other sections in simple quadruple (**C** – equivalent to $\frac{4}{4}$).

> There was really no choice of time signature at 'O zittre nicht', as simple
> quadruple metre was the rule for recitatives.

In No. 5, the key signature is 𝄵 – 'cut common', with two minim beats per bar: a minim beat is much more convenient than a crotchet beat in the faster tempo here. The slower concluding section (Andante) reverts to 𝄴 and a crotchet beat.

Features of rhythmic interest in No. 4 include:

- Offbeat quavers in the upper parts of the orchestral introduction – against the onbeat crotchets of the bass. In the Classical period this was a common way of adding tension (the Queen's arrival at this point in the opera was dramatic and had been heralded by thunder and the sound of rocks splitting apart)
- Considerable diversity of rhythms and note values in the aria:
  - The long tied note in bars 34–35 emphasises the first syllable of 'Bösewicht' ('scoundrel') – it lasts for almost four beats in a slowish tempo (Larghetto)
  - Minims in bars 47 and 48 (again in the Larghetto) make the Queen's cries of 'helft!' ('help!') dramatic
  - The solid minims at the end of the Queen's part (in an Allegro tempo) give a really firm ending, especially after...
  - ... the astonishing vocal display in bars 79–94 with its semiquaver melismas.

The note values and rhythms in No. 5 are less diverse, but note:

- The syncopations in the First Lady's part in bars 188 and 189
- The alternating notes and rests in the Andante (bars 217–221) – an effect somewhat similar to staccato, and useful for clearly articulating text *sotto voce*.

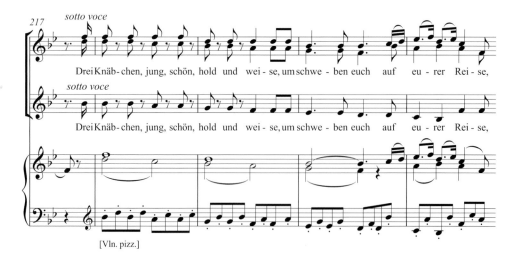

> The Anthology includes a 'vocal score' in which all the voice parts are shown,
> but only a reduction of the orchestral parts suitable for playing on the piano.
> (A 'full score' would include all the orchestral parts.)

Set work:
On Wenlock Edge, Nos. 1, 3 and 5: 'On Wenlock Edge', 'Is My Team Ploughing?' and 'Bredon Hill')

Ralph Vaughan Williams

A LEVEL

Musical context

Composer

Ralph Vaughan Williams (1872–1958) was one of the leading British composers of his time. His work included nine symphonies, several concertos, major choral works and solo songs.

By the time that Vaughan Williams composed *On Wenlock Edge* in 1909, some European composers – notably Arnold Schoenberg (1874–1951) – were abandoning the system of major–minor tonality used by their 18th- and 19th-century predecessors. Vaughan Williams did not do this, but neither did he limit himself to traditional tonality. He was influenced by music from outside the dominant Germanic tradition – notably traditional English folk music, the music of Tudor England, of Debussy, and of Ravel (who was briefly his teacher).

***On Wenlock Edge* shows such influences, including:**

- Some vocal melodies that resemble folk song
- Use of modes (ancestors of major and minor scales)

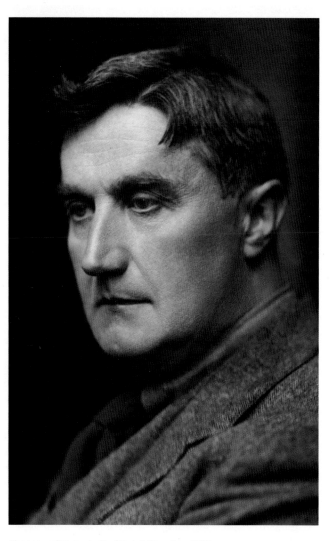

Photographic portrait of Ralph Vaughan Williams, taken by E. O. Hoppé in 1921

- False relations
- Parallel movement between parts, sometimes involving perfect 5ths, of the kind banned in (for example) Bach chorale harmonisation.

On Wenlock Edge: the poems

On Wenlock Edge consists of six poems from *A Shropshire Lad* by A. E. Housman (1859–1936).

> The work is a 'song-cycle' – a collection of songs in the Western Classical tradition that share similar subject matter, or all have texts by the same poet. There is a list of all six songs in the Anthology

'On Wenlock Edge'

> Wenlock Edge is a limestone escarpment in the Shropshire Hills Area of Outstanding Natural Beauty, covered with an ancient deciduous woodland.

The poet imagines gales lashing the young trees on Wenlock Edge, and realises that the same storms were experienced in Roman times. Likewise, people then must have faced the same struggles (the 'gale[s] of life') as in his own time. However, just as the storm is brief, so modern sufferings will soon be over, as now those of the Romans are.

'Is My Team Ploughing?'

This poem is a dialogue between the ghost of a young man and a friend who is still alive.

At first the dead man receives reassurance. But when he asks if his girlfriend is happy, he is told that she no longer grieves, but is 'well contented'. He then enquires after his friend, and the answer – although enigmatic – is devastating.

'Bredon Hill'

'Bredon Hill' tells of young love defeated by death.

> Bredon Hill is near Tewkesbury on the Worcestershire–Gloucestershire border, not in Shropshire as the title 'A Shropshire Lad' might imply.

On summer Sunday mornings, a young man and his girlfriend would lie on Bredon Hill, listening to the bells calling people to church. The girl in particular would ignore the call, but the young man promised that they would obey the bells' summons on their wedding day.

At Christmas, however, the girl 'went to church alone' – she had died – and just one bell tolled. In the final stanza the young man hears the bells as in happier days. He replies that he 'will come' – but, although this is not explicit, it will be to his own funeral.

Musical elements

Sonority

On Wenlock Edge was composed for tenor, string quartet and piano.

There is considerable variety in the use of these forces. For example, 'Is My Team Ploughing?' begins with the three highest string parts (see box below), while for maximum contrast, the setting of stanza 2 is for piano and cello. In 'Bredon Hill', stanzas 3 and 4 are for piano only, while stanza 5 focuses largely on the strings.

> The small notes in the piano part at the beginning of 'Is My Team Ploughing?' are played only in an alternative version of the work for tenor and piano without strings.

The piano part

The piano part is not easy, but neither is it virtuosic or showy in the manner, for example, of a piano concerto.

Special effects include:

- Quiet demisemiquaver flourishes (with ***ppp*** echoes) in bars 31–32 and 43–44 of 'On Wenlock Edge', followed by extended trills
- Tremolos from bar 67
- Full textures in 'Bredon Hill', including:
  - Bars 20–23 – large (but extremely quiet) chords (with hands widely separated) together with chains of parallel 4ths, all sustained (and blurred) by pedal
  - Bars 100–113 (Largamente) – the right hand plays a melody doubled at the 4th and octave above, while the left hand plays low block chords and higher octaves alternately. From bar 105 there is an octave legato melody in the bass, which involves more leaps for the left hand.

The string quartet

Important features in 'On Wenlock Edge' include:

- Tremolo, with
  - Rapid repetition of notes to represent storm and turbulence (e.g. bars 1–3)
  - Alternation between two notes a 3rd or more apart (e.g. bars 57–64)
- Long trills, which intensify the atmosphere created by the tremolos

- *Sul ponticello*, with the player bowing very near to the bridge in order to create a thin, rather strained tone:
  - Usually quietly, as in bars 57–61
  - But momentarily in bar 57 loudly with a much more aggressive effect (to represent the force of the gale).

The indication '*Naturale*' in bar 62 cancels '*sul ponticello*'.

'Is My Team Ploughing?' involves muted strings (*con sord*[*ino*]) for much of the time, to enhance the mysterious, distant effect of the music that sets the dead man's words.

A **MUTE** is a small device placed on the instrument's bridge to dampen the vibrations and give a less resonant sound. At bar 37, where dynamics are mostly loud, the mutes are removed ('*senza sord*[*ino*]' means 'without mute').

'Bredon Hill' features:

- *Con sord.* until bar 115, the muted effect helping to suggest distance – both in time and geography (some of the bells are in far-off steeples) – and the hazy atmosphere of summertime
- Double stopping (as in bars 1–34), which, together with *con sord.* and constant use of 7th, 9th and 11th chords, has a broadly similar effect
- *Sul D* in violin I and viola and *sul G* in violin II and cello (bar 115) – meaning 'play on the D [or G] string' instead of on the string that the player might normally use. These directions create a richer and more powerful effect, especially during the *molto cresc.* (bars 121–122) that leads up to the climactic line 'Come all to church, good people'
- Natural harmonics on open strings (bars 144–145), with the symbol ° above each note. The player touches the string lightly to produce a thin 'ghostly' sound at the notated pitch.

Dynamics

Dynamics are varied, to reflect the changing character of each text.

In 'On Wenlock Edge' the gale and the wood's 'trouble' are matched by the opening *f*, while the frequent use of *crescendo* and *diminuendo* mark variations in the gale's speed and ferocity.

Extremely quiet dynamics are common in the other two songs (even down to ***pppp*** in 'Bredon Hill', bar 20), although there are loud outbursts. Quietness can suggest remoteness (the ghost in 'Is My Team Ploughing?' and the far-off steeples in 'Bredon Hill') or death (notably in 'Bredon Hill' for the setting of stanza 5).

Texture

Textures are homophonic, but with considerable variety. For example:

- In bars 6–10 of 'On Wenlock Edge', cello and piano (left hand) double the voice, an octave lower, while the piano right hand maintains continuous broken-chord semiquaver sextuplets. There are long trills in inner string parts, and occasional ornamental details in violin I

- In stanzas 1 and 3 of 'Is My Team Ploughing?' a single chord sustained by the upper strings provides the simplest possible harmonic background for the voice (and yet is so effective and atmospheric)

- For stanzas 2 and 4 the piano has repeated-note triplet chords almost throughout (to reinforce the animated and agitated character of the vocal part). The cello has a countermelody, although this mostly doubles the bass or the piano's right-hand melody

- In stanza 2 of 'Bredon Hill' the voice is accompanied by dense parallel semibreve and minim chords in the piano, together with more sparse parallel chords in the strings.

The beginning and ending of 'Is My Team Ploughing?' are homorhythmic (all parts have the same rhythm): simple, but most effective.

Structure

The structure of each song is a blending of strophic and through-composed, as suggested by the development of the text.

A **STROPHIC** song has the same music for every stanza. A **THROUGH-COMPOSED** song has little or no repetition

'On Wenlock Edge'

Bars	Text, etc.	Comment
1–6	Introduction	Descending parallel $^6_3$ (first-inversion) chords, with chromaticism and false relations (theme **a**)
6–16	Stanza 1: 'On Wenlock Edge…'	Vocal melody **b** is mostly pentatonic, but chromatic from bar 14
16–21	Interlude	Almost exactly the same as bars 1–6
21–31	Stanza 2: ''Twould blow like this…'	Similar to bars 6–16, but with some changes in the tenor part to suit the new words
31–33	Interlude	Flourishes in piano against long trills in strings
34–43	Stanza 3: 'Then, 'twas before my time'	New chromatic motif **c** (strings, bars 35–36). Then (at bar 39) descending parallel $^6_3$ chords in piano (different from those in the Introduction)
43–44	Interlude	= bars 31–33
45–55	Stanza 4: 'There, like the wind through woods in riot'	Similar to music for stanza 3, but partly a semitone higher (e.g. see bars 39 and 50)

55–57	Interlude	Based on the Introduction
58–68	Stanza 5: 'The gale, it plies the saplings double'	Largely new vocal line. Piano, left hand from 62, develops bars 6 to 10 of **b**, then compare bars 65–66 with 11–12
69–77	Postlude	**c** is combined with the opening rising 4th of **b**

'Is My Team Ploughing?'

1–4	Introduction	Theme **d** – modal, with violin I circling around A (see music example, page 105)
5–9	Stanza 1: 'Is my team ploughing'	Bars 5–6 developed from bar 2 of **d**
9–19	Stanza 2: 'Ay, the horses trample'	Themes **e** (cello, descending chromatically) and **f** (tenor)
19–22	Interlude	= bars 1–4, plus G in cello
23–27	Stanza 3: 'Is my girl happy'	= Music for stanza 1, but with new text
27–37	Stanza 4: 'Ay, she lies down lightly'	Music begins as for stanza 2, but high notes on 'No change' are avoided in favour of a gentler tone at 'your girl' (bar 33)
37–38	Interlude	A shorter, more agitated version of the introduction (also an octave higher, with tremolo, *f* dynamic and pizzicato cello)
39–44	Stanza 5: 'Is my friend hearty'	The dead man, clearly agitated, refuses to 'be still … and sleep.' The melody begins a 4th higher than for stanzas 1 and 3 – it is *f*, but *misterioso*
45–55	Stanza 6: 'Yes, lad … I lie easy'	Partly modelled on bars 9–19 (stanza 2), with **d** reappearing before the final devastating line
55–62	Postlude	**d** descends through four different octaves, ending *tranquillo*, an octave lower than in the Introduction

Stanzas 3–6 of 'Is My Team Ploughing?' are *stanzas 5–8* of the poem. Vaughan Williams avoided Housman's rather lame stanzas about football.

'Bredon Hill'

1–24	Introduction	Very quiet, with many superimposed 7th chords
24–35	Stanza 1: 'In summertime'	Theme **g** – a simple folksong-like melody 'to be sung freely' over an almost static chordal accompaniment
35–38	Interlude	Similar texturally to bars 5–8, but harmonically different
39–48	Stanza 2: 'Here of a Sunday morning'	Tenor part largely as in bars 24–35. Accompaniment a little more active
48–51	Interlude	= 5–8 from Introduction
52–66	Stanza 3: 'The bells would ring to call her'	A big contrast in texture, rhythm, sonority and tempo. Unity is maintained because the melody shares with **g** an initial repeated note and the stepwise rise through a 3rd
66–83	Stanza 4, with postlude: 'But here my love would stay'	Vocal part quieter and lower than in stanza 3, but broadly similar in style. The postlude is similar to the end of the Introduction
84–100	Stanza 5: 'But when the snows', preceded by the start of the new accompaniment pattern	The atmosphere darkens. The melody circles round G (tonic of G minor), and then, rather chillingly, around B♭ (tonic of B♭ minor). Slow chords in the accompaniment, separated by rests
100–114	Stanza 6: 'They tolled the one bell only'	Repeated Gs recall the 'one bell'. The melody is similar in character to that of stanza 5
114–135	Stanza 7: 'The bells they sound on Bredon'	The atmosphere of the early part of the song is recalled when the opening vocal phrases from stanzas 1 and 2 reappear. A loud and hectic passage accompanies the bells' grim summons, then the music becomes gradually calmer
136–146	Postlude, and repetition of 'I will come'	Compare Introduction, bars 8–14. The unaccompanied 'I will come' (all on G) is stunning in its simplicity

Tonality

'On Wenlock Edge'

The key signature (in conjunction with the first notes in the piano, left hand) indicates G minor.

G is clearly the key note in bars 3^3–10, where all pitches belong to the five-note (pentatonic) set G–A–C–D–F. There is some major–minor ambiguity because neither the B♭ of G minor nor the B♮ of G major is present – but we are likely to hear G minor in the light of the earlier B♭s. Also, the F♮s probably suggest G minor rather than (a modal) G major.

Until bar 14^2, the voice continues with the G–A–C–D–F pentatonic set. However, from bar 11 cello and piano have A♭s and are actually in A♭ major. The bitonal effect (with two keys simultaneously) intensifies the sense of stress and conflict.

A public path on Bredon Hill, Worcestershire

The A♭s return for stanza 2 (bar 26) and lead to further flatward moves (notably D♭s from bar 31). They are quite persistent, even being reinforced near the end by the enharmonic equivalent G♯.

At the end of the song, G minor is firmly – and traditionally – established by repeated octave D–G (V–I) movements in the bass.

'Is My Team Ploughing?'

The introduction and the music for stanzas 1 and 3 can be described as *either* in the Dorian mode *or* in D minor (see the key signature) with Dorian 'inflections' (B♮s and C♮s regularly replacing B♭s and C♯s).

Opening of 'Is My Team Ploughing?', showing violin 1, violin 2 and viola parts in short score

The Dorian mode (whose scale is D–D without any flats or sharps) is common in British folk music. The influence of such music on Vaughan Williams has already been noted.

The settings of stanzas 2 and 4 are *not* modal – to help differentiate the friend's replies from the dead man's questions. Initially the tonality in these stanzas is D minor with the bass descending chromatically, but later it is less clear, not least because of the insistence on the note A♭, a disruptive tritone away from the tonic.

The Dorian-mode music is re-used for the interlude before stanza 5. Later, the note A♭ is emphasised as part of a brief excursion to the 'distant' key of F minor.

The tonality at the end of stanza 6 suggests a blurred and inconclusive E major (with G♯ enharmonically equivalent to the previous A♭).

'On Bredon Hill'

The tonality of 'On Bredon Hill' is blurred throughout. Vaughan Williams superimposes different 7th chords, or sets up deliberate conflicts involving dissonant A♭s (as at bar 85).

In all three songs, A♭s are used to increase harmonic tension.

We can speak of G as a 'tonal centre' because:

- It is rarely absent and so much gravitates around it
- The melody used for stanzas 1 and 2 is clearly 'in G', as indicated by:
  - The pentatonic set G–A–B–D–E
  - The F♮ from the Mixolydian mode on G (or as a Mixolydian inflection within G major)
  - In bars 33–34, the B♭ and F♮ from the Aeolian mode on G (or from G minor with an unraised 7th degree).

> Minor tonality, an unexpected response to 'A *happy* noise to hear', perhaps hints at future *un*happiness.

However, some passages (notably, much of bars 1–51) seem closer to E minor, or to a much blurred A minor, because of the strong emphasis on E minor and A minor 7th chords.

Organisation of pitch: melody

The tenor's range is a 12th, from the D below middle C up to A. The highest notes are at points of special drama or tension – for example, in 'Bredon Hill' the line 'Oh, noisy bells, be dumb' centres around top G, with top A on 'bells'.

Generally there is one note per syllable, but there are some slurred pairs of notes and a few short melismas for emphasis (as on 'ring' and 'hap-(py)' in bars 29 and 33 of 'Bredon Hill').

As suits the voice, there is much stepwise movement and use of small leaps. Leaps larger than a perfect 5th are reserved for intense moments, as in the *agitato* second stanza of 'Is My Team Ploughing?' with several descending major 6ths, and a rising major 7th (bars 14–15). Naturally, the instrumental parts are freer in their use of large intervals.

Organisation of pitch: harmony

Vaughan Williams chiefly used chords that were common well before the 20th century, but sometimes employed them in quite new ways.

A leading principle of pre-20th-century functional harmony was *contrary motion*, with bass and melody moving in opposite directions. Vaughan Williams is fond of *parallelism*, all parts employing *similar* motion.

> Vaughan Williams's fondness for parallelism was partly the influence of recent French music, particularly Debussy's.

For instance, at the beginning of 'On Wenlock Edge' (see music example on the opposite page) he wrote a number of parallel $\frac{6}{3}$ (first-inversion) chords. In bar 1 (starting from the second triplet quaver), and in the corresponding part of bar 2, each part always moves by a major 2nd (to produce an *exact* parallelism).

In traditional harmony, parallel scalic movement normally involves a mixture of major and minor 2nds according to a given major or minor scale.

Opening of 'On wenlock Edge', showing the piano part, which is doubled by the strings

Exact parallelism generally involves false relations (e.g. the D♭ and D♮ in bar 3). The C and C♭ (bars 1 and 2) still produce a false-relation effect even though there is a chord in between.

False relations were common in some Tudor music, which Vaughan Williams admired, but these did not result from parallelism.

Other points of harmonic interest, not all involving parallelism include:

- Three parallel minor $\frac{5}{3}$ (root position) triads that effect the shift from Dorian D minor to F minor in bars 40–41 of 'Is My Team Ploughing?' (with deliberate consecutive 5ths)
- Superimposed minor 7th chords in 'Bredon Hill' (initially Em[7] and Am[7]), together with:
  - Parallel $\frac{6}{4}$ (second-inversion) triads, some major, some minor, in the strings (bars 10–14)
  - Parallel 4ths in the piano (from bar 16)
- More straightforward quartal harmony in bars 3–10 of 'On Wenlock Edge' (piano part, with the pentatonic set G–A–C–D–F).

> **QUARTAL HARMONY** is based largely on 4ths (unlike traditional harmony, with its 3rds-based triads and 7th chords).

In 'Bredon Hill' (bars 52–77):

- Parallel 8ves divided into 5th + 4th or 4th + 5th in piano, right hand initially (from the pentatonic set B♭–C–D–F–G) – representing bells – over 7th chords and triads with at least some conflicting pitch(es)
- From bar 64 a mixture of 6ths, 5ths and 4ths (using the set D–E–F♯–A–B)
- Other parallelisms (including successions of perfect 4ths and 5ths).

The above harmonic features are characteristic of the early 20th century, and in many cases of Vaughan Williams in particular. However, in 'Is My Team Ploughing?' the composer reverts to a relatively old-fashioned style of chromatic harmony when the friend is singing. Note the chromatically descending bass, the half-diminished 7th chords (e.g. bars 11[1-3] and 12), and the French augmented 6th chord (bar 15[2-4]).

Tempo, metre and rhythm

In all three songs, the rhythm of the tenor part is always in keeping with the stress patterns of the text.

Other points concerning tempo, metre and rhythm include the following.

'On Wenlock Edge'

'On Wenlock Edge' is marked 'Allegro moderato', which is surprising for a 'stormy' piece, but tremolos, trills and other short notes help to provide plenty of rhythmic activity.

This song is in simple quadruple metre ($\frac{4}{4}$) throughout, but the introduction has so many triplet quavers and sextuplet semiquavers that the music could almost be heard as compound quadruple ($\frac{12}{8}$) rather than as $\frac{4}{4}$. The 'real' metre is clarified when the voice (doubled an octave lower by cello) enters. Listen also for the 'ordinary' semiquavers in violin I.

Syncopation in the piece chiefly involves the motif heard first in the strings in bar 35, and trills that begin on weak beats (e.g. violin I, bar 3).

'Is My Team Ploughing?'

Changes of tempo are made in response to the shape of the text. For example, the dead man's first two questions are slower ('Andante sostenuto ma non troppo lento') than the replies of the living friend ('Poco animato', after a transitional 'animando'). Later, there are several changes, with a sense of resolution at the final 'Tempo I tranquillo'.

Changes of metre are also part of Vaughan Williams's detailed response to the text. For example, bar 8 (in $\frac{3}{4}$) would have been too drawn out if it were 'stretched' to $\frac{4}{4}$ (the prevailing metre), and too abrupt if it had been 'squeezed' down to $\frac{2}{4}$. The 'short' $\frac{2}{4}$ bars just before stanzas 2 and 4 perhaps suggest the friend's eagerness or impatience, and his final response is mostly in $\frac{3}{2}$, again with a sense of urgency.

The opening of this song shows a rhythmic flexibility characteristic of much of Vaughan Williams's music, with its mixture of dotted rhythms, triplet quavers (the first of each group tied to a crotchet), ordinary quavers, and offbeat crotchets (e.g. bar 4).

Concerning the repeated-note triplet quavers in stanzas 2 and 4, see 'Texture'.

'Bredon Hill'

Here again changes of tempo reflect changing situations in the text.

The song is in simple duple time with minim beats ($\frac{2}{2}$) until bar 84 (apart from the $\frac{3}{2}$ bar at 71 for the sake of the word-setting). The change to $\frac{4}{4}$ for bars 84–114 reflects the slower tempo, where a minim beat would be impractical. There is a return to $\frac{4}{4}$ at bar 123, in preparation for the 'Più lento' (bar 127).

Features of rhythmic interest include:

- Increased activity in the Introduction – from heavy semibreves, through movement in minims and crotchets and a triplet crotchet group to quavers (in the piano)
- Continuous triplet crotchets in the piano (representing bells) in the settings of stanzas 3 and 4 – these lead smoothly into the (slightly more rapid) quavers in the piano

- Syncopation in the accompaniment to stanza 6 (from bar 100) – the dotted minim chords and crotchet octaves that represent the bells fall on the second and fourth beats of the bar

- Bar 127–132, where the voice part is 'sung quite freely – irrespective of the accompaniment' while the (ostinato-based) accompaniment is 'in strict time regardless of the voice part' – to suggest the clangour of the bells and their reverberation

- What might be termed the 'notated rallentando' in bars 134–5 – while the beat remains unchanging, semiquavers give way to triplet quavers, then to quavers and finally to triplet crotchets, all of which leads on effectively to the minims at the beginning of the postlude.

Musical language

The direction *colla voce* ('with the voice') appears several times (e.g. in 'Is My Team Ploughing?', bar 50). The players must keep with the singer, who must have scope for rhythmic freedom at particularly intense moments.

Test yourself

Below are five short questions on each set work. These are not 'exam questions' but are intended to help you get to know each work better.

Most questions use the command words listed in Appendix 5 of each specification (with which you will need to be familiar when preparing for exams).

For each set work there is also a sample essay question for each level. These correspond to Question 6 in Pearson's Sample Assessment Materials.

Essays at the two levels are marked from different assessment grids, as may again be seen from the Sample Assessment Materials. The allocation of marks is different, with fewer marks at AS implying the need for less information. At A Level there is greater emphasis on saying *how* and *why* particular things happen in the music, and relatively less on just saying *what* happens.

When answering the questions below, you should refer to the printed score of the relevant work or movement.

In your exam you will have a special booklet containing the scores you need. You will not be allowed to take a copy of the anthology or other printed music into the exam room.

Cantata 'Ein feste Burg ist unser Gott' BWV 80, Movements 1, 2 and 8 (Bach)

Short questions:

a. Explain the original purpose and intention of Bach's Cantata 'Ein feste Burg ist unser Gott'.

b. Describe how bars 3^3–6^1 of the alto part in Movement 1 differ from bars 1–3^3 of the tenor part.

c. Compare the instrumental parts and the vocal parts in bars 1–30 of Movement 1.

d. Explain how the chorale melody is used in Movement 2.

e. Discuss Bach's setting of words in Movement 2.

Question 6 practice:

AS

Evaluate the use of melody and rhythm in Movement 1 of Bach's Cantata 'Ein feste Burg ist unser Gott'. Relate your discussion to other relevant works. These may include set works, wider listening or other music.

A Level

Evaluate the use of melody, rhythm and structure in Movement 1 of Bach's Cantata 'Ein feste Burg ist unser Gott', with reference to the treatment of the chorale melody. Relate your discussion to other relevant works. These may include set works, wider listening or other music.

The Magic Flute, Act 1 Nos. 4 and 5 (Mozart)

Short questions:

a. Give a definition of *Singspiel*.

b. Compare the recitative and aria sections of No. 4 ('O zittre nicht') in terms of texture and rhythm.

c. Describe the use of dynamics in No. 4.

d. Describe the structure of No. 5 (the quintet), making appropriate reference to tonality.

e. Discuss Mozart's writing for voices in No. 5.

Question 6 practice:

AS

Evaluate Mozart's use of structure and tonality in 'O zittre nicht' (bars 1–103) from *The Magic Flute*. Relate your discussion to other relevant works. These may include set works, wider listening or other music.

A Level

Evaluate structure, tonality and harmony in 'O zittre nicht' (bars 1–103) from Mozart's *The Magic Flute*, to show how these three elements are used to underline the dramatic situation at this point in Act 1. Relate your discussion to other relevant works. These may include set works, wider listening or other music.

On Wenlock Edge: Nos. 1, 3 and 5 (Vaughan Williams)

Short questions:

a. Explain the terms 'Dorian mode' and 'Mixolydian mode'.

b. Explain how Vaughan Williams creates atmosphere in 'On Wenlock Edge'.

c. Compare the vocal writing in 'On Wenlock Edge' and 'Bredon Hill'.

d. Compare the role of the piano in 'Is My Team Ploughing?' and 'Bredon Hill'.

e. Evaluate the effectiveness of Vaughan Williams's setting of the poem 'On Wenlock Edge'.

Question 6 practice:

A Level only

Evaluate the use of melody, rhythm and texture in creating an effective setting of the poem 'Is My Team Ploughing?'. Relate your discussion to other relevant works. These may include set works, wider listening or other music.

Instrumental music

OVERVIEW

The Instrumental Music set works introduce you to three important categories: concerto, symphony and chamber music.

(AS) (A) **Concerto in D minor Op. 3 No. 11, RV 565 (Vivaldi)**

(AS) (A) **Piano Trio in G minor Op. 17, Movement 1 (Clara Schumann)**

(A) ***Symphonie fantastique*, Movement 1 (Berlioz)**

Set work:
Concerto in D minor Op. 3 No. 11, RV 565
Antonio Vivaldi

AS LEVEL

A LEVEL

Musical context

Composer

Antonio Lucio Vivaldi (1678–1741), a major late-Baroque composer, was born in Venice (then an independent city-state). He was particularly important in developing the concerto.

His work was much admired by many at the time, including J. S. Bach. He also composed operas and church music.

The concerto

From the Classical period onwards, a concerto has generally been a three-movement work for a single instrumental soloist (commonly a pianist or violinist) and orchestra. Soloists' parts have generally been technically very challenging, with opportunities for players to 'dazzle' their audiences with showy passages.

In the Baroque period, many concertos featured more than one soloist. A concerto for two violins, cello and strings is usually referred to as a concerto grosso (Italian: 'grand concerto'). In concerti grossi soloists' parts were often more difficult than those of the orchestral players, but not massively so as a rule.

> The various meanings of 'concerto' are summarised in *Baroque Music in Focus* by Hugh Benham (Rhinegold Education, 2010), page 58.

At its simplest, a concerto grosso involved an alternation between the following:

- The soloists on their own (the 'concertino')
- Everyone ('tutti'), the soloists being doubled by the other players (the 'ripieno')...

... with no sections for ripieno only. The ripieno would have been a small group of players rather than an 'orchestra' in the present-day sense (see 'Sonority' below).

Vivaldi was largely content with the above arrangement in Op. 3 No. 11, but he departed from it occasionally and began to demand considerably more of the soloists than his important predecessor Corelli (1653–1713) had done.

Concerto Op. 3 No. 11 in D minor

In Vivaldi's day, composers usually gave an opus number to each published collection of instrumental works. Vivaldi's third opus (or 'Op. 3'), contains 12 concertos and was published in Amsterdam in 1711.

Vivaldi's Op. 3 was entitled *L'estro Armonico*, which means something like 'the harmonic fancy' or 'harmonic inspiration'. The title was probably intended as an eye- or ear-catching phrase to help generate good sales. Certainly the publication was very successful and influential.

In Op. 3 No. 11 the solo group consists of two violins (marked Violino I and Violino II in the Anthology score) and a cello. This was a favourite concerto grosso grouping (although in Op. 3 Vivaldi employs it only twice).

Antonio Vivaldi

Musical elements

Structure and tonality

Vivaldi's concertos often have three movements – quick, slow, quick – a pattern that J. S. Bach generally followed. On the other hand Corelli, in his concerti grossi, had favoured four movements – slow, quick, slow, quick – or sometimes more, as in his Op. 6 No. 8 (the 'Christmas Concerto') in G minor with six. This work has appeared in a previous Edexcel Anthology, and is scored for the same forces as Vivaldi's Op. 3 No 11.

There are differing opinions about the number of movements in this set work.

The Anthology edition sees the work as having four, and we shall adopt this view in these notes.

- Movement 1 (Anth. page 98): Allegro (D minor)
- Movement 2 (Anth. page 99): Adagio e spiccato *and* the following Allegro (D minor)
- Movement 3 (Anth. page 104): Largo e spiccato (D minor)
- Movement 4 (Anth. page 106): Allegro (D minor).

All movements are in the same key. There are, of course, modulations, but these are mainly to minor keys. This may seem like a recipe for monotony, even dreariness, but Vivaldi is brilliant at getting a great deal out of limited tonal and harmonic material, largely through rhythmic vitality and memorable melodic ideas, and this music is full of life.

> Op. 3 No. 11 is not unique among Vivaldi's concertos in having the same key for each movement – see for example Op. 3 No. 2 in G minor. Bach and later composers of concertos preferred some tonal contrast, notably with a middle movement in a different key from the outer movements. See for example Bach's Brandenburg Concerto No. 5 in D, whose second movement is in B minor.

Movement 1

The opening Allegro (entirely in D minor) divides into:

- A canon for the solo violins (unaccompanied): bars 1–20
- A passage for solo cello (with continuo): bars 20–31.

Movement 2

The three-bar Adagio:

- Provides contrast of texture (it is all in block chords) and tempo
- Provides big harmonic contrast (see 'Harmony', below)
- Introduces the sound of the tutti (soloists and ripieno together) for the first time, well before the following Allegro uses the full forces in bar 16.

The Allegro alternates tutti and solo passages (see the table below). In many of Vivaldi's concertos some or all of the music of the opening tutti (known as the 'ritornello') is repeated near the end in the tonic key, and, in between, once or more in a different key or keys (following ritornello form). In our Movement 2 the three tuttis share melodic material, but the second and third are not literal repeats or transpositions of the first. However, it is still useful to employ the word 'ritornello', and to refer to the solo sections as 'episodes'.

Movement 2 is not entitled 'fugue', but begins with a four-part fugal exposition and employs the same melodic material in fugal style so much that the term 'fugue' is often applied.

> It is a measure of Vivaldi's flair that his music does not always fit with conventional structural and textural 'templates'.

Bars	Section	Key(s)	Comment
4–23	Ritornello 1 ■ Tutti (gradual build up from one to four parts at bar 16)	■ Mainly Dm ■ Am at bars 16–20	■ Bars 4–20: four-part fugal exposition with **a** (see music example, opposite) as the main theme (or 'subject') accompanied by **b** and **c** ('countersubjects') first entering in bars 8 and 13 respectively
23–32	Episode 1 ■ Soloists (plus continuo)	■ Dm ■ Am (from 27)	■ Use of part of **a** (in vln I) in bar 23 helps to integrate this solo section and the previous tutti ■ The second part of **a** (crotchets) is embellished – compare bars 5–7 (cello) and 24–27 (vln I) ■ **c** is prominent in bars 24–27
32–48	Ritornello 2 ■ Tutti	■ Am to Gm (but with cadences in Dm at 35–36 and 42)	■ **a** in continuo part at first, with **b** and **c** ■ Part of **a** at bars 36–37 (violas), leading into **b**, with **c** inverted (cello and continuo) ■ Further reappearances of **a** (inexact and incomplete) and **c** (no longer inverted)
48–56	Episode 2 ■ Soloists (plus continuo at beginning only)	■ Starts in Gm ■ Moves to Dm almost immediately ■ Touches on major keys (briefly F, C, B♭) before cadencing in Dm	■ Further use of **c** and the start of **a** ■ The major keys touched on are the three most closely related to D minor
56–73	Ritornello 3 ■ Tutti	Almost entirely Dm	■ Free use of previous melodic material (e.g. the crotchets moving in 5ths re-appear without the first part of **a**) ■ New semiquaver patterns (bars 62–64) ■ Long dominant pedal A (see box, above right) in bars 58–69 (more than 10% of the whole movement!)

A dominant pedal commonly signals the approaching end of a section or piece, keeping the listener in suspense. There is a wonderfully prolonged dominant pedal, full of suspense, in the harpsichord cadenza from Bach's Brandenburg Concerto No. 5, Movement 1

The following music example illustrates themes **a**, **b** and **c** from Movement 2.

It is acceptable to refer to musical themes by letters, as in the table above and in the music example, provided that it is completely clear what each letter refers to.

Movement 3

Movement 3 has a simple ternary structure (which could alternatively be labelled tutti-solo-tutti or ritornello-episode-ritornello). Only violin I has a solo part.

Bars	Instrumentation	Key(s)	Comment
1–3^2	Tutti	Dm	Homophonic phrase (in siciliana style)
3^3–17^2	Solo: Vln I, accompanied by Vln II (solo and ripieno) and violas	Starts in Dm, before passing through several other keys, including (in bars 5–8) Gm and Fm	Relatively long middle section, shaped by the repetition of ■ bars 3^3–5^2 at 11^3–13^2 ■ bars 13^4–15^3 at 15^4–17^2 (to provide finality)
17^3–20	Tutti	Dm	Repeat of opening Tutti

Movement 4

In Movement 4 the emphasis is even more clearly on the soloists than in Movement 2; the tutti passages are brief. Whereas Movement 2 is unified by references to one or more of themes **a**, **b** and **c**, Movement 4 has some repetition of entire textures.

It is simplest to think of the movement as having the four main sections, shown in the table below in blue. A ritornello is most commonly scored for the tutti, but here it is convenient to consider the ritornello as beginning for soloists and ending with the tutti.

Bars	Instrumentation	Key(s)	Comment
1–14		Dm	Ritornello 1
1–11^2	Soloists: ■ bar 1: vlns I and II, later joined by cello (without continuo) ■ 7: solo cello with ripieno	Dm	■ Descending chromatic movement in bass is important in Movement 4 ■ This first occurs in the cello (bars 4–6)
11^3–14^1	Tutti	Dm	Descending chromatic movement in continuo (different in rhythm and pitch from bars 4–6)
14–30		chiefly Am	Ritornello 2
14–27^3	Soloists: ■ 14–22: soloists without continuo ■ 23–27^3: just vln I with ripieno	Dm, to Am (from bar 18)	■ Bars 14–19 are new ■ Bars 20–22 = 4–6, but in Am ■ Bars 23–27 = 7–11, but in Am
27^3–30^1	Tutti	Am	= bars 11^3–14^1, but in Am
30–53		various	Episode
30–42	Soloists: ■ 30: vlns I and II with ripieno ■ 35: vln I, with other violins and violas (no cello or continuo)	Begins and ends in Dm. Gm (bars 35–40)	New material
43–46^3	Tutti	Dm–Am	New

46³–53	Soloists (without continuo) alternating with tutti	Traces of Gm and F. Then Dm (with repeated imperfect cadences)	New. ■ From bar 46³: sequential passage for soloists ■ From bar 50: tutti, echoing start of soloists' passage ■ From bar 51: soloists repeat tutti phrase (adapted for reduced forces) ■ From bar 52: tutti round off section with repeat of their previous phrase (bar 50)
53–73		Dm	Ritornello 3
53–67	Soloists: ■ 53: all three, without continuo ■ 59: vln I with continuo (doubled by cello)	Dm	■ From bar 53: an ornamented version of bars 1–3 ■ From bar 56: repeat of bars 4–6 ■ From bar 59: new
68–73	Tutti	Dm	■ From bar 68²: repeat of material beginning in bar 11⁴ ■ From bar 70³: repeat of bars 68–70² down an octave (for greater weight)

Organisation of pitch: melody

Vivaldi's melodic style features:

■ Motivic writing: short melodic patterns frequently recur to provide musical unity. See, for example, the ascending pattern of two semiquavers and quaver heard twice (in melodic sequence) in theme **a**, or the dotted quaver, semiquaver, quaver pattern (first heard with the pitches D–E–D) in Movement 3

■ Fairly frequent repeated-note patterns, for example:

  ■ The repeated Ds in the opening duet of Movement 1, and the quavers in the short Adagio at the start of Movement 2

  ■ Simple accompaniment patterns, especially in bars 35–42 of Movement 4 (to provide a simple, slowly-changing harmonic background)

■ Stepwise movement, notably in scalic writing (particularly in the semiquaver figure **c**)

■ Leaps

  ■ Arpeggio patterns (chiefly at the beginning of Movement 1)

  ■ Many small leaps of up to a 5th (especially see the 5ths in theme **a** which generate 'circles of 5ths')

  ■ Occasional larger leaps such as octaves from a higher to a lower dominant in the bass at a perfect cadence (e.g. Movement 2, bars 47–50).

Note the juxtaposition of leaps and repeated-note patterns in the solo part at Movement 4, bars 35–42. The melodic line is effectively divided into melody and accompanying notes, as the following musical example shows.

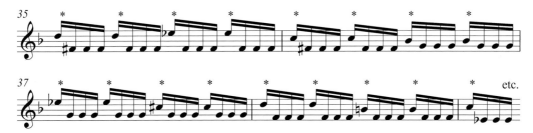

* = 'melody' note

Organisation of pitch: harmony

Vivaldi's chord vocabulary consists of:

- Triads in root position (very widely used), especially chords I and V (see box, below)
- Triads in first inversion, including the 'Neapolitan 6th'
- Seventh chords, mainly in root position, but sometimes in first or third inversion.

> The opening of Movement 1 shows extreme harmonic economy: for five bars we hear just arpeggiations of D minor chord I (the main musical interest being the expansion in melodic range from one octave to two).

One of Vivaldi's harmonic fingerprints is the circle of 5ths. In bars 5–7 of Movement 2, for example, he goes full circle round the key, using a root position chord on each scale degree, with the bass leaping alternately down a 5th and up a 4th. Each chord except I is a 7th chord.

The harmony is frequently embellished with passing notes.

Suspensions are quite common, sometimes (a convention of the time) on chord V at a perfect cadence (e.g. Movement 2, bar 15^4). In Movement 4, the passage first heard at bars 11–13 has two consecutive 7–6 suspensions in bar 12, which add harmonic strength and tension, especially alongside the 7th chords in bar 13 (V^7 on beat 1 and II^{7}b on beat 3).

The most colourful passage harmonically is the Adagio at the start of Movement 2.

A title page from the 1711 Amsterdam edition of *L'estro armonico*

Bar, beat(s)	Key	Chord	Comment
1, 1-2	D minor	V^7 of V	Contains the first note in the piece that is outside the D minor scale – G♯. In isolation, the chord (E–G♯–B–D) sounds like V^7 in A minor, but it is really a 'secondary dominant' in D minor – V^7 of V, or the dominant of the dominant (see box below).
1, 3-4	D minor	V^7	Note the beginning of a striking chromatic descent in the top part.
2, 1-2	D minor	V^7 of IV	A chord of D as expected after V^7, but with F♯ and C♮ – another secondary dominant.
2, 3-4	D minor	IV^7 with raised 3rd (B♮)	The passage up to this point is an incomplete circle of 5ths (bass E-A-D-G), with each chord a root position seventh chord.
3, 1	D minor	♭IIb (Neapolitan 6th)	Bass G still, but it is no longer the root of a chord (so that the passage no longer sounds like a circle of 5ths).
3, 2		C minor chord	This chord is difficult to label in Roman numeral terms (a system that post-dates Vivaldi) unless we call it ♭VII (minor) in D minor.
3, 3-4	D minor	V^7	V^7 is a(n attractive) surprise after the preceding chord – with its double false relation (C♮/C♯ and E♭/E♮). It is the perfect choice for leading on to the chord I that begins the following Allegro

On secondary dominants, see *AS Music Harmony Workbook* by Hugh Benham (Rhinegold Education, 2008), pages 47-48.

Texture

Movements 1 and 2

The first two movements can be conveniently considered together. They show considerable textural variety:

- Movement 1 begins with canon (a contrapuntal device), and is followed by homophony (cello and continuo) and the chordal passage at the start of Movement 2. The rest of Movement 2 is contrapuntal

- Movement 2 employs contrasts between solo and tutti passages.

The use of canon helps to make it clear that the two solo violin parts are equal partners (at least in this section): the second part is not consistently below the first as in much music with two violin parts, but is equally often on top.

To start with, the canon is at the unison at one beat's distance – that is, both solo violins play the same notes in the same octave, but with the second starting one beat after the other. From bar 7 the second part is a whole bar behind the first, which makes it easier for the descending scales to be clearly heard.

Bars 20–31 are homophonic – there is a melodic part (for solo cello) with a simple bass for the continuo. Although the music looks as if it is in two parts, the keyboard player adds an improvised accompaniment which 'fills out' the two-part outline to make complete harmony.

Bars 1–3 of Movement 2 are in chordal (or homorhythmic) style – that is, each of the parts has the same rhythm.

Bars 4–23 of Movement 2 are based principally on fugal imitation of theme **a**. The four imitative entries, beginning successively on D, A, D and A, together make up a 'fugal exposition' (i.e. with subject, answer, subject, answer) and subsidiary themes **b** and **c** recurring in the manner of fugal countersubjects. Much more material is in fugal style, and the whole movement is often referred to as a fugue.

Movement 3

The melody in the first violin(s) is the main focus, and the texture is melody-dominated **homophony**. The accompaniment is rhythmically very simple, particularly in the central section with even quavers in all parts.

Movement 4

Movement 4 employs a good deal of melody-dominated homophony, but with some variety.

Bars	Comment
7–11	Cello solo. The accompaniment has crotchet chords, each followed by a crotchet rest
14–19	The melody in violin I is doubled in 3rds by violin II. The solo cello provides the bass (there is no continuo)
23–27	Compare 7–11, but the solo is in violin I
35–42	Violin I solo. The accompaniment is in continuous quavers
59–67	Violin I solo. Accompaniment just in continuo (doubled by solo cello) with the repeated rhythm quaver rest, quaver, crotchet

Elsewhere there is some contrapuntal interest. At the start there is imitation between the violins, and then between violin I and cello from bar 3³, with the violin leading:

Note also the **imitation** between the two solo violins in bars 30–33.

Sonority

The solo group (or 'concertino') has two violins and cello, accompanied by strings ('ripieno'), although only one of the violins has a solo role in some passages, notably in Movement 3.

In the anthology score the music for the solo violins is printed on the top two staves, which are labelled 'Violino I' and 'Violino II', with the direction 'Soli' or 'Solo' when one or both of them play without the ripieno. The music for the ripieno violins is on the staves labelled 'Violino III' and 'Violino IV'. When these ripieno violins are playing, the soloists mostly double them (they do not stop playing). It is possible that in Vivaldi's time the parts for Violino III and IV were each taken by a single player.

The two violas (presumably there *were* just two of them) always play the same music as each other, and share a single stave in the Anthology score. The solo cello does not appear right next to the solo violins (as in some editions of this concerto), but just above the continuo part for

Canal streets in the Castello area of Venice, where Vivaldi was born

'Violone e Cembalo'. The violone was a stringed instrument, probably with a similar range to the modern double bass. 'Cembalo' means harpsichord, although a fretted instrument such as an archlute can be used instead: the purpose of either is to provide harmony as indicated by the figuring (7, ♯, etc.)

The essence of the work is the contrasting of different forces. The main distinction is between the concertino and the other instruments. But at the beginnings of Movements 1 and 4 the two solo violins are clearly opposed to the solo cello and continuo. The first violin alone is soloist at times – chiefly in Movement 3 (with the second violin playing as part of the ripieno).

> Contrasting of different forces was one of the crucial innovations of the early Baroque – notably in the music of composers from Vivaldi's own city-state of Venice, such as Giovanni Gabrieli (c. 1555–1612).

Dynamics

Vivaldi, following the convention of his day, supplied few dynamic markings. The loud-soft dynamic contrasts that he employed (without, for example, any indication of crescendo or diminuendo) are known as 'terraced dynamics'.

- The indications p ('piano') and f ('forte') occur towards the end of Movement 2, to indicate echo effects. The first p is at bar 59 (followed by f at bar 60). The dynamic level before the first p was presumably f. It may well be therefore that f is always the default dynamic

- In Movement 3, the pp ('pianissimo') in the accompanying parts is to make really sure that the solo part (no dynamic marking) is not over-shadowed

- There is a similar use of pp and f in Movement 4 (from bar 35)

- Finally, note the p and f markings near the end of Movement 4. The p marking reinforces the quieter effect likely to be produced when some of the music is repeated an octave lower (from bar 70³). The closing f ensures a robust ending.

Tempo, metre and rhythm

As with many concertos from Vivaldi's time onwards, the first and last movements are fast ('Allegro'), while there is slower music in between (Movement 2 begins 'Adagio', and Movement 3 is 'Largo').

> The Adagio is headed in full 'Adagio e spiccato'. The word 'spiccato' (Italian for 'separated') probably indicated just 'staccato' in the early 18th century (whereas today it refers to short bow-strokes in which the bow is made to bounce lightly onto the string). Here it obviously applies to the quavers, not to the pause-marked minims. In Movement 3 ('Largo e Spiccato'), it presumably refers chiefly to the accompanying parts, especially in the middle section where the solo melody requires a more sustained delivery (and even has a few slurred groupings).

Movements 2 and 4 are entirely in $\mathbf{C}$ time (equivalent to simple quadruple time or $\frac{4}{4}$, with a crotchet beat). Contrast is provided by the simple triple time ($\frac{3}{4}$) of the opening solo section and the compound quadruple time ($\frac{12}{8}$) of Movement 3.

As with much late Baroque music, there is, above all, rhythmic continuity in Op. 3 No. 11 – for example, note how the music keeps going in the opening duet. In places, as in the latter part of that duet and in the following cello solo, there is constant semiquaver movement in at least one of the parts.

Most of the Allegro from Movement 2 is based on a small number of rhythmic patterns, which are all worked very hard.

Look again at themes a, b and c, noting particularly the patterns of:

- Quaver rest, two semiquavers and two or more quavers
- The chain of crotchets
- The descending semiquaver scale passages.

Movement 3 is in the style of a siciliana and features characteristic rhythms, most importantly the pattern dotted quaver, semiquaver, quaver, which is widely heard in the tutti sections and in the solo violin I part.

> A **SICILIANA** was normally slow, and in compound time, with lilting rhythms. It was sometimes associated with pastoral scenes (idealised country scenes with shepherds, etc.) For instance, Handel's siciliana-style 'Pastoral Symphony' from Messiah suggests the shepherds of the Christmas story.

Movement 4 is broadly similar in general rhythmic character to the main (Allegro) section of Movement 2. Striking moments include:

- The change from the opening continuous quaver movement to the cello's semiquavers at bar 7
- The clear differentiation between the cello's semiquavers here and the rhythmically very sparse accompaniment.

Musical language

Tasto solo (Movement 2, bars 58–69 of the continuo line) means that a continuo keyboard player should not add any chords here (and indeed there are no figured bass indications in these bars).

> **TASTO** can mean 'key' (on a keyboard instrument), or 'fingerboard' (on a stringed instrument). 'Tasto solo' might mean that the keyboard player must stop altogether and that only the continuo instrument(s) with fingerboard continue to play the bass part.

Set work:
Piano Trio in G minor Op. 17, Movement 1
Clara Schumann

Musical context

Composer

Clara Schumann (1819–1896) is described in *The New Grove Dictionary* as a 'German pianist, composer and teacher'. She was referred to as the 'Queen of the Piano', and the instrument features in all of her compositions.

There are many solo works (which would have featured in her recitals), a sizeable number of songs with piano accompaniment, and two piano concertos. The Piano Trio in G minor, Op. 17 (1846) is widely regarded as her most important work. It is often tense and melancholic, apparently reflecting the personal troubles in her life at the time of composition.

Portrait of Clara Wieck-Schumann, painted by Franz von Lenbach in the late 1870s

The composer was known as Clara Schumann after her marriage, but today she is sometimes referred to as Clara Wieck-Schumann to emphasise that she had established a career as a pianist, and had composed a large number of works, before she was married. She is not known as just 'Schumann' because of possible confusion with her husband, the composer Robert Schumann, who is normally referred to in this way.

The piano trio

A **piano trio** is a work in several movements for piano and two other instruments, normally violin and cello. The work is really a sonata for these instruments, and it is just convention that the term 'piano trio' is preferred.

The piano trio is an important type of 'chamber music' – that is, music for a small number of performers, generally each with an undoubled part (as opposed, for example, to orchestral music, where all the string parts and most or all of the wind parts are taken by more than one player). 'Chamber music' is music for a chamber or room in the sense that it is most suitable for relatively small performance spaces rather than for large concert halls. The most important chamber music genre is the string quartet – two movements from Op. 59 No. 3 in C by Beethoven, a leading exponent of the string quartet, are recommended for wider listening.

The earliest piano trios were composed in the Classical era. They were the descendants of Baroque sonatas for violin plus a continuo section of cello and keyboard. Standard Baroque practice was to provide the keyboard player with only the bass part and figuring, but in piano trios the piano part is written out in full. At first the cello still did little more than double the piano left hand, but in Mozart's late works (e.g. K.542 in E) and in Beethoven's (e.g. his 'Archduke' Piano Trio in B♭, Op. 97) each instrument increasingly played an independent part. This set work, written 35 years after Beethoven completed his Op. 97, is from the Romantic period.

Piano Trio in G minor Op. 17

Clara Schumann's piano trio is in four movements.

The overall plan is as follows:

- Movement 1: Allegro moderato
- Movement 2: Scherzo – tempo di menuetto
- Movement 3: Andante
- Movement 4: Allegretto.

In the late 18th and early 19th centuries, and frequently afterwards, a similar 'sonata plan' was usual for works entitled sonata, for large-scale chamber works (trios, quartets, and so on), and for symphonies. A sonata plan might, however, lack a scherzo and span three movements rather than four. Normally the first movement (and occasionally one or more other movements) followed a pattern known as sonata form, on which see further below. The 'slow movement' (in Clara Schumann's case, the movement marked 'Andante') was more commonly the second movement than the third. Beethoven's four-movement String Quartet in C, Op. 59 No. 3, has a Minuet (rather than Scherzo) as third movement, which runs into the finale without a break. Movement 1 begins with a slow, questing introduction before the sonata-form Allegro vivace. Compare the slow introductions that head Haydn's Symphony No. 6 in D (short) and Berlioz's *Symphonie Fantastique* (much longer).

The comments that follow concern Movement 1 only.

Musical elements

Sonority

The ranges of the three instruments are typical for the early to mid-19th century – that is, a little larger than was often the case in the 18th century and smaller than in some 20th-century music:

Violin:

Cello:

Piano:

The violin and cello parts both have a range of nearly three octaves, with the violin part going down to the instrument's very lowest note. The piano part has a range of five and a half octaves – at a time when many pianos had a range of about six and a half octaves.

> The treble clef that appears in the cello part in the Anthology, and in many editions of this work, is a 'false' treble clef: meaning that the notes should be played down an octave. For example, in beats 2, 3 and 4 of bar 122 in the Anthology edition, the cello plays a 3rd lower than the violin, not a 6th above it.

The string parts are played almost entirely arco and one note at a time, but the cello plays pizzicato in bars 238–246, and the violin has occasional double stopping, notably to add intensity to the figure first heard in bar 22.

The piano part is active and quite challenging, partly because of some unusually wide and awkward stretches towards the end of the movement, especially from bar 276.

Pedalling is rarely indicated, but special blurred effects are specifically required in bars 56, 117–118 and 121–122 (where the pedal has to be held down to sustain one harmony against another).

Texture

The movement has a range of **homophonic** textures. Although there is considerable **contrapuntal** interest in parts of the **development** section (notably from bar 115, with the interplay between violin and cello), the texture is still fundamentally homophonic with the piano providing harmonic support to the two melodic parts.

The main melodic interest generally alternates between the violin and the right hand of the piano – a principle clearly established at the start of the movement (compare bars 1–8 with the bars that follow).

Violin and cello are active for most of the time, but occasionally:

- They rest simultaneously, as in bar 59 where a linking passage in the piano re-establishes the tempo after a *poco rit.*
- The violin alone presents a melody with piano accompaniment (as in bars 1–8).

The cello occasionally has independent melodic interest, but it also:

- Provides an ornamented or simplified version of the piano's bass line (e.g. from bar 9)
- Doubles an inner part (as in bars 37–41)
- Strengthens a melody by doubling the violin at the octave (as in bars 61–69) or in (compound) 3rds (bars 17–20).

The pianist is busy almost all the time, with plenty of textural contrast to sustain interest. For example:

- Bars 1–8 contain:
  - A broken-chord accompaniment in the right hand (the violin having the melody) over a slower bass line
  - Offbeat chords in the right hand with a left hand part that is *on* the beat (See bars 127–138 for a more extended use of this device)
- In bars 9–16, the piano has the melody in the right hand with a broken-chord accompaniment in the left. No single accompaniment pattern is over-used – compare the left-hand part of bars 9–11 (mostly alternating two notes on the beat and a single note off the beat) with the simple broken-chord pattern in bar 12
- In bars 22-23 there are *ff* chords with octaves in both hands plus some 'filling-in' notes in the right. (Left-hand octaves are quite widely used to strengthen the bass line and give depth to the texture – especially in bars 149–153).

Dynamics

Dynamics range from *ff* to *p* – these extremes being dramatically juxtaposed in bars 22–28, after the long crescendo from bar 14. Plentiful crescendos and diminuendos add emotional intensity elsewhere, and the directions *sf* and *fp* sometimes underline important or harmonically intense chords (as in bar 59, where they also highlight the syncopation).

There is only one *mf* marking (piano, bar 250) and no *mp* – surprisingly, as these more subtle dynamics were common by the mid 19th century.

Structure and tonality

The movement is in **sonata form**. The **tonic key** is G minor, and the 'complementary key' (in which the **exposition** ends) is the conventional choice: B♭ major (the **relative major** of G minor).

The table below provides a guide to the whole movement, but note first the principal components:

- **Exposition** (with its progression from G minor to B♭) – from bar 1
- **Development** (with some excursions to other keys and the manipulation of ideas previously heard) – from bar 91
- **Recapitulation** (with G as the tonic most of the time, including music previously heard in B♭), followed by Coda – from bar 165.

Before working through the detail in the table, make sure you are familiar with the following:

> **Sonata form** developed gradually from rounded binary form in the 18th century, and, as we have already seen, it was regularly used to structure one or more movements of piano sonatas, chamber works such as trios and quartets, and symphonies. Remember that 'sonata form' refers to the form or structure of a single movement, not to a whole sonata.
>
> The terms **first subject** and **second subject** in the table below are widely used as names for the main parts of the exposition that are in, respectively, the tonic key and a complementary key. The **bridge passage** (or **transition**) between the two subjects has the modulation from the tonic to the complementary key.
>
> In sonata form, a subject may contain more than one theme.

Exposition (bars 1 to 90)

The exposition is clearly balanced – with first subject and bridge passage equal in length and together balancing the second subject and brief codetta (second subjects in sonata-form movements were usually relatively long in this way). The exposition is marked to be repeated – see bar 90.

Bars	Section	Main key(s)	Comment
1–21	First subject	Gm	There is one principal song-like theme in the first subject ■ 1–8 (melody in violin: and brief music example on page 133) ■ Repeated in 9–14 (melody in piano, right hand) and is freely extended
22–45^1	Bridge passage	Gm to B♭	The bridge passage begins with a striking idea, marked $\boldsymbol{f\!f}$ in the piano part, followed by a quiet answering phrase. The music at bars 30 and 32 (starting with repeated notes) may be deliberately related to the $\boldsymbol{f\!f}$ idea. ■ Bars 22–25: firmly Gm ■ 26–30^1: begins the same, but moves to a fairly weak cadence in B♭ (V^{7}b–I) ■ 30^2–45^1: firmly in B♭, with three strong perfect cadences. (there is occasional chromaticism – the F♯s, for example, do not re-establish Gm)

Bars	Section	Key	Notes
45²–85¹	Second subject	B♭	Opens with a syncopated descending idea, followed by a quaver figure in the piano based partly on repeated-note patterns. These two ideas dominate for some time, after which there are various other ideas that are hardly distinctive or persistent enough to be termed 'themes': ■ Bars 45–49¹ are repeated a tone lower – suggesting A♭ before a perfect cadence in (surprisingly) D major at bars 56–57 ■ A return to B♭ leads to a modified repeat of bars 45–57 from bar 61, in which a unison passage for violin and cello in quavers is now combined with the syncopated chordal passage for piano ■ Firm perfect cadence in B♭ at bars 84–85
85²–90	Codetta (see box)	Back to Gm	■ The return to Gm prepares for the repeat of the Exposition

> A **CODETTA** ('little coda') is a passage that rounds off an exposition, often with repeated cadencing in the complementary key – whereas the coda is a more substantial conclusion to the whole movement, after the recapitulation.

Development (bars 91 to 164)

Bars	Section	Key	Notes
91–164	Development	Principal key is Cm, with some Fm, and Gm (especially from 146, to prepare for Recapitulation)	■ From bar 104, the development is largely based on the first subject, with imitation between the violin and cello parts and broken-chord figurations in piano ■ See also the statement in piano left hand at 149

Recapitulation (bars 165 to 249)

The recapitulation is in Gm, with G major for the second subject.

Bars	Section	Key	Notes
165–185	First subject	Gm	An exact repeat of the first subject from the exposition.

186–210[1]	Bridge passage	Gm to G major, having passed through Cm and E♭ (in bars 192–196), and Gm again	■ Begins by repeating the original Bridge Passage, but 191 is different, with a Neapolitan 6th chord (see 'Harmony' below) ■ Bars 191–210[1] are a transposed, varied repeat of bars 27–44[1]. This passage is one bar longer than in the exposition (19 rather than 18), and obviously we do not end in B♭ as the original bridge passage did)
210[2]–249	Second subject	G major (not Gm)	■ As far as bar 238, a transposed repeat of the exposition second subject ■ It was common in a minor key movement (as here and in, for example, Beethoven's Symphony No. 5 in C minor, Movement 1) for the recapitulation of the second subject to be in the tonic *major* key (so that a major key second subject from the exposition did not have to be rather artificially made minor)
250–288	Coda	Gm	■ Begins by repeating the codetta, and then extends this in sequence ■ Further descending phrases in the violin part lead to a chromatic descent (violin and cello in octaves) at bar 262 ■ Then the first subject theme is restated at bar 266 (again, in octaves) ■ Imitation of the descending part of this theme from 276 ■ Final perfect cadence in Gm is at 275–276 ■ Long tonic pedal and plagal cadence conclude the movement

Schumann's movement as set out above is a good example of 'textbook' sonata form (whereas Movement 1 of Berlioz's *Symphonie Fantastique* shows a more original treatment).

For example, in the recapitulation there is considerable repetition of music from the exposition. Some of this is note-for-note, but there is also transposition from the complementary key to the tonic (major), because a recapitulation traditionally avoids the complementary key in order to emphasise the tonic.

Organisation of pitch: melody

The first subject begins with an attractive eight-bar melody with two balancing four-bar phrases (an example of the 'periodic phrasing' that underlies much **Classical** and early-**Romantic** music), as shown in the music example at the top of page 133.

The climactic top G in the second phrase (a major 3rd above the high point of the first phrase) is approached by a strong upward leap of an octave:

There is plenty of rhythmic variety and a carefully controlled balancing of ascending and descending motion, stepwise movement and leaps. The interval of a 3rd between the D and B♭ in bar 2 provides additional character – a straight stepwise descent might have been expected here.

The first phrase cadences on A (implying chord V and an imperfect cadence), and the listener may expect a balancing V–I perfect cadence at the end of the second phrase. However, Clara Schumann cadences onto chord V again, thus keeping things open for the repeat of the melody in the piano right hand.

At times chromaticism contributes significantly to the emotional intensity of the music, especially the darkly descending semitonal movement in bars 18–20.

Melodic sequence is an important means of extension and development in this movement, as in much Baroque, Classical and Romantic music. Such writing can sound predictable, but here it is sometimes treated with freedom to excellent effect.

For example, in the violin:

- Bars 27–30, where the size of the descending leap changes each time (compare the more 'regular' sequence in bars 24–25):

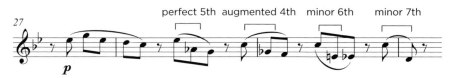

- Bars 92–103, with some rhythmic and melodic irregularity:

Organisation of pitch: harmony

The harmony is functional, with strong reliance on chords I and V$^{(7)}$ to define the key, especially at perfect cadences.

Characteristically for its time, the movement uses mostly triads and 7th chords in root position and inversion; but there are fairly frequent chromatic chords, and some striking dissonances, prepared (suspensions) and unprepared (appoggiaturas).

The chord at bar 191, beat 2 in the recapitulation (bridge passage) is particularly effective. The listener may well be expecting a repeat of the chord heard in bar 187 (C–E♭–G–A), as happens in the exposition bridge passage (compare bars 23 and 27).

> In bar 23 the chord C–E♭–G–A is clearly G minor II7b, but in bar 27 the same chord is the **pivot chord** that initiates the **modulation** to B♭ (in which key it is VII7b).

However, in bar 191 the G is omitted and the A becomes A♭ – a clearly audible first indication that the recapitulation cannot indefinitely follow the same course as the exposition. The resulting chord is A♭ major in first inversion. The most likely interpretation, given the approach in the key of G minor, is chord ♭IIb in that key (the Neapolitan 6th chord).

But Clara Schumann provides another surprise by taking this chord instead as VIb in C minor (which she follows with chords VII7b, II7, V7, V7b and I in that key) before returning to G minor via E♭ major.

The dark atmosphere of the movement is strengthened by fairly frequent diminished 7th chords. There are several, for example, in the first subject, including those in the music example opposite.

> The diminished 7ths in the first subject are brief and on weak beats – they are handled gently rather than aggressively. There is greater boldness in the development section, with longer and more heavily accented diminished 7ths: this deliberately raises the harmonic temperature in what was traditionally the most tense part of a sonata-form structure. See for example bars 110 and 114.

Bar 11 (see example below) contains a half-diminished chord (E♮ G B♭ D(♮)), but with the G replaced for most of the second beat by a poignant F♯ appoggiatura, followed by a (French) augmented 6th chord: E♭–G–C♯–A (all four notes present at beat 4).

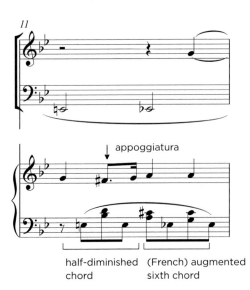

half-diminished   (French) augmented
chord   sixth chord

Bars 17⁴–20¹ (see example below) involve a (nearly exact) harmonic sequence, with bar 19 a 3rd lower than bar 18. The chromatic descent is an even more powerful indicator of a dark emotional scenario than the diatonic descent in the bass at the start of the movement. Each beat is dissonant. See for example:

- Bar 18¹: the suspended C♯ (an upward-resolving **suspension**, or '**retardation**'), clashing with its note of resolution, D. This type of clash is less than common in functional harmony, because it will sound rough and crude if mishandled

- Bar 18²: the C♮ appoggiatura (or 'accented passing note') leading to the B♮ harmony note

- Bar 18³: the D appoggiatura (clashing with its note of resolution, C).

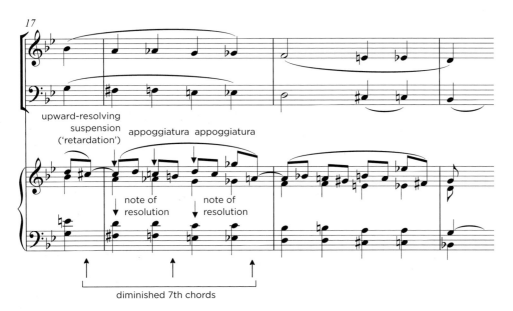

Tempo, metre and rhythm

The first movement of a piano trio or other sonata-like structure is normally fast or moderately fast: this movement is labelled 'Allegro moderato'.

The direction *poco rit.* highlights a delightful tonal surprise – the brief excursion into D major at bars 56–59¹. The same temporary holding back of the tempo marks the corresponding passage in the recapitulation (bars 221–224¹): this is in B major, a key very distant from the tonic key of G minor.

The metre is 𝄵 throughout.

Syncopation is used from time to time to help maintain rhythmic variety and vitality within the constant 𝄵 metre. For example, note how:

- The second note of the bridge passage main theme (bar 22) is placed on the last (weak) semiquaver of the third crotchet beat

- The first three chords of the second subject (bars 45–46) begin on a *weak* crotchet (each chord is two crotchet beats long).

There is a fairly wide range of note values and rhythmic figurations, with much continuous quaver movement, but the only semiquavers follow dotted quavers, and there are no triplets.

Set work:
Symphonie fantastique, Movement 1 'Rêveries – Passions'
Hector Berlioz

Musical context

Composer

Hector Berlioz (1803–1869) was the most important and influential French composer of the first half of the 19th century (his most important work being in the fields of opera, song and orchestral music). He was also a conductor and a prolific writer about music.

Berlioz was highly unusual for a composer at the time in not being a keyboard player (his instruments were flute and guitar). All this and a sensitive and imaginative temperament led to a highly individual approach to composition.

Symphonie fantastique

Berlioz's *Symphonie fantastique*, probably his most widely known work, was composed when he was in his late twenties. It was 'fantastic' in the sense that it has a large element of fantasy.

A Painting of Berlioz by Ernst Hader

If today we say 'fantastic' to mean 'brilliant' or 'wonderful', we use the word in a different, more recent sense.

'Fantasy' in music often features images and events far removed from ordinary experience, and was typical of a great deal of Romantic music. Berlioz was the arch-Romantic, and *Symphonie Fantastique* is almost as Romantic as it is possible to be.

Romantic music (more than earlier music) often:

- Goes to extremes (e.g. in terms of instrumental colour, technical display, length, emotionalism, tonal and harmonic adventurousness)

- Features the supernatural (as opposed to the religious) and/or the world of nature (as in the fifth and third movements respectively of *Symphonie Fantastique*)

- Is written not just to please and entertain but also to challenge and express the composer's individuality

- Mainly from the second half of the 19th century, features nationalistic elements (especially to give a voice to oppressed peoples – e.g. works by Dvořák that celebrate his Bohemian inheritance).

It is impossible to give exact dates for the Romantic period of music history – it did not suddenly begin and end in particular years. The A Level specification associates Romanticism with 'c.1820 to c.1900', which is very reasonable, but some people would argue for starting a little earlier and ending a little later (e.g. from about 1810 to about 1910).

For a detailed discussion of Romanticism, see *The Oxford History of Western Music (College Edition)* by Richard Taruskin and Christopher H. Gibbs (2013), pages 464–477.

Berlioz thought of his work as a symphony because it was a large-scale orchestral work with several movements, but he was well aware that he was breaking away from the traditional largely 'abstract' approach favoured by Haydn and Mozart, and at times Beethoven (as in Symphonies Nos. 1 and 2). Beethoven (one of Berlioz's musical heroes) was to some extent a model, however. Beethoven had already expanded the symphony in length and weight and had widened its scope in terms of 'subject matter' – as in No. 6 ('Pastoral') with its evocations of nature and its use of *five* movements, and in No. 9 ('Choral') where the philosophical message could not be fully conveyed without words and voices.

Exceptionally for his time, Berlioz supplied his audiences with a programme note that outlined the 'plot' of *Symphonie fantastique* – rather as the synopsis of an opera might be provided – in fact, he regarded the work as an 'instrumental drama'. The *main* part of his title for the work was initially 'Épisode de la vie d'un artiste' ('Episode in the life of an artist'): 'Symphonie fantastique' was almost a subtitle.

The 'story' concerns a young musician who falls in love (hopelessly, of course) with a beautiful woman. Whenever he thinks of her, a particular musical theme comes to his mind (this is the *idée fixe*, as first heard in Movement I, at bar 72).

At the time Berlioz himself was passionately in love with Harriet Smithson, whom he worshipped from a distance (he had seen her on stage, but had not yet met her). Berlioz's term *idée fixe* indicates a fixed or obsessive idea – here the composer's obsession with his beloved. The term later came to be used in the medical world to describe an abnormal preoccupation with a (probably dangerous) notion.

The subject of Movement 1 is, to paraphrase Berlioz, various emotional states – dreamy melancholy, brief episodes of unfocused joy and delirious passion, moments of fury and jealousy, returning tenderness, tears and consoling religious thoughts.

Only the first movement is for study as a set work, but the rest of the work would make valuable wider listening. Read Berlioz's programme note (available online and in print), and listen for the reappearances of the *idée fixe* in the other movements.

Symphonie fantastique was composed in 1830 at a time of considerable political upheaval in France – the latest revolution had brought Louis Philippe to the throne. Berlioz was optimistic about the outcome for the arts generally and for his career. Indeed, the first performance of *Symphonie fantastique*, at the end of this momentous year, was a success.

Musical elements

Sonority

By early 19th-century standards, Berlioz wrote for exceptionally large forces in *Symphonie Fantastique*. Page 128 of the Anthology shows that in Movement 1 Berlioz expected:

- 'At least' 60 strings (see the instructions to use 'au moins' ('at least') 15 first violins, 15 seconds, 10 violas ('altos'), 11 cellos, and nine double basses)
- Four (rather than two) bassoons
- Two *cornets à pistons* as well as two trumpets.

Cornets à pistons are cornets – valved brass instruments that were new in Berlioz's day. They were useful in allowing the composer some chromatic notes not available then from trumpets (which in France at this time were commonly without valves). Note also that the second flute player is required to play the piccolo instead from bar 409, to give additional brilliance to the orchestral sound.

> Additional instruments are required later in the work, as you can see from a complete score – and can hear easily enough from a recording. An informative remark about, say, the additional brass and percussion in Movement 5 would qualify as a reference to 'other music' in an examination essay (if relevant to the question).

As a non-keyboard player, Berlioz had to think orchestrally, and his scoring was sometimes very original. He realised that his writing could sometimes be difficult – see, for example, his lengthy note on page 129 of the Anthology warning conductors about bars 17–27 (the violin writing in particular).

> Berlioz's *Treatise on Instrumentation and Orchestration* (1844) is a remarkable survey of his own and contemporary practice. See www.hberlioz.com, where there are various editorial references to the first movement of *Symphonie fantastique*.

Among examples of distinctive scoring are:

- Bars 12 and 14. Note here, as sometimes elsewhere, how the double bass part moves away from its conventional role of doubling cellos at the octave. Accordingly the string writing is in more than the previously customary four parts

- Bar 72 onwards. The *idée fixe* is played at first – unaccompanied – by unison first violins and solo flute. Then it is accompanied by pairs of quaver chords in the other strings (perhaps suggesting the agitated heartbeat of the artist as he thinks of his beloved)

- Bar 410 onwards. A massive tutti with divisi first and second violins and cellos. The *idée fixe* is ornamented by the violins, which present successive fragments of the theme antiphonally.

> A string part is marked 'div[isi]' when temporarily divided into two (or occasionally more) separate parts (e.g. the first violins divide to play two different parts). Such division was a novel idea at the time. Incidentally, in bars 7 and 10, the second violins do not play divisi – everyone plays both notes (this is 'double stopping', a well-established device widely used by Berlioz).

Dynamics

Berlioz, as one would expect in a movement that explores such varied states of mind, explores a wide range of dynamics – from *ppp* (notably in bar 2, and at the end for the peaceful 'consolations of religion') to *ff*.

The extreme changes in bars 304–311 reflect the mental turmoil suffered by the protagonist.

Texture

The movement is varied texturally, although it is chiefly homophonic. For example, note:

- Much use of 'melody-dominated' homophony, notably in bars 3–14 (from the slow introduction), in most of bars 72–110 (the first appearance of the *idée fixe*) and at bars 156–166 (with much doubling of the melody)

- Chordal homophony (homorhythm), notably in bars 64–67, 187–190 and at the end in the closing 'Religiosamente' passage.

Other types of texture include:

- Dialogue in bars 176–179 between lower strings (parts of the *idée fixe*) and 'sighing' melodic fragments in the woodwind

- Monophony – at the beginning of the *idée fixe* (bars 72–77 and 80–83).

And just as one demonstration of Berlioz's textural inventiveness, look at bar 358 onwards:

- The solo oboe plays an expressive melody

- This is accompanied by fragments from the *idée fixe* in imitation (cellos and violas)

- Double basses mark out some of the main beats

- Clarinets and bassoons play a consistently off-beat chordal pattern

- First violins play repeated-note crotchet triplets.

Tempo, metre and rhythm

Movement 1 begins with an extended slow introduction, marked 'Largo' ('broadly'), but as you would expect in such highly emotional music, there are many tempo adjustments.

The main part of the movement (from bar 64) is marked 'Allegro agitato e appassionato assai' ('Fast, agitated and very passionately'). One bar here is to be equivalent to approximately a quarter of a bar previously (i.e. the music is effectively four times as fast as before).

The time signature changes from **C** ('common time' or $\frac{4}{4}$, with a crotchet beat) to **¢** ('cut common' or $\frac{2}{2}$, with a minim beat) for the much faster music at bar 64.

Rhythmically the movement is varied. For example, note:

- The wide range of note values – e.g. in bars 1–3 (quaver or triplet quaver movement juxtaposed with the semibreves of bar 2)

- Successions of rapid notes in the Allegro – e.g. the quavers in bar 111 are really fast (and 'con fuoco' = 'fiery') and even the crotchets in bars 198–228 move swiftly

- Triplets and sextuplets – e.g. triplets right at the start so that the first bar *sounds* as if it is compound time, and, in the 'difficult passage' at bar 17, semiquaver sextuplets (six notes per crotchet beat)

- Syncopation – e.g. in the accompanying woodwind at bar 359 and in many parts (including clarinets and bassoons) from bar 410

- Dotted notes – e.g. the dotted crotchet–quaver and dotted minim–crotchet pairs that are so prominent in the *idée fixe*.

Structure and tonality

In broad outline, Movement 1 consists of:

- The Largo (bars 1–63), an extended slow introduction beginning in C minor (corresponding to the 'Rêveries' in the movement's title 'Rêveries – Passions')

- The Allegro (bars 64–end, the 'Passions'), the mostly fast 'main part' of the movement in a (freely interpreted) sonata form beginning and ending in C major.

This overall slow introduction and sonata-form Allegro structure has important precedents in the work of Haydn and Beethoven (e.g. in the latter's Symphonies 1 and 2).

The slow introduction

In the slow introduction, after two introductory bars, there is a roughly ternary structure (A B A[varied]), plus a coda or free extension:

- A: bars 3–16. First violins play a melody borrowed from a (now lost) song that Berlioz had composed some years previously (see box below). Keys: C minor, briefly through G minor, ending with C minor IVb, but eventually cadencing onto I in C *major* in bar 18

- B: bars 17–27. This is the 'difficult passage' referred to earlier. At first it is positively cheerful (C major), but it becomes more pensive (and moves back into C minor) at bar 24 with a melody for solo flute. The music moves to E♭ for...

- ... A[v]: bars 28–42. The melody of A returns, re-harmonised to begin in E♭ major, not C minor. The accompaniment is now fuller and more complex, with woodwind sextuplets

- Free extension, much of it over an A♭ pedal in cellos and basses. To start with (bar 46), the A♭ is the submediant of C minor, but later it is really G♯ (see all the sharps in the upper parts), leading to an A♮ (bar 60) and from there to the dominant of C major.

The composer said in his autobiography that the melody in the introduction expressed perfectly the terrible sorrow of a young man feeling for the first time a hopeless love. The words of the lost song upon which it is based began 'Je vais donc quitter pour jamais / Mon doux pays, ma douce amie' ('I am going therefore to leave for ever / My sweet country, my sweet (girl) friend').

The beginning of the idée fixe is another self-borrowing, from the cantata *Herminie* (1828). The borrowed melody comes at the start of the cantata, and reappears later, although without the pervasiveness of its later extended version in *Symphonie fantastique*. The melody is instrumental, helping to set the scene for the opening recitative (words translated as 'What trouble pursues you, unhappy Herminie?').

The Allegro

See the section on Clara Schumann's Piano Trio for a brief explanation of sonata form.

Berlioz clearly regarded sonata form as a highly flexible ground plan, not as a more or less standardised pattern (as Clara Schumann appears to have done in the first movement of her G minor Piano Trio).

The description of Berlioz's movement in the table below is one possible way of attempting to square what happens with what the listener with a knowledge of traditional sonata form might *expect* to hear.

An alternative interpretation would be acceptable if it were supported by equally strong (or stronger) evidence (see for example the paragraph following the table). Ultimately Berlioz is more likely to have been guided by the demands of his 'plot' than by any pre-existing structural pattern.

Bars	Section	Key(s)	Comment
64–71	(Introductory)	C	
72–167	**Exposition**	C to G, but at times tonality is unsettled (e.g. in bars 137–145)	■ 72–111: in C (first subject) ■ 111–149: moves to G (chord V^7 at bar 146) – a transitional section (or 'bridge passage'). There is new thematic material here – although bars 119–124 are broadly similar in character to the *idée fixe*. ■ There is no clear break between the bridge passage and the second subject, which appears to begin at bar 150 150–167 (first-time bar): in G (second subject). Hints of *idée fixe* initially. Then a descending idea beginning with a dotted minim and two quavers (and a brief hint of E minor; see music example on page 144). In relation to the whole exposition, the second subject is uncommonly brief – but there is more G major (dominant key) material later on to compensate!
	Exposition repeated		The Anthology CD recording includes this repeat, but it is omitted in some performances.
166 (2nd-time bars) –231	**Development**	See next column	Music very chromatic, but fairly narrow tonally, being essentially anchored to main C–G tonality area by means of: ■ G and D inverted pedals (bars 166–190) ■ C major V–I (bars 197–198) ■ Chord V^7b of V in G (bar 228) What is 'developed'? ■ Clear references to *idée fixe* (rising sequentially, by semitones G, A♭, A, B♭) in lower strings (bars 166–178)

■ First four notes of *idée fixe* (as straight crotchets, again rising sequentially, with chromaticism), in bars 179–186

■ Second subject (bars 191–198) in C (the D♯s and F♯s are chromatic). It is unusual to emphasise the tonic in the development so far ahead of the recapitulation

232–328	**Recapitulation**	Much is in G	■ Full statement of first subject *idée fixe* – but considerably rescored. A recapitulation usually begins in the tonic key (C major in this movement) rather than G (the dominant) ■ The exposition bridge passage is not repeated. Much chromatic writing, initially descending from bar 275 ('depths of despair'), then ascending. Three V–I cadences in G (from bar 290) ■ Second subject returns at 311 – also in G, contrary to 'standard' practice (but we did hear this – unexpectedly – in C during the development where it began with G–F♮ rather than G–F♯). This passage is not an exact repeat from the exposition – which for Berlioz would have been too uninteresting
329–525	Coda	Chiefly in C	■ If we accept that the coda begins as early as this, Berlioz must have been (consciously or otherwise) following Beethoven, who liked long codas (as in the finales of Symphonies 5 and 8) ■ The firm re-establishment of the tonic, normally achieved in the recapitulation is delayed (although anticipated in the development). Note the long C pedal starting at 329 ■ Bars 329–357 are based principally on the theme first heard in the bridge passage (bar 119), which gets progressively lower in the texture (see the indication 'canto' ('song') at bars 344 and 352) ■ Bars 358–409: fragments of the *idée fixe* are worked against a song-like oboe theme, which at times seems to recall the melodic and rhythmic character of some of the later parts of the idée fixe. Note the restless effect of the chromatic bass, which rises an octave and a 5th from low G at 369 ■ Bars 410–438: *ff* presentation of *idée fixe* for full orchestra (not a literal repeat of the theme, especially towards the end; much more syncopated and more urgent (e.g. fewer rests). In C ■ Bars 439–450: brief respite (*mf*, with reduced scoring), then a rising chromatic passage (with repeated quavers in strings, *crescendo*) to a tutti C V with $\frac{4}{3}$ suspension at bar 449 heralding…

- ... Bars 451–491: fragments of the *idée fixe,* followed by a more fully scored repeat of the material beginning at bar 439. Then the bass circles round the dominant (bars 475–482) before a climactic V–I (bars 487–491)

- Bars 492–510: final glimpses of the *idée fixe,* first with repeated statements of the four-crotchet pattern (compare from bar 179) against a slow chromatic descent in the oboe, with touches of C minor

- Bars 511–525: Religiosamente ('Religiously') – the 'consolations of religion', with the orchestra directed to play as quietly as possible. Homorhythmic texture in semibreves, with two clear plagal cadences ('Amen-like' and conventionally suggestive of church and religion), with the final I much prolonged. The first of these is preceded by an inverted plagal progression in bars 511 to 514 with chords IV (with flattened 3rd, A♭ not A♮) and Ib

The beginning of the 'second subject' (skeleton score); annotations indicate the key, followed by the chord within that key

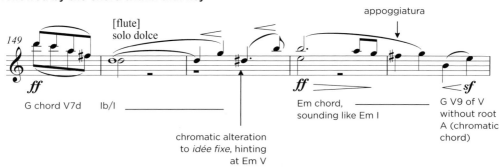

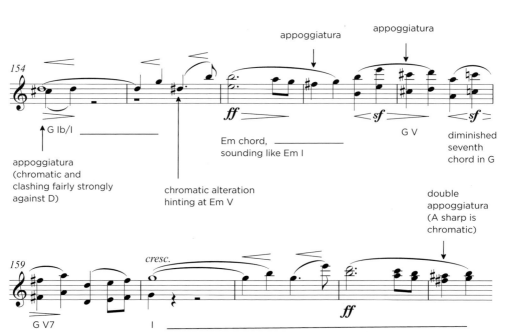

Coloured lithograph of Berlioz conducting one of his typically grand orchestrations

It would be possible to consider that the recapitulation begins at bar 410, where the tonic key and a return of the *idée fixe* coincide. In this case, the recapitulation in the table above may be part of an extremely extended development section. Or the re-appearances of the first and second subjects (in the dominant key) might be a kind of false recapitulation (deliberately deceptive?) preceding a second development section.

Organisation of pitch: melody

The main melodic themes are identified above.

For comments on the treatment of the *idée fixe* melody, see the table above.

Generally, Berlioz's melodic writing is varied, including:

- Urgent repeated-note patterns (notably bar 1, and bars 187–190)
- Much repetition of short motifs (as in bars 56 and 58, horns)
- Song-like melodies combining stepwise movement and small, easily singable leaps (hardly surprising as important melodic material is borrowed from vocal works)
- Chromatic ascents (less often descents) at different speeds to increase tension and excitement, notably in the passage beginning at bar 198 and the section beginning at bar 439 (first violins, and, more rapidly, second violins from bar 443)
- Some irregular phrase lengths (e.g. the seven-bar phrase in the *idée fixe* at 79[4]–86, introducing a note of urgency as the succeeding phrase begins 'early')
- Melodic sequence (as in bars 86[4]–98, both within and between phrases).

> See the reference to 'regular' periodic phrasing under 'Melody' in the notes on Clara Schumann.

Organisation of pitch: harmony

Berlioz's harmony is essentially functional (tonality being defined in particular by V–I perfect cadences). Pedals are used from time to time, the most striking being the prolonged A♭ in the Largo (bars 46–59 – about one minute in duration at a metronome marking of 56!).

> It is interesting how the bass A♭ at bars 46–59 is made to form part of a series of different chords. The A♭ eventually 'means' G♯, but Berlioz stuck to A♭ probably because a change to G♯ might have unsettled the intonation of the lower string parts.

Parallel chromatic movement can create spectacular effects, for example, with the parallel first-inversion triads ($\frac{6}{3}$ chords) in the passages beginning in bars 198 (see box below) and 439.

> These passages use sharps or flats to suit individual orchestral parts rather than to facilitate score reading – see, for example, bars 208–209, where a B♭ chord in first inversion is spelt D F A♯.

Almost all chords are triads or 7th chords (and their inversions), including diminished 7ths. In other words, unusual harmonic effects result from surprising juxtapositions of 'ordinary' chords, as, for example, in bars 52–53.

The dominant 9th chord in C minor (V^9) in bar 10 is an interesting case, not least because the 7th and 9th above the bass (F and A♭) are neither prepared nor resolved.

Here, and sometimes elsewhere, as in bars 97–98, Berlioz is happy to disregard the 'rules' of harmony and part-writing, and navigate by (a generally very sound) instinct. This is hardly something which should surprise us.

Musical language

Berlioz uses a fairly extensive vocabulary – Italian and French.

Among the less common terms are:

- 'I, II unis.' (bassoons, bar 1). Only bassoons I and II play (without bassoons III and IV), and in unison
- 'A punta d'arco' (see violin I, bar 17). At the point of the bow (for a delicate effect)
- 'Baguettes' (see timpani, bars 64 and 329). Drumsticks. At bar 64 Berlioz asks for 'baguettes de bois recouvert en peau': wooden sticks covered with skin, for a harder effect than 'baguettes d'éponge' (sponge-headed sticks) at bar 329, which create a *pp* roll.

Test yourself

Below are five short questions on each set work. These are not 'exam questions' but are intended to help you get to know each work better.

Most questions use the command words listed in Appendix 5 of each specification (with which you will need to be familiar when preparing for exams).

For each set work there is also a sample essay question for each level. These correspond to Question 6 in Pearson's Sample Assessment Materials.

Essays at the two levels are marked from different assessment grids, as may again be seen from the Sample Assessment Materials. The allocation of marks is different, with fewer marks at AS implying the need for less information. At A Level there is greater emphasis on saying *how* and *why* particular things happen in the music, and relatively less on just saying *what* happens.

When answering the questions below, you should refer to the printed score of the relevant work or movement.

In your exam you will have a special booklet containing the scores you need. You will not be allowed to take a copy of the anthology or other printed music into the exam room.

Concerto in D minor Op. 3 No. 11 (Vivaldi)

Short questions:

a. Define 'continuo'.

b. Describe the texture of Movement 3 (Largo e spiccato).

c. Compare Vivaldi's understanding of a 'concerto' in Op. 3 No. 11 and the general understanding of 'concerto' in the Classical and Romantic periods.

d. Compare Movements 3 and 4 in terms of tempo, metre and rhythm.

e. Discuss the notion that the first solo violin part is much more demanding and showy than the two other solo parts.

Question 6 practice:

AS

Evaluate Vivaldi's use of structure and tonality in the short Adagio and the following Allegro that comprise Movement 2 of his Concerto in D minor Op. 3 No. 11. Relate your discussion to other relevant works. These may include set works, wider listening or other music.

A Level

Evaluate Vivaldi's use of texture, structure and tonality in the short Adagio and the following Allegro that comprise Movement 2 of his Concerto in D minor, Op. 3 No. 11, with particular reference to the amount of contrast involved. Relate your discussion to other relevant works. These may include set works, wider listening or other music.

Piano Trio in G minor Op. 17, Movement 1

Short questions:

a. Identify, in bars 137–163
   i. a diminished seventh chord;
   ii. five consecutive chords belonging to a circle of fifths;
   iii. a suspension.

b. Give a definition of 'parallel motion', and locate three contrasting examples.

c. Compare the texture of bars 1–8 and bars 9–20.

d. Discuss the role of the cello.

e. Discuss Clara Schumann's handling of sonata form in this movement.

Question 6 practice:

AS

Evaluate Clara Schumann's use of melody and harmony in the first movement of her Piano Trio in G minor Op. 17. Relate your discussion to other relevant works. These may include set works, wider listening or other music.

A Level

Evaluate Clara Schumann's use of melody, harmony and dynamics in her Piano Trio in G minor, Op. 17, Movement 1 to show how these are typical of highly expressive Romantic writing. Relate your discussion to other relevant works. These may include set works, wider listening or other music.

Symphonie Fantastique, Movement 1 (Berlioz)

Short questions:

a. Describe the structure of the Largo (bars 1–63).

b. Explain why Berlioz considered bars 17–27 so difficult for the performers.

c. Compare any two presentations of the *idée fixe*.

d. Discuss Berlioz's approach to sonata form in the Allegro (from bar 64 to the end of the movement).

e. Evaluate Berlioz's musical response to the programme that he wrote for the Movement 1 of *Symphonie Fantastique*.

Question 6 practice:

A Level only

Evaluate Berlioz's use of sonority, dynamics and rhythm in Movement 1 of *Symphonie Fantastique*, with particular reference to their variety and dramatic impact. Relate your discussion to other relevant works. These may include set works, wider listening or other music.

Music for Film

OVERVIEW

The Music for Film set works introduce you to
a broad range of styles and techniques, used to
score three very different films:

AS **A** **Cues from *Batman Returns* (1992)
(Danny Elfman)**

AS **A** **Cues from *The Duchess* (2008)
(Rachel Portman)**

A **Cues from *Psycho* (1960)
(Bernard Herrmann)**

Introduction

Silent black-and-white films became popular from the end of the 19th century.

Initially, they were often presented with an accompaniment provided by mechanical musical instruments – organ or player piano – whose primary function was less the creation of mood than the drowning of the projection sounds. Very soon, however, live musicians were employed to create a more flexible and sensitive soundtrack to the events pictured on screen. At first this mood music relied heavily on the improvisatory skills of a pianist. In some cinemas small bands were also employed, and their repertoire frequently drew on well-known classical works or popular songs of the day, selected by the leader of the group. To ensure that there was as systematic an approach as possible in the selection and placing of musical material, film producers, starting with Edison Pictures in 1909, issued cue sheets, which enabled local musicians to choose appropriate works ahead of the screening.

CUE is the term still applied to the portion of music intended for inclusion at a specific point of the film's narrative. For example, cue 17 of *Psycho* is the music for the famous shower scene.

Over time, anthologies of music deemed suitable for particular types of scene were independently published, notably *Kinothek* (Berlin, 1919) and, as late as 1929, near the close of the silent film era, *Allgemeines Handbuch der Filmmusik* (*General Handbook of Film Music*). It is clear from the contents of these volumes that generally Romantic styles and idioms prevailed, and that a number of well-worn clichés were in common use, such as tremolo diminished 7ths for villains and their dastardly deeds, weepy solo violin music for love scenes and the Bridal March from Wagner's *Lohengrin* for weddings.

Though it would certainly be true to say that most film music at the start of the 20th century was cobbled together from pre-existing sources, there were a number of examples of specially composed scores. The first of these was by Saint-Saëns, who provided a score for *L'assassinat du duc de Guise* in 1908, and other notable examples include the American composer Victor Herbert's soundtrack for *The Fall of a Nation* (1916), and in France, Honegger's music for *La Roue* (1923) and *Napoléon* (1927) and Milhaud's music for *L'inhumaine* (1924). Other notable 'silent film' scores included Gottfried Huppertz's music for Fritz Lang's *Metropolis* (1927), Meisel's music for Eisenstein's *The Battleship Potemkin* (1925) and Shostakovich's music for *The New Babylon* (1929).

The problem of synchronisation continued to exist until the development of a film-sound technology, first used for a 15-minute passage of dialogue in Howard Hawks's now lost film *The Air Circus* (1928). It involved the recording of sound waves on the film, running in parallel with the images, so enabling sound and vision to be aligned throughout.

Opposite: Keira Knightly in *The Duchess* (2008)

With the introduction of synchronised sound, a number of specific features and approaches can be seen in film music:

- Use of diegetic music, that is, the use of music which has its source in the action on screen. This approach was often used in Hollywood's early sound films where the specially composed musical score was often limited to just opening and closing credits, any other music being restricted to what was an intrinsic part of the action

- Increasing use of an underscore, or background music, which created a mood or emotional atmosphere to underline the screen action

- Mickey-mousing, that is, the very precise synchronisation of musical gesture with on-screen action, most evident in comic cartoon films.

One of the most celebrated Hollywood composers of the inter-war period was Max Steiner, whose *King Kong* (1933) made extensive use of leitmotifs and dissonance to portray terror. His other film scores included *Gone with the Wind* (1939) and *Casablanca* (1942).

> A **LEITMOTIF** is a motif that is associated with a particular character, object or idea and which recurs throughout a work, subject to development as appropriate. It was originally used in connection with Wagner's music dramas.

Steiner was Viennese and brought to Hollywood the styles and techniques of Romantic music. Another 'Romantic', originally Viennese, composer at work during this era was Erich Wolfgang Korngold, whose best-known scores are *Captain Blood* (1935), *The Adventures of Robin Hood* (1938) and *The Sea Hawk* (1940).

During the middle years of the century, a number of major composers whose reputation is built on their work in other fields composed film scores, notably Prokofiev (*Lieutenant Kijé*, 1934), Arnold Bax (*Malta GC*, 1942; *Oliver Twist*, 1948; *Journey into History*, 1952), Vaughan Williams (*49th Parallel*, 1941; *Scott of the Antarctic*, 1948), William Walton (*Henry V*, 1944; *Hamlet*, 1948; *Richard III*, 1955) and Leonard Bernstein (*On the Waterfront*, 1954).

Film music has done much to familiarise audiences with styles and advanced musical techniques that might otherwise seem 'difficult' and distinctly 'non-popular'. *On the Waterfront* contains passages of bitonality and Jerry Goldsmith's score for the original 1968 *Planet of the Apes* film drew on serial techniques.

> **SERIALISM** is the compositional technique associated with Schoenberg and the Second Viennese School, generally chromatic, atonal and dissonant.

More recently, minimalist composers including Philip Glass and Michael Nyman, and post-minimalist composers such as Max Richter, have created outstanding film scores using the same musical language that they use to create concert music.

There has also been an increasing tendency for film music to become the province of composers who specialise in the genre – for example, John Williams, James Horner and Bernard Herrmann.

Set work:

Batman Returns: 'Birth of a Penguin Part 1', 'Birth of a Penguin Part 2', 'Batman vs the Circus' and 'The Rise and Fall from Grace'

Danny Elfman

AS LEVEL

A LEVEL

Musical context

Composer

Danny Elfman (b. 1953) is a singer and composer who, in the earlier part of his career, was associated with the rock group Oingo Boingo, which he led from 1976 to 1995.

He has had a long association with the director Tim Burton, providing the scores for many films, including *Beetlejuice* (1988), *Edward Scissorhands* (1990), *The Nightmare Before Christmas* (1994), *Sleepy Hollow* (1999) and *Charlie and the Chocolate Factory* (2005) and two Batman

Danny Elfman

films, *Batman* (1989), and *Batman Returns* (1992). He has provided scores for numerous television series, of which *The Simpsons* and *Desperate Housewives* are probably the best known. He has cited Bartók, Glass, Prokofiev, Ravel, Satie, Stravinsky and Tchaikovsky as important influences on his musical style, while in the field of film music he acknowledges a debt to Bernard Herrmann, Erich Wolfgang Korngold and Max Steiner, among others.

For *Batman Returns*, Elfman provided the basic score, which was then orchestrated by Steve Bartek, with some additional help from Mark McKenzie. Elfman likened the experience of scoring his second Batman film to a 'visit to an old friend', adding that the Batman theme remained one of his favourite creations. He also 'loved the Penguin...

so tragic'. In the event he was disappointed by the final result. In composing the score, he had been mindful of dynamic contrast, but found everything was levelled in the course of dubbing: 'In the end result, I believe that if 25% of the score and 25% of the sound effects had been dropped, the entire soundtrack would have been infinitely more effective than the busy mess it became.' He told *Film Score Monthly* in 1995 that most directors 'don't have good ears, even the brilliant ones. With Tim Burton, I had my best and worst dubs back to back. I've never had a better dub than on *Edward Scissorhands*, and I've never had a worse dub than on *Batman Returns*'.

Batman Returns

Batman (1989) and Batman Returns (1992) are the first two in a series of Batman films produced by the Warner Brothers studio.

The plot of *Batman Returns* is particularly complicated and implausible. It is enough to know that the Batman character, a superhero dedicated to the defeat of evil, is the *alter ego* of Bruce Wayne, a wealthy playboy and businessman. Here he is pitted against the Penguin, the deformed and rejected offspring of Tucker and Esther Cobblepot, who is reared by the emperor penguins of Gotham City Zoo. Intent on being recognised as a citizen of Gotham City by whatever means, the Penguin and his Red Triangle Circus Gang kidnap Max Shreck, a corrupt businessman who is blackmailed into assisting the Penguin in his devious schemes. An additional complication arises when Shreck's secretary discovers that her boss's proposed power plant will in effect drain Gotham City of its electricity. She is thrown out of a window and after suffering a nervous breakdown assumes the role of Catwoman. Batman, needless to say, vanquishes the foes of Gotham.

The four prescribed extracts accompany the tossing of the infant Cobblepot into a river ('Birth of a Penguin Part 1'), the main titles ('Birth of a Penguin Part 2'), a scene in which Batman defeats the gang of circus performers sent by the Penguin to disrupt a city meeting ('Batman vs the Circus') and preparations to introduce the Penguin into Gotham society ('The Rise and Fall from Grace').

Musical elements

Sonority, texture and dynamics

Elfman and his collaborators required a full symphony orchestra with organ, children's choir, synthesiser and a large percussion section including xylophone, marimba and vibraphone. Other additions include whistle, accordion and fairground steam organ.

To save repetition of titles of sections, the following abbreviations are used in the following bullet lists:

B1   Birth of a Penguin Part 1

B2   'Birth of a Penguin Part 2' (Main theme)

C   Batman vs the Circus

R   The Rise and Fall from Grace

Some examples of the more arresting timbres include:

- Horns in low register, as in the Batman motif (B1, bars 1–2)
- Tutti orchestra, organ and vocalising choir (B1, bars 5–6)
- Organ solo in contrast with strings (B1, bars 7–10)
- Celesta chords with tremolo strings (B1, bar 11)
- Tuba, low woodwinds and timpani in low register combined with synthesiser in high register (B1, bar 22)
- Tutti choir and orchestra with sleigh bells (B1, bar 26)
- Brass and strings with detached chords in choir (B1, bar 38)
- Low strings and harp (B1, bar 46)
- Choir, widely spaced strings, harp and celesta broken chords (B2, bar 53)
- Xylophone, temple blocks and low percussive piano line with snare drum (C, bar 26)
- Xylophone, piano bass, timpani, marimba and muted trumpet (C, bar 30)
- High string cluster chord (R, bars 7–9)
- Accordion with flute and harp (R, bar 20)
- Contrabass clarinet with celesta, trumpet and string tremolo (R, bar 37).

A wide range of performing techniques can also be observed:

- Tremolo strings (see above)
- Pizzicato strings (B1, bar 14; R, bars 1–2)
- Harp glissandi (B1, bar 25)
- Muted brass, e.g. trumpets (B1, bar 21)
- Tam-tam roll (B1, bar 6)
- Cymbal roll (B1, bars 13, 25)
- Stopped horn notes (B2, bar 13; C, bar 15)
- Flutter-tongued flute (B2, bar 101)
- Violin glissandi (C, bar 25)
- Horn glissandi (C, bar 42)
- Trumpet extreme lip trill (C, bar 50)
- Oboe extreme vibrato (C, bars 57–58).

The choir vocalises throughout the 'Birth of a Penguin Part 1', changing from 'Ah' (B1, bar 3) to 'La' (B1, bar 26) and 'Oo' (B1, bar 34).

Textures draw on a variety of homophonic layouts throughout:

- Drone supporting harmonised melody occurs at B1 (bar 1) with the portentous announcement of the Batman motif, and again at the opening bar of 'Batman vs the Circus'
- Predominantly chordal textures appear from bar 7 of B1, first in strings then on organ. At bar 11 they are overlaid with three-note celesta chords
- B1, bar 28: block chords are decorated with falling broken-chord figures in violins
- B1 (bar 22): a passage of octaves
- B2 (bars 1–20): layers of ostinati over pedal notes and with drawn-out high notes on violin. The layered texture supports statements of the Batman theme and trumpet fanfares

- B2 (bar 27): melody-dominated homophony with pounding triplets supporting statements of the Batman theme
- C (from bar 13): 'Circus'-inspired music with comic accompanying trombone figures and fragmentary texture made up of short rapidly contrasted interjections from different sections of the orchestra
- C (bar 26): prominent percussive elements (xylophone and piano octaves with temple blocks and side drum)
- R (bar 1): single note pizzicato cello line
- R (bar 8): high strings cluster with widely spaced octaves and sustained dominant pedal beneath
- R (bar 20): accordion with 'waltz' accompanying figure and long sustained notes for flute and harp in octaves.

Dynamics span the full available range. Besides the more conventional contrasts and effects, particular use is made of the quick-acting *crescendo* (e.g. B1, bars 5–6, 14–15, 38–39).

Tempo, metre and rhythm

Speeds are shown by way of metronome marks rather than terminology. A wide range of tempi is to be found in the four extracts, often changing rapidly from one to another. In broad terms, 'Birth of a Penguin Part 1' is slow to moderate; Part 2 moves from moderate to brisk; 'Batman vs the Circus', after a slow introduction, moves into a fast passage at bar 18 (170 crotchets a minute), while 'The Rise and Fall from Grace' is relatively moderate.

Metres are changed on occasion. 'Birth of a Penguin Part 1' settles into a steady quadruple time after the slow triple time introduction. There is one interpolated bar of $\frac{3}{8}$ at bar 13. Part 2 is in $\frac{4}{4}$ throughout apart from one bar of $\frac{5}{4}$ at bar 20.

'Batman vs the Circus' is mainly in quadruple time, but there are frequent bar changes to reflect the zany action. In contrast, 'Rise and Fall', though mainly in quadruple time, contains a distinctive triple-time waltz section.

Rhythm is handled in traditional terms, but 'Birth of a Penguin Part 1' is characterised by its ponderous steady crotchets (e.g. bar 3) and the brief lively dance-like theme at bar 26.

Rhythms in 'Birth of a Penguin Part 2' are more distinctive, with ostinati composed of running semiquavers or repeated short patterns (see bar 5). Triplets also play a more important role here, most notably in the main part of the movement where a strong feeling of propulsion is created in the heavily accented accompaniment to the Batman theme, which also incorporates triplets. Another technique used here is the (loose) augmentation of the Batman theme at bar 65, with the triplet quavers changed to minim and crotchets. High energy in 'Batman vs the Circus' is created through the near-constant quaver movement and the bursts of semiquaver–semiquaver–quaver figures on Temple Blocks from bar 26. Motifs are often breathless, with frequent rests and placing of the same motif on a different beat of the bar (see bars 20–22). The hectic feel to the music is further intensified by sudden sextuplet semiquavers (bars 69 and 70).

Organisation of pitch: melody

The melodic writing of *Batman Returns* draws in part on a number of leitmotifs (which will be referred to as 'motifs'), notably those associated with Batman himself, the Penguin and Catwoman, though the Catwoman motifs are not used in the prescribed extracts. The Batman motif is heard at the start of 'Birth of a Penguin Part 1', its distinctive shape resulting from the conjunct rising line, outlining the first three notes of the minor scale, and the succeeding upwards leap of a fourth and semitone fall to the dominant note (although notated with a key signature of four flats, the key is clearly B♭ minor at this point).

Batman motif in 'Birth of a Penguin Part 1'

The next appearance of this motif is in 'Birth of a Penguin Part 2' at bar 8 where it is in D minor, and then at bar 13 where the presence of a triplet hints at the imminent appearance of the 'Batman theme' proper, as seen at bar 27:

Batman motif in 'Birth of a Penguin Part 2' (the 'theme proper')

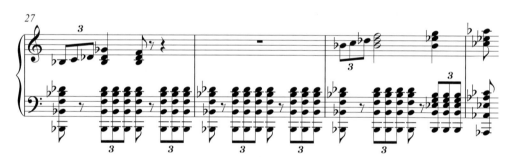

This 'triplet' version gives way to an extensive treatment of the motif in longer note-lengths, beginning in bar 34.

Further Batman motif in 'Birth of a Penguin Part 2'

As you can see above, the fifth note of the motif rises in bar 35 (as in bar 29).
In the subsequent statement of the motif (from bar 38) it follows the original form.

'Batman vs the Circus' opens with a reference to the Batman motif in bass instruments in B minor, and throughout the rapidly moving circus action it appears as follows:

Bars 47–48	C♯ minor	First four notes in bass instruments with answering trumpet fanfare, the second note of which is a diminished 4th above the tonic
Bars 52–53	C♯ minor	First four notes in brass
Bars 56–57	B minor	Triplet rhythm
Bars 64–65	B minor	First four notes in trombone and tuba, augmented
Bars 82–84	E minor	First four notes in brass, augmented rhythm
Bar 88	A minor	First three notes; trombone and tuba

Two motifs that are closely related to each other are associated with the Penguin. The first one, Penguin motif **a**, consists of four crotchet notes, circling around the dominant.

It first appears in bar 3 of 'Birth of a Penguin Part 1' in F minor:

Penguin motif a at the beginning of 'Birth of a Penguin Part 1'

Then, with an abrupt switch into the key of A minor, it is heard in rhythmic augmentation in bar 7. It underpins the whole of 'Birth of a Penguin Part 1', resurfacing in various keys, and at bar 26 is transformed into a folk-like dance, accompanied by sleigh bells:

'Folk-like' use of Penguin motif a in 'Birth of a Penguin Part 1'

A further folk-style continuation of Penguin motif **a** occurs at bar 32.

Further 'folk-like' use of Penguin motif a in 'Birth of a Penguin Part 1'

The second Penguin motif – motif **b** – appears at bar 34 and spans two bars. Notice, however, that it is closely linked to the previous motif with its prominent stepwise descent:

'Penguin motif b in 'Birth of a Penguin Part 1'

As we have seen, 'Birth of a Penguin Part 2' is given over mainly to a working out of the Batman motif, but there is reference to Penguin theme **a** in B minor at bar 85, its fourth note raised by a semitone to E♯. It also appears disguised in 'Batman vs the Circus' within a moto perpetuo line: notice the shape created by the first of every four-quaver group of notes in piano and xylophone:

Penguin motif a 'disguised' in 'Batman vs the Circus'

Further ingenious re-workings of both Penguin motifs are embedded in the texture of 'The Rise and Fall from Grace':

Bars 4–7	Penguin theme **a**: cellos (unevenly augmented note-lengths)
Bars 8–16	Penguin theme **b**: harp and marimba (broken octaves)
Bars 17–18	Penguin theme **a**: harp and marimba (broken octaves)
Bars 20–22	Penguin theme **a** (extended): accordion (first note of bar), flute and harp
Bars 26–28	Penguin theme **a**: cellos (unevenly augmented note-lengths)
Bar 29	Penguin theme **a**: harp (two crotchets and two quavers)

In general, the melodic writing of 'Batman vs the Circus' is fragmentary and sometimes chromatic, as in the brief oboe solo at bars 57–58. A reference to Penguin motif **b** can be heard at bars 62-63.

Organisation of pitch: harmony

Elfman draws on a fundamentally functional harmonic language, involving use of cadences. In fact, imperfect cadences frequently occur to aid continuity, such as 'Birth of a Penguin Part 1', bars 5–6, 12–13, 21, 31 and 37.

The effect of a perfect cadence is created at 'Birth of a Penguin Part 1', bars 45–46, in spite of the marked change in texture at this point. Occasionally, conventional cadences are avoided altogether, such as at the close of 'Birth of a Penguin Part 2' on, where a second inversion C♯ minor chord reduces to an open chord of G♯ and C♯.

In the first few bars, root position, first and second inversion chords are employed, though it soon becomes clear that some of the finer points of traditional harmonic practice are disregarded, notably in the relaxed approach to part-writing.

Some characteristic features of the harmonic vocabulary include:

- Tonic pedal (B2, bars 1–6)
- Accented passing note (B1, bar 12^3)
- Dominant 7th (B1, bar 13)
- Diminished triad (B1, 34^3)
- Supertonic 7th (B1, bar 36^3)
- Diminished 7th (B1, bar 37^2)
- Side-shifting of chords, such as B2, bars 20–21, with B♭ minor moving to C major; bars 66–67, A♭ minor moving to B♭ major; C, bars 6–7: B minor to C♯ major)
- Half-diminished chord (B2, bar 59)
- Augmented triad (B2, bar 71; R, bar 51)

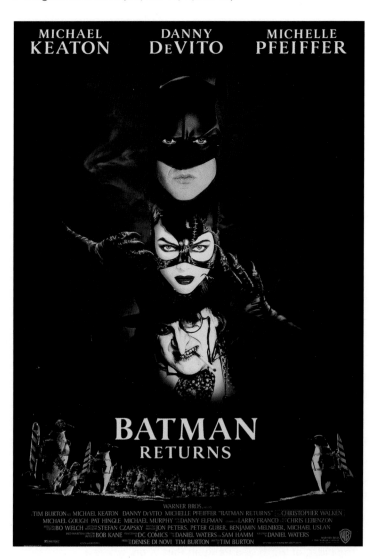

The poster for *Batman Returns*, showing, top to bottom, Batman, Catwoman and The Penguin

- False relation (B2, bars 93–96: E♯–E♮; G♯–G♮)
- Added sixth chord (C, bar 5⁴, where notes 1, 3, 4 and 5 of the Batman motif are verticalised to form a chord)
- Cluster chord (C, bar 62 and R, bars 7–9)
- 'Neapolitan' harmony (R, bar 45)
- Appoggiatura (R, bar 49)
- Whole-tone chords (R, 50–52).

Structure and tonality

All the prescribed extracts are through-composed, the succession of material clearly dictated by the course of the on-screen action. Keys for the most part are clearly defined, either by pedal points or functional chord progressions.

'Birth of a Penguin Part 1'

Bars	Key	Comment
1–2	B♭ minor	Batman motif
3–6	F minor	Penguin motif **a**
7–10	A minor	Penguin motif **a** augmented, melodic minor bass line
11–13	G minor	Penguin motif **a** with significant bass motif
14–21	C minor	Penguin motif **a** augmented
22–25	C minor	Octaves, with C major harp glissando in bar 25
26–31	D minor	'Folk'-style version of Penguin motif **a**
32–33	F♯ minor	Second bar related to bass of bar 11 and anticipating Penguin motif **b**
34–37	G minor	Penguin motif **b**
38–41	C minor moving to V of G minor	Penguin motif **b** in bar 39 (bass)
42–47	D minor	Penguin motif **a**

'Birth of a Penguin Part 2'

Bars	Key	Comment
1–10	D minor	Layered ostinato; Batman motif
11–20	B♭ minor	Batman motif
21–24	C major	
25–52		Batman 'march' theme, passing through the keys listed below
25	B♭ minor	
30	A♭ minor	
34	F♯ minor	
38	C♯ minor	
40	E♭ major	
42	B minor	
44	D♭ major	Choir enters with falling 3rd motif
53–62	F♯ minor – A♭ major	Falling 3rd motif continued
63–84		Batman theme merged with falling 3rds, passing through the keys listed below
63	A♭ minor	
73	C♯ minor	
80	B minor	
85–92	B open 5th, latterly B minor	Augmented Penguin motif 1; Pedal point on B
93–102	C♯ major/minor	Alternating mediant-related chords of C♯ major and E minor, closing on C♯ minor 2nd inversion reducing to an open chord of G♯ and C♯

'Batman vs the Circus'

Bars	Key	Comment
1–6	B minor	Batman motif
7–12	C♯ major	Alternation of C♯ major and E minor
13–17	E minor–G minor	Begins with whole-tone chord
18–25	C minor/major	
26–44	C minor – dissolves in whole-tone figures	Moto perpetuo based on Penguin motif **a**
45–46	B♭ minor	
47–55	C♯ minor	Batman motif
56–65	B minor	Batman motif; Penguin motif **b** (at bar 62 on steam organ)
66–70	E♭ major	
71–95	E minor	Occasional Batman references; material from moto perpetuo quavers

'The Rise and Fall from Grace'

Bars	Key	Comment
1–7	C minor	Incorporates Penguin motif **a** (bar 4, cellos)
8–19	C minor	Penguin motif **b**; then Penguin motif **a** at bar 17
20–25	C minor	Penguin motif **a** in waltz rhythm
26–39	C minor	Penguin motif **a**; descending lines from bar 31
40–46	C minor	Broken chord melodic patterns, often based on diminished 7th
47–54	C minor/major	Bars 49–52 use whole-tone harmony; the last two bars are in the tonic major

Set work:
The Duchess: 'The Duchess (Opening)', 'Mistake of Your Life', 'Six Years Later', 'Never See Your Children Again', 'The Duchess (End Titles)'

Rachel Portman

AS LEVEL

A LEVEL

Musical context

Composer

Rachel Portman (b. 1960) has built her career mainly on the composition of film music. She studied music at The University of Oxford, where she was involved in writing incidental music for student film and theatre productions, and made her professional debut with her music for *Privileged* (1982), a film directed by Michael Hoffman for the Oxford Film Foundation.

Since then, she has composed over 100 television, film and theatre scores, of which some of the best known are *Emma* (1996), for which she won an Academy Award in the category of Best Musical or Comedy Score, *The Cider House Rules* (1999), *Chocolat* (2000), *The Manchurian Candidate* (2004), *Oliver Twist* (2005), *The Duchess* (2008) and *Never Let Me Go* (2010). Her other works include *The Little Prince* (2003), a children's opera based on the book by Antoine de Saint-Exupéry, and *Little House on the Prairie* (2008), a musical which draws on the story by Laura Ingalls Wilder.

Rachel Portman

Portman has said that some of the main influences on her composition are Ravel, Erik Satie, and above all, Bach. She has also stated that her music is influenced predominantly by composers of the classical tradition rather than other film composers. In general, her scores are notable for a preference for 'natural' sound-sources rather than synthesised effects.

See Portman's interview with Bob Jones (February 2011) on Classic FM, accessible on www.classicfm.com/composers/rachel-portman.

The Duchess

The Duchess is an account of the life of Georgiana Cavendish, Duchess of Devonshire (1757–1806), focusing in particular on her unhappy marriage with William Cavendish, 5th Duke of Devonshire, her betrayal by her friend Bess Foster who becomes the Duke's mistress, and her own affair with Charles Grey, 2nd Earl Grey, which resulted in the birth of a daughter, Eliza Courtney.

Charles Grey (1764–1845), one of Britain's most historically important political figures, steered the Reform Act of 1832 through parliament, a measure which marked the start of the process leading to universal suffrage. The historical Georgiana was celebrated in her day both for her beauty and unfortunate love life. She was an active political campaigner, and an unflattering cartoon by Rowlandson portrays her trading kisses for votes for the Whig cause. There are many more sympathetic portrayals, however, including one by Joshua Reynolds and another of her, with her brother and sister, by Angelica Kaufmann. She was an inveterate gambler, and at her death left a debt in the region of £3,720,000 in modern terms. Her tomb and memorial can be found in Derby Cathedral.

The music

The film score consists of 18 cues, two of which draw on historically appropriate material: Beethoven's German Dance No. 10 in D (Cue 7) and the Adagio from Haydn's String Quartet in D, Op. 1 No. 3 (Cue 14). In the remaining cues, Portman avoids specific pastiche, producing instead an underscore which is deliberately light in terms of content but provides, for the most part, attractive background music that is vaguely suggestive of the refinements of past times.

As one commentator has remarked (see box below), the music is exactly what is to be expected from a Portman film score: 'lush string writing augmented by soft woodwinds, a generally light and romantic tone, a slightly upbeat bounce in the tempo, and an overall sense of florid "Englishness"'.

See Jonathan Broxton's review, dated 19 September, 2008, accessible at http://moviemusicuk.us/tag/the-duchess/.

An appropriately darker atmosphere is, however, created in two of the prescribed cues: 'Mistake of Your Life' and 'Never See Your Children Again'.

The cues selected for study are:

1. 'The Duchess (Opening)'
2. 'Mistake of Your Life'
12. 'Six Years Later'
15. 'Never See Your Children Again'
18. 'The Duchess (End Titles)'

Musical language

In the Anthology, all cues are notated in short score with indications regarding scoring as required. Tempi are indicated by metronome marks, with some Italian terms used (e.g. *accel., poco a poco, rit., a tempo*).

Although instrumentation is given in English, some Italian terminology is employed (e.g. tacet, tutti) as well as traditional dynamic marks.

'The Duchess (Opening)': musical elements

Tempo, metre and rhythm

This cue is notated in simple quadruple time, with a tempo of 116 crotchets per minute (a moderate speed). A *ritardando* is indicated at bar 13 for two bars, after which there is no fluctuation of tempo.

Rhythms are characterised by:

■ Continuous quavers

■ Syncopation in both accompaniment (e.g. bar 1) and melody (e.g. bar 10)

■ Long note lengths in both bass and melody

■ Occasional triplets (bar 22) and semiquavers (bar 37).

Organisation of pitch: melody

The melody is in D major with Mixolydian inflections (e.g. the C♮ in bar 7).
Notice the following:

■ Transposition up an octave of part of the first theme at bar 10

■ Auxiliary notes (e.g. bars 2 and 35)

■ Frequent stepwise movement interspersed with leaps of 3rd, 4th and 6th

■ Appoggiaturas (e.g. bar 18). The strict definition of appoggiatura is a dissonant note which is resolved by step, upwards or downwards, but which is unprepared, that is, normally approached by leap. However, it is also used in such instances as bar 18, where the dissonant note (here a G) is sounded in the same part immediately before

■ Stepwise descending and ascending line, twice moving down from tonic to dominant and back again (bars 37–43).

Keira Knightley in *The Duchess* (2008)

Organisation of pitch: harmony

The harmonic language is functional, with some perfect cadences (e.g. bars 41–43). 'Functionality' is not strong, however, as the entire cue is built on an alternation of the two basic chords of tonic (D major) and 'modal' dominant (A minor), and consequently the drive towards cadences is weak.

> A 'MODAL' DOMINANT is one in which the leading note is lowered a semitone, so that here in place of the expected A major chord with C$\sharp$, a Mixolydian-derived chord of A minor with C$\natural$ is used. The device can occasionally be found in some 19th-century works (for example Brahms's Piano Quintet in F minor Op. 34, movement III, bar 19, in the 'old' Anthology). In 'Mistake of Your Life', a modal dominant in a minor key is used (i.e. D minor dominant in G minor).

Variety in this cue comes from:

- Use of (non-cadential) second inversions (bars 8, 12–14)
- Introduction of (unprepared and unresolved) 7ths (e.g. bar 11)
- Use of A^7 over pedal D (bar 21).

Tonality

The cue is in D Mixolydian throughout; there is no modulation.

Structure

The cue consists of three separate themes laid end to end. There is no development.

Bars 1–16 contain Theme A:

Theme A

Bars 17–34 contain Theme B (heard twice, i.e. bars 17–26 (10 bars) and 27–34 (8 bars):

Theme B

Bars 35–43 contain Theme C (notice the motif **x** beginning at bar 37 which is heard extended in the 'End titles')

Theme C

Texture and sonority

The texture is melody-dominated homophony, with pedals and quaver rhythmic ostinato.

The instrumentation is gradually built up as the movement progresses:

Bars 1–16	Strings and harp
Bars 17–34	Violin solo; the quaver figure is transferred from violin and harp to viola; timpani and cello punctuate with two-note V–I every two bars
Bars 35–43	Tutti, that is, full woodwinds and horns added

Mistake of Your Life

This cue reflects the deteriorating state of the Duchess's marriage.

Tempo, metre and rhythm

The music here is in a slow (69 crotchets per minute) triple time. The introduction is characterised by a long, sustained dominant pedal and ominous patterns on timpani:

Continuous quavers in the accompaniment are heard in bars 43–67.

Organisation of pitch: melody

The introduction consists of a series of sustained sounds, each lasting two bars, moving up and down through a minor 2nd. Following this, there are two main motifs, both of which bear some similarity to themes from the first cue. The first motif (at bar 19) is a rising, conjunct line in G minor, the basic shape of which relates to theme B (see above):

Notice that both melodies rise from tonic to dominant, and share a distinctive two-quaver figure, with appoggiatura, at the highest point (compare the second bar of theme B with the third bar here).

An almost complete sequential repetition of bars 19–26, taking the original melody from G minor up a tone into A minor, starts at bar 27.

The second theme, appearing for the first time at bar 35, adopts the auxiliary note figure from bar 2 of theme A. The motif is now heard in a minor mode and the original falling 3rd is replaced by a descending minor 6th:

This melody is also treated sequentially, this time appearing down a step at bar 39.

Organisation of pitch: harmony

The introduction consists of a dominant pedal, supporting first a single line, then 3rds from bar 9.

Other features include:

- 'Modal' dominant (i.e. dominant chord in minor key with unraised leading note, bar 21)
- Ascending harmonic sequence (see bars 27–34)
- Descending harmonic sequence (compare bars 39–42 with 35–38)
- Functional dominant chord beginning in bar 57 (that is, an 'ordinary' chord V with raised leading note)
- Open 5ths chord at bar 73
- Final chord (bars 81–82) is an unstable tonic in second inversion.

Tonality

The key is G minor, reinforced by a dominant pedal, using both a 'modal' and a functional dominant. There are brief excursions to A minor (bars 27 and 51).

Structure

The cue is built on two alternating themes with introduction:

Bars 1–18	Introduction
Bars 19–34	Theme I
Bars 35–42	Theme II
Bars 43–59	Theme I (modified at close; expanded orchestral texture)
Bars 60–69	Theme II (lengthened; expanded orchestral texture)
Bars 70–82	Theme I (first phrase repeated, now with sustained chordal accompaniment)

Texture and sonority

The texture is mainly melody-dominated homophony, although the introduction opens with a dominant pedal and a single-line melody.

Low strings and timpani are used at the start. Harp and violins are added at bar 19, and woodwinds, horn and piano at bar 35.

From bar 43 an additional line is added in the inner parts, and cello and harp provide continuous quavers. Tutti is employed at bar 60.

Six Years Later

The music for this cue falls into two clearly defined sections, the second of which is built on material from the first cue ('The Duchess (Opening)').

Tempo, metre and rhythm

The first section sounds like a brisk waltz, in spite of its notation in compound duple time with 60 dotted crotchets per minute. The main theme makes use of three quavers followed by a longer note, answered by a semiquaver motif.

For information about the main features of the second section (from bar 30), see the comments on the first cue. Note, however:

- The slightly faster tempo (120 crotchets per minute)
- The insertion of a single $\frac{2}{4}$ bar at bar 34
- The *ritardando* at bar 61, leading to a close at a slower tempo (72 crotchets per minute), and the breakdown of the quaver pattern.

Organisation of pitch: melody

The main melodic element of the 'waltz' is a rising broken chord of D major, balanced by a falling broken chord of A minor, clearly referring back to the music of 'The Duchess (Opening)':

The figure in bar 6, shown above, might be regarded as a diminution of bar 2 of the first cue, with chromatic alteration.

Organisation of pitch: harmony

Bars 1–28 draw mainly on the chords of D major and A minor, sometimes in second inversion.

The augmented triad on D is used in bars 25 and 27, giving some slight variation to the basic vocabulary.

Tonality

The key is D major throughout.

Structure

Bars 1–2	Introduction
Bars 3–15	'Waltz' theme
Bars 16–28	Part repetition of 'waltz' theme
Bar 29	Link bar
Bars 30–34	Theme A from 'The Duchess (Opening)'
Bars 35–36	Theme B from 'The Duchess (Opening)'
Bars 37–63	Theme C from 'The Duchess (Opening)'
Bars 64–66	Coda, based on quaver pattern.

Texture and sonority

The texture is again melody-dominated homophony, reducing to a single note at bar 29, and bass pedal with melody at the coda.

The orchestral writing requires pizzicato strings and harp at the start, and cello and harp at the end. There is a tutti at bar 16 and also for the appearances of Theme C.

Never See Your Children Again

Tempo, metre and rhythm

This cue is in slow (66 crotchets per minute) triple time.

Following the opening long, sustained note, the first section is marked by the use of repeated slurred quavers, producing a 'dragging' effect, while the melody is presented in long, drawn-out notes.

The ominous timpani rhythm from 'Mistake of Your Life' is heard again from bar 22.

Organisation of pitch: melody

From bar 7, there is a drawn-out line, rising by step. As such it bears some resemblance to the first theme from 'Mistake of Your Life', which in turn is derived from Theme B from 'The Duchess (Opening)':

There is no melodic element as such in the passage from bar 22.

Organisation of pitch: harmony

A pedal D is present throughout, and is heard in an inner part from bar 8. Harmony is dissonant in the first part of the cue, incorporating a persistent added E throughout: notice in particular the clashing F and E in bars 5-10.

The closing chord is G diminished over the pedal D♮.

Tonality

Non-functional D minor.

Structure

The cue is in two through-composed sections separated by a four-bar link and rounded off by a four-bar coda.

Bars 1–21	Section 1: Melody with dissonant accompaniment
Bars 22–25	Link: D minor chord with timpani rhythm
Bars 26–33	Section 2: Repeated passage, built on descending 3rds over pedal
Bars 34–37	G diminished chord over pedal D♮

Texture and sonority

After the single note at the beginning, the texture is melody-dominated homophony.

It is scored for strings with prominent parts for timpani (from bar 22) and harp (from bar 26).

End titles

This cue closely resembles the opening credits. Significant departures are given below.

Tempo, metre and rhythm

Tempo is now very slightly faster at 120 crotchets per minute.

The semiquavers at bar 37 of the opening are changed to quavers (bar 25)

Organisation of pitch: melody

The variations and extensions here involve:

- Introduction of F♮ (bar 14)
- Variant of Theme B from bar 17, involving a contraction (here it takes five bars as opposed to the original nine)
- More extensive treatment of the motif at the end of Theme C (opening, bar 37) from bar 25
- Theme C extended by descending sequential repetition at bar 43.

Organisation of pitch: harmony

Whereas the opening cue was based entirely on the chords of D major and A minor, the vocabulary is here expanded to also include F major, G major (first inversion) and Em^7.

The harmonic pace remains slow, but a suspension is added at bar 43.

Tonality

The music is in D with modal inflections (C♮, F♮). There is no modulation.

Structure

Bars 1–8	Theme A
Bars 9–24	Theme B varied
Bars 25–40	Theme C, motif **x** (see page 168)
Bars 41–50	Theme C first part, varied and repeated
Bars 51–60	Theme C, motif **x**

Texture and sonority

The texture is melody-dominated homophony and, as before, a violin solo is used for Theme B and tutti for Theme C.

Set work:

Psycho: 'Prelude', 'The City', 'Marion', 'The Murder' (Shower Scene), 'The Toys', 'The Cellar', 'Discovery', 'Finale'

Bernard Herrmann

A LEVEL

Musical context

Composer

Bernard Herrmann (1911–1975) trained at New York University and the Juilliard School, before joining CBS where he worked in Radio Theatre, perfecting his economical, powerfully suggestive style. His breakthrough came in 1940 when he wrote the score for Orson Welles's *Citizen Kane*, but he is perhaps best known for his collaboration with Alfred Hitchcock at Paramount and MGM Studios, in the course of which he composed scores for *Vertigo* (1958), *North by North West* (1959) and *Psycho* (1960). Subsequently he collaborated with Truffaut (*Fahrenheit 451*, 1966) and Martin Scorsese (*Taxi Driver*, 1976).

Unusually, Herrmann took responsibility for the entire score and unlike many film composers, he orchestrated his own works. In this respect, he was extremely innovative, and here it is also worth mentioning *The Day the Earth Stood Still* (1951), which requires two theremins, electronic violin, bass and guitar, four harps, four pianos, percussion and brass.

Bernard Herrmann

His style is unusual in that he avoided leitmotifs or extended melodic lines in favour of short motifs and frequent ostinati, often used to indicate obsessions. He was not afraid to employ extreme dissonance and chromaticism.

Though most of his work was in the field of incidental music, he left a number of works in other genres: Sinfonietta (1935), from which he quoted a motif in the course of *Psycho*, and most importantly, the opera *Wuthering Heights*, which he worked on between 1943 and 1951.

Psycho

Psycho, released in 1960, is one of Hitchcock's most famous films. It was based on Robert Bloch's novel of the same name, published in 1959, with a screenplay by Joseph Stefano. After the opening scenes in Phoenix, Arizona, it is set in a Gothic-style motel (the set was based on a painting by Edward Hopper, *The House by the Railroad*, dating from 1925), and develops into a thoroughly bleak and chilling investigation of the mind of a murderer.

Though filmed on a low budget in black and white, marking a radical departure from the opulence of Hitchcock's previous films, it broke box-office records. This was in part a consequence of skilful marketing and a 'no late admission' rule which led to lengthy queues outside cinemas, thus attracting further publicity. Eventually it came to enjoy enormous critical acclaim, and in no small measure, the film's success can be attributed to the impact of Herrmann's score, Hitchcock himself remarking that '33 percent of the effect of *Psycho* was due to the music'.

Working within the bounds of budget restrictions (which interestingly did not extend to the composer's own fee), Herrmann scored the music for strings only rather than a full symphony orchestra or the jazz band for which Hitchcock originally asked. The reduction of performing forces to a single family of instruments (14 first violins, 12 seconds, 10 violas, 8 cellos and 6 double basses), albeit employed with considerable ingenuity, reflected the monochrome on-screen images, and this limitation is further intensified by the use of mutes throughout, except in the shower scene.

Cue 1: 'Prelude' (Titles): musical elements

The score is written in staff notation with conventional Italian terminology for tempi and instrumental techniques. Explanations of these are given below as they occur.

The title sequence, by Saul Bass, an abstract design consisting of interlocking horizontal bars moving back and forth, was intended to suggest clues coming together. Its mechanical quality is underpinned by Herrmann's relentlessly moving music.

Sonority, texture and dynamics

Aggressive double-stopped chords at the opening have a Bartókian quality.

Béla Bartók (1881–1945) was a Hungarian composer who fused folk music with a sophisticated harmonic and tonal idiom. For examples of his, at times, savage style of string writing, see String Quartets Nos. 4 and 5.

String writing in this number includes combinations of arco (bowed), pizzicato (plucked) and occasional tremolandi. Notice also the relatively high cello line at bar 111, producing a particularly intense timbre.

Textures vary from:

- Chords (homophony), as in bars 1 and 21
- Ostinati and pedals supporting short motifs (bar 5)
- Melody with tremolandi and chordal accompaniment, i.e. melody-dominated homophony (bar 37).

Dynamics span the full range from *ff* at the opening to *pp* at bar 31. Further contrasts are obtained by reducing the forces at various points.

Tempo, metre and rhythm

The Prelude is labelled 'Allegro (molto agitato)' (Fast (very agitated)) – and is cast in a constant, unremitting duple time, which only slackens at the close, where a pause is included before the final bar. Much of the music's drive and urgency comes from:

- Almost constant quaver movement, with quavers slurred in pairs for additional emphasis
- Energetic triplet figures (see Motif 2, bars 5–6, opposite)
- Dotted rhythms and suddenly broken rhythms (see Motif 3, bars 21–22, opposite)
- A recurring rhythm, associated with the opening chords (see Motif 1, bars 1–3, below).

The only contrast with the driving quavers comes with the more extended wisps of melody (e.g. bar 37) in crotchets.

Organisation of pitch: harmony, melody and motifs

The Prelude is based on three motifs and a more extended melody.

The first motif, shown below in skeleton short score, is in reality a series of repeated chords: a B♭ minor triad in second inversion with additional major 7th. This chord returns in subsequent cues in various positions and transpositions, and its markedly dissonant quality immediately suggests aggression and violence.

Motif 1

Motif 2 (violin 1, see upper stave) is heard over a semitonal ostinato (in viola, C♯ to D, slurred) and B♭ pedal, and its melody also involves semitonal figures. Notice that the second bar consists of the same pitches, but now in even quavers.

Motif 2

Motif 3 is characterised by its jagged dotted rhythm and sudden rest. It is chordal, the harmonic structures consisting of 13ths and simultaneous false relations. This one-bar figure is extended by sequential repetition, initially a perfect fourth higher.

Motif 3

The final thematic element is a melodic line that appears three times in the course of the Prelude. It is mainly conjunct, and so forms a marked contrast with the fragmentary preceding material, the more so as it consists of three clearly defined four-bar phrases. In its early stages it also has a more diatonic feel and is composed almost entirely of crotchets. The first phrase starts on B♭ and the second on E, making it sound as if the first four bars are lodged on the tritonal dominant of the second phrase, another rather Bartókian feature (see the box at the top of page 178). The supporting harmony consists of an added 6th on E♭ minor for four bars, followed by E major with added second, triggering false relations with the G♮ in the melody.

A typical feature of Bartók's harmonic and tonal system in his mature work was the frequent replacement of the traditional dominant (a perfect 5th above the tonic) with a dominant lodged on the augmented 4th above the tonic (e.g. B♭–E), dividing the scale into two halves.

Structure and tonality

The Prelude consists of varied presentations of all three motifs listed above, the whole held together by a driving ostinato consisting of slurred pairs of quavers. Tonally, the Prelude takes as its starting-point an expanded B♭ minor, suggested by the opening chord. There are few digressions. The main landmarks are as follows:

Bar	Musical material	Notes
1	Motif 1	B♭ minor plus major 7th (in second inversion)
3	Ostinato	B♭ pedal
5	Motif 2	B♭ pedal and ostinato
9	Ostinato varied	Four-part texture, with original semitone figure appearing in violas in minor 3rds and in an inverted form in violin 2 in major 3rds. Notice that the second chord is a transposition up a semitone of motif 1.
11	Motif 2	Supporting harmony changed to E♭ minor plus minor 6th
15	Development of bar 9	The material from bar 9 is transposed down a 3rd, but notice that the major 3rds in violin 2 are replaced by minor 3rds and vice versa in the viola part.
17	Motif 2	B♭ pedal and ostinato
21	Motif 3	C♯–F♯
25	Motif 1	Varied spacing and octave shifts
29	Variant of Motif 2	Note-order: F–E–G♯–E
31	Motif 2 + bar 9 variant at bar 35	

37	Melody 1st appearance	B♭/E♭ minor–E major/minor
49	Motif 3	Varied distribution of parts
53	Motif 1	
57	Motif 2	
63	Motif 3	
67	Motif 1	
69	Ostinato modified	C♯ and D sounded simultaneously
71	Motif 2	
77	Melody second appearance	Harmony as before
89	Motif 1	
91	Variant of Motif 2 (from bar 29)	C♯ pedal
97	Motif 2	Changing harmonisation, from B♭m^7 to E^7 to enharmonic B♭m^7 again (i.e. C♯ and A♯ in supporting chords)
103	Motif 3	
107	Motif 2	
111	Melody third appearance	Redistribution of parts with melody in cello, harmonic support in upper parts
121	Motif 1	
123	Coda (repeated)	Built on Motif 2 and chord of opening. Final note is an unrelated D♮, giving an alienating effect

Cue 2 – 'The City': musical elements

Captions indicate time and place: Phoenix, Arizona; Friday December 11 at 2.43 pm. The shot homes in on a hotel window, through which Marion Crane and Sam Loomis can be seen after making love.

Tempo, metre and rhythm

In obvious contrast to the Prelude, this section is in slow quadruple time, 'Lento molto sostenuto' (slow, very sustained), and consists of steadily moving crotchets, with crotchet-slurred-to-quaver pairs every third bar.

The only exception is the final bar, which consists of a semibreve in each part.

Sonority, texture and dynamics

The movement alternates between eight-part divisi upper strings (without basses) and the usual four-part writing every third bar (reinforced by isolated double bass notes). Bars 6 and 12 are scored for divided violins alone.

Texture is homophonic throughout.

Dynamics are generally low, never rising above *mf*.

Organisation of pitch: melody and harmony

The overall effect of the cue is almost akin to wave motion, with descending lines answered by ascending ones. Furthermore, the opening descending line outlines notes which form the basic harmonic structure of the cue.

The melody in fact consists of five three-bar phrases (two bars plus one), the opening descent answered by an inexact inversion. A similar pattern is used in the remaining phrases.

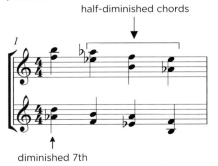

Notice that the particular distribution of parts deprives the opening diminished 7th of its usual sinister quality. The movement closes with the same diminished 7th that appeared at the opening, but in a much lower position.

Most of the remaining chords are different positions of a widely spaced half-diminished chord, that is, F–A♭–B–E♭, where the B is enharmonic C♭.

The few chords which do not fit the diminished/half-diminished scheme are:

- Bars 3, 9 and 15, beats 2 and 4: A minor with added 6th
- Bar 6: G♯ minor moving to V7 of D, 3rd inversion
- Bar 12: A♭ minor (enharmonic B♮), first inversion moving to B♭ minor.

Structure and tonality

The structure of this brief cue is dictated by the melody (five three-bar phrases plus a concluding chord) and the tonality is best described as an unrealised A minor (listen to the last two bars).

Cue 3 – 'Marion': musical elements

This section incorporates a figure that anticipates Cue 14 ('The Madhouse') and also the closing bars of the score where Herrmann quoted a motif from his Sinfonietta.

Tempo, metre and rhythm

A slow quadruple-time movement – 'Lento assai' (very slow) – with repetition of a syncopated figure throughout.

Sonority, texture and dynamics

A quiet arco throughout, only rising to *mf* in the last bar with its sinister dissonance.

The texture is homophonic, initially in three parts and expanding to the full ensemble in the final stages with some division of parts.

Organisation of pitch: melody and harmony

The movement is built on a sequentially descending three-note figure featuring a falling perfect 5th. The melody is cast in diatonic C major, supported at first by a chromatically descending line in viola and a sustained inner part in Violin II, which is gently dissonant with the melody. Suspensions are formed between the outer parts.

With the introduction of a fourth part in bar 9, the harmony clarifies to G^{13} moving to $Dmin^7$ (which happens twice in bars 9–12). The succeeding bars are a four-part version of the opening four bars, leading to an unexpected close on G minor plus major 7th, a transposed version of the chord that started the Prelude.

Structure and tonality

This relatively lyrical portion of the score is through-composed, consisting of balanced phrases (four sets of four bars) with additional concluding dissonance. The key is C major throughout, though the final chord is a threatening inconclusive expanded dominant.

> **EXPANDED** here refers to the way the final chord includes a major 7th. It also contains a B♭ instead of the expected B♮.

Cue 17 – 'The Murder' (Shower Scene): musical elements

Herrmann ignored Hitchcock's instruction not to compose music for this scene and instead produced one of the most celebrated cues in the history of the cinema.

On realising just how forceful this music was, Hitchcock reversed his decision, later telling Herrmann that his original directive was an 'improper instruction'.

Sonority, texture and dynamics

This is the only cue in which the strings are unmuted. Some thought at the time that Herrmann used electronic resources, such as amplified bird screeches, to create the vicious slashing sound, but the only recording 'trick' was the placing of microphones close to the instruments to produce a harsh sound.

Additional playing techniques contributing to the overall effect were the use of down bows on every beat, and shrieking glissandi from bar 9. Savage bow strokes are used at first, but from bar 17 chords are heard alternately arco and pizzicato. The texture is homophonic throughout, with a dissonant structure building down from the opening high note. From bar 17, a chord on the first beat in upper strings is followed on the off-beat by octaves in the lower strings.

Dynamics are very loud throughout (with each note marked *sffz*).

Tempo, metre and rhythm

The indication is Molto forzando e feroce (very forceful and fierce).

The time signature is triple time (three minims to a bar), with steady minims at the beginning. From bar 9, the minims are replaced with crotchets followed by crotchet rests.

Longer durations occur from bar 17 onwards.

Organisation of pitch: melody and harmony

It is impossible to speak of melody here. The dissonant harmonic structure in the opening eight bars consists of an accumulation of high tension major 7ths and diminished octaves.

The passage from bar 17 is composed of two alternating chords on strong beats with only one note different. The prominent syncopated bass part moves by semitones (F–E; B♭–A), before closing on a tritone chord (F♯–C).

Structure and tonality

In spite of the prominence of particular notes, this section is virtually non-tonal.

Structurally it consists of two eight-bar sections, the second varied by use of glissandi, and a 21-bar coda built on the two chords (death of Marion).

Cue 37 – 'The Toys': musical elements

Marion's sister, Lila, searches for traces of Marion.
She discovers toys in Norman's room.

Sonority, texture and dynamics

This movement is homophonic throughout, with both Violin I and Violin II divided into four parts, Violin II intermittently reinforcing Violin I chords. The cellos play pizzicato and violas down-bowed crotchets.

Dynamics are consistently quiet (*ppp*–*pp*) except for the final *f* octaves.

Tempo, metre and rhythm

Slow simple quadruple (54 crotchets per minute) with steady crotchets in violas and cellos throughout. Longer note values in upper strings (minims and semibreves) and double basses (dotted minims tied to quavers).

Organisation of pitch: melody and harmony

The melody is a descending conjunct line, composed of three three-bar phrases.

The harmony consists of parallel descending 7ths supported by a pedal E and dissonant minor 9th (F) in viola. The music is entirely non-chromatic, and in this case could be described as 'white-note' harmony.

> **WHITE-NOTE HARMONY** is an expression referring to music which could be played entirely on the white keys of the piano without actually being in C major. An example occurs in the Danse Russe from Stravinsky's *Petrouchka*.

Structure and tonality

Although the upper parts are lodged on an E pedal, there is an avoidance of functional relationships. The extract could be regarded as being in the Phrygian mode, that is, the church mode based on E.

The music is so brief that, other than the three-bar phrasing, it is unhelpful to speak of structure as such.

Cue 38 – 'The Cellar': musical elements

Lila rushes to the cellar.

Sonority, texture and dynamics

A forceful opening in octaves with trills leads to pp, scurrying tremolandi on divisi strings. From bar 47, half the ensemble is directed to play *sul ponticello*, the other half normally.

The main part of the movement is reminiscent of a fugue (see Structure), giving way to octaves in upper parts supported by sustained bass from bar 47, and finally soft, sustained chords, though with a sudden crescendo in the final bar.

Tempo, metre and rhythm

Hectic 'Allegro molto' (very fast) in duple time. The 'fugal' passage consists of constant quavers. The final bars consist of long drawn-out chords.

Organisation of pitch: melody and harmony

The pitch outline in bars 1–4 (D–A–A♭, marked in the score below as 1, 2 and 3) anticipates the chromaticism of the fugal subject from bar 5. There are also hints here of a prominent motif from the Prelude (compare intervals of bars 6–7 with those of bar 6 of Prelude).

The 'subject' (beginning in bar 5 in the cello and double bass line) initially moves by step, but latterly expands intervallically to embrace major and minor 3rds and wider intervals, including a diminished 4th and various types of 5th and 6th. Here are the opening few bars of the cello and double bass line, showing the introduction and opening of the subject:

At bar 32, the subject is heard in the bass, but fragmented by the insertion of quaver rests:

The harmony is dissonant, and vertical structures result from the free play of the contrapuntal lines. The final dissonance is essentially an augmented triad (D♭–F–A), clouded by the temporary addition of a diminished triad (C♯–E–G) in bars 72–76.

Structure and tonality

Broadly the music of this cue could be described as a short introduction and fugue or fughetta, that is, a short, relatively undeveloped fugal movement, though it should be stressed that Herrmann does not follow traditional fugal procedures, particularly with regard to tonic–dominant entries.

Bars	Description
1–4	Introduction, with D acting as 'dominant preparation'
5	'Fugue subject', starting on G, in cello and double bass. The line is initially split between different instruments (passed from one to the other).
13	Second entry of 'subject', in viola, on the G an octave higher, with countersubject 1 in cello and bass
21	Third entry of subject, still on G and at the same pitch as viola, in violin II, with counter-subject 1 in viola and countersubject 2 in cello and bass
28	Fourth entry of subject, on G and still at the same low pitch in violin I. This entry is a bar earlier than expected. Countersubject 1 eventually appears in violin II, and countersubject 2 in viola
32	Rhythmically dislocated entry of subject in cello and bass
40	Rhythmically dislocated subject on viola
47	Subject in unison in three upper parts with sustained notes in bass
58	Fugue breaks down with chromatic descent, derived from countersubject 1
68	Concluding chord (augmented triad on D♭)

Cue 39 – 'Discovery': musical elements

Lila finds the clothed skeleton of Norman's mother.

Sonority, texture and dynamics

Pizzicato bass emphasises accented notes in opening bars. Pizzicato bass and cello can also be heard in the cross-rhythmic passage from bar 19 before changing to arco at bar 23.

> The cross-rhythmic passage here involves the combination of eight semiquavers and triplet crotchets.

Texture varies as the cue progresses:

- Opening is entirely homophonic
- At bar 19, there is differentiation between the chords in the upper parts and the triplet crotchet bass
- At bar 26, bass notes are more sustained
- Single chord for last four bars.

Dynamics are $f\!f$ throughout.

Tempo, metre and rhythm

Marked 'Allegro feroce' (fast and fierce) this furious movement opens in duple time ($\frac{2}{4}$) before moving into a frenzied whirlwind in triple time ($\frac{3}{8}$). The opening motif has a distinctive syncopated figure, followed by steady streams of semiquavers with main quaver pulses accented.

From bar 19, continuous semiquavers are heard against triplet crotchets.

Bars 26 to 36 are composed entirely of semiquavers (except for the bass notes), the only long sustained sound being the final chord in the last four bars.

Organisation of pitch: melody and harmony

Semitones, tritones and perfect 4ths are prominent, relating to material of the preceding cue (the first three pitches are a retrograde of the opening motif of 'The Cellar').

Typical melodic devices include:

- Sequential repetition
- Inter-cutting of component motifs (see Structure)
- Octave shifts.

Harmony often consists of a vertical presentation of the (horizontal) melodic line. Here is the first bar of the cue:

Notice how the first chord...

... is constructed from the melodic pitches of the first bar:

Other features include:

- Extreme dissonance
- Parallel movement (see bar 3)
- Reappearance of the opening chord (transposed) of the prelude (bar 23)
- Repositioning of dissonant chords: compare bars 26 and 28, where the same letter-names are employed but differently distributed.

Structure and tonality

This section is atonal and through-composed, with component bars reappearing in contrasting combinations – for example, bars 8–9 are very similar to bar 1 followed by a transposition of bar 6.

Cue 40 – 'Finale': musical elements

Norman is shown in a white-walled cell.

The music to this scene relates to Cue 14 ('The Madhouse', touching on Norman's relationship with his mother), Cue 38 ('The Cellar') and, more distantly, to Cue 3 ('Marion').

Sonority, texture and dynamics

This lean-sounding movement involves some relatively high string writing. After a monophonic start, it is freely contrapuntal until the concluding homophonic bars. The dynamic is almost entirely pp until the final f bars.

Tempo, metre and rhythm

The direction is 'Adagio e mesto' (slow and sad), and in metre it shifts between triple and quadruple time. The viola line at bars 12–14 is syncopated, as are the final chords.

Organisation of pitch: melody and harmony

The melody is characterised by:

- Chromaticism
- Angular intervals, especially augmented 4ths and diminished 5ths
- A three-note motif (F–E♭–D) quoted from Herrmann's own Sinfonietta for Strings (see bars 15 and 16 and the example below), as well as his cantata *Moby Dick*.

Harmony:

- Freely dissonant (augmented octaves, major 9ths, etc.)
- The viola part at bar 12 contains seemingly deranged suspensions which do not follow conventional procedures (contrasting with those in 'Marion')
- Closes with a minor 9th chord, spanning D to E♭, the last two pitches of the Sinfonietta motif mentioned above.

The following example shows the last repeat of the Sinfonietta motif and the final chord. The bottom stave shows the cello and double bass parts.

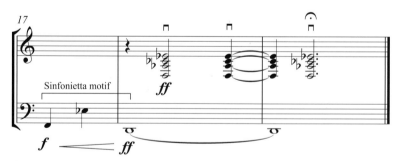

Structure and tonality

The cue is through-composed. The melodic and harmonic writing is so chromatic that it is not possible to define a key, and the final dissonance leaves matters unresolved.

Test yourself

Below are five short questions on each set work. These are not 'exam questions' but are intended to help you get to know each work better.

Most questions use the command words listed in Appendix 5 of each specification (with which you will need to be familiar when preparing for exams). For each set work there is also a sample essay question for each level. These correspond to Question 6 in Pearson's Sample Assessment Materials. Essays at the two levels are marked from different assessment grids, as may again be seen from the Sample Assessment Materials. The allocation of marks is different, with fewer marks at AS implying the need for less information. At A Level there is greater emphasis on saying how and why particular things happen in the music, and relatively less on just saying what happens. When answering the questions below, you should refer to the printed score of the relevant work or movement.

In your exam you will have a special booklet containing the scores you need. You will not be allowed to take a copy of the anthology or other printed music into the exam room.

Cues from *Batman Returns* (Danny Elfman)

Short questions:

a. Name the percussion instruments used in *Batman Returns*.

b. List and locate the principal motifs.

c. Explain how circus effects are created in *Batman vs the Circus*.

d. List the keys used (with bar numbers) in *Birth of a Penguin Part 1*.

e. Discuss the string writing in *Birth of a Penguin Part 2*.

Question 6 practice:

AS

Evaluate Elfman's use of resources and texture in 'Birth of a Penguin Part 1'. Relate your discussion to other relevant works. These may include set works, wider listening or other music.

A Level

Evaluate Elfman's use of resources, texture and motifs in 'Birth of a Penguin' Parts I and II, with particular reference to their dramatic significance.Relate your discussion to other relevant works. These may include set works, wider listening or other music.

Cues from *The Duchess* (Rachel Portman)

Short questions:

a. Identify the modal aspects of the harmony in 'The Duchess (Opening)' and 'Mistake of Your Life'.

b. Describe the texture of 'Never See Your Children Again'.

c. Explain how the harmony of 'The Duchess (End Titles)' differs from that of 'The Duchess (Opening)'.

d. Describe the instrumentation of 'Six Years Later', bars 1–28.

e. Explain how the melodies of 'Mistake of Your Life' relate to those of 'The Duchess (Opening)'.

Essay questions:

AS

Evaluate Portman's use of melody and rhythm in 'Six Years Later'. Relate your discussion to other relevant works. These may include set works, wider listening or other music.

A Level

Evaluate Portman's use of melody, rhythm and harmony in 'Six Years Later' and 'Never See Your Children Again' with particular reference to the changing circumstances in which the heroine finds herself. Relate your discussion to other relevant works. These may include set works, wider listening or other music.

Cues from *Psycho* (Bernard Herrmann)

Short questions:

a. Describe the harmony of 'The Murder'.

b. Describe the texture of 'The Cellar'.

c. Explain how rhythm contributes to the driving quality of the *Prelude*.

d. Explain how Herrmann uses melody to evoke the character of Marion in *Marion*.

e. Discuss Herrmann's approach to instrumentation.

Essay question:

A Level only

Evaluate Herrmann's use of dynamics, melody and harmony in *Prelude, Marion* and *The Murder*, with particular reference to the creation of contrasting moods. Relate your discussion to other relevant works. These may include set works, wider listening or other music.

Popular music and jazz

OVERVIEW

The set works in this Area of Study include some of the most important and durable works in a period marked by a diversity of approaches.

AS **A** **Tracks from** *Back in the Day* **(Courtney Pine)**

AS **A** **Tracks from** *Hounds of Love* **(Kate Bush)**

A **Tracks from** *Revolver* **(The Beatles)**

Introduction

As in other Areas of Study, you are required to study three set works. There are three groups of numbers from different albums (plus of course the works suggested for wider listening).

The earliest of these wider listening albums is Bix Beiderbecke's *Jazz Me Blues*, Dixieland jazz from 1927, and the most recent is Jay Z's *The Blueprint 3* from 2009. In contrast, the set works span a period of only 34 years, from the Beatles' *Revolver* (1966) to Courtney Pine's *Back in the Day* (2000).

The set works include some of the most important and durable pieces released in a period marked by the diversity of approaches within these genres.

Some of the most important trends are:

- An increasing reliance on studio production and electronics, which in some cases led bands such as the Beatles to abandon live performance
- Increasing sophistication in the forms employed, whether building on existing popular music structures or moving away from them altogether
- The merging of different genres.

Opposite: Kate Bush on tour in 1979

Above: The Beatles in 1964

Set work:

Back in the Day: 'Inner State (of Mind)', 'Lady Day and (John Coltrane)' and 'Love and Affection'

Courtney Pine

AS LEVEL

A LEVEL

Courtney Pine

Musical context

Composer

Courtney Pine was born in London in 1964. He initially learned clarinet, but subsequently focused on saxophone, and also plays flute, bass clarinet and keyboards. He is now regarded as one of Britain's leading modern jazz musicians, responsible for reviving the genre from the 1980s onwards. His style draws on soul, rhythm and blues, reggae, urban and hip hop as well as more traditional elements.

Leading jazz expert John Fordham has described him as a 'phenomenal technician, drawing together styles from early jazz to experimental and avant-garde. His playing can be amazingly abstract, atonal, dissonant, but with such a strong underlying groove it makes sense to a non-specialist audience.'

Back in the Day, issued in September 2000, was his eighth album. It was produced by Pine himself, who remixed it 'like a DJ, thinking about tempo and beats, not just scales and keys'. The album is regarded as more of a personal statement than the preceding albums, and incorporates the influence of soul music of the 1970s. It includes cover versions of numbers by Gil Scott-Heron ('Lady Day and (John Coltrane)'), Curtis Mayfield ('Hardtimes') and Joan Armatrading ('Love and Affection'). Two of these cover versions are among the set works, the other prescribed piece being 'Inner State (of Mind)'.

You will find it useful to listen to the original versions to assess the extent of Courtney Pine's creative contribution, although you won't be questioned on them in the exam. You can find both of them on YouTube.

Besides Pine himself (playing saxophones, bass, keyboard and 'drum program'), there are parts at various times for lead and backing vocals, rappers, guitars, horns, alto sax, trumpet and trombone.

'Inner State (of Mind)': musical elements

This number is an example of contemporary jazz. It is characterised by a blend of elements: notably jazz rap, an off-shoot of hip hop, with a tight drumming program built on hip hop-style rhythms. There are two rap sections that expand on the message of the verse ('so know yourself, mankind').

Sophisticated production techniques are also indicative of this type of music, as is the relatively restricted range of harmonies and tonal scheme, and the prominence given to riffs. Hip hop is generally more focused on rhythm, but there is considerable melodic invention here.

Hip hop can be traced back to late 1960s New York where it originated in African and Latino American gang and street culture in the Bronx. It is characterised by rap (spoken or chanted text with a strong rhythmic accompaniment), 'turntablism' (manipulating sounds using turntables and DJ mixing systems) and dynamic dance styles. You may find it useful to examine the rap style of Jay Z in *The Blueprint 3*.

Musical language

The song is notated using staff notation, with chord names given above the top stave. Tempo is given in terms of (114) beats per minute, and there is a *Repeat ad lib* (i.e. repeat if desired) sign at the close.

Structure and tonality

The key is Dorian C minor, hence the key signature of two, rather than three, flats. There is no modulation as such.

Try to grasp the overall structure as outlined in the table below. Because of the improvisational nature of the performance, material is freely varied, extended and interwoven. Further details regarding musical content are given subsequently.

Bars	Section	Details
1–2	'Inner state of mind' motif	Pentatonic line, rising a sixth
2–9	Instrumental introduction	Sax solo with supporting chords of alternating Cm^7 and Dm^7
10–21	Verse	Riff introduced, chords now largely alternate between Cm and F
21–35	Rap	Sax fills, with supporting chords of alternating Cm^7 and Dm^7
36–53	Verse extended	Riff resumed; 'Inner state' motif incorporated at bar 44; Additional vocal line introduced; Scat starts at bar 52; Chord selection broadened at bars 52–53
54–70	Rap	Riff; Chords of Cm^7–F–Cm^7–Dm^7; Additional female vocal (not in score)
70–71	Link	Homophonic partially quartal harmony (i.e. use of chords made up of intervals of a fourth, e.g. bar 70^4)
72–90	Verse	Opens with first eight bars supported by riff and chords; Bar 80 onwards is an extension of bar 18 with broken rather than block chords and different vocal line; Scat from bar 82
90–93	Link	Glissando
93–94	'Inner state' motif	
94–107	Mainly instrumental	Riff modified; Chords as at bar 54; 'Inner state' motif at bar 101
107–117	Coda	Riff and chords continue Scat Fades out with sax trill

Tempo, metre and rhythm

Tempo throughout is a brisk quadruple time, moving at 114 crotchets a minute.

A steady drum program in hip hop style is maintained throughout, except in:

- The first bar
- Bars 18–21, where the reduced dynamic involves much lighter percussion
- Bars 52–53 (a scat section)
- Bar 62, first beat (a punctuation point midway through the second rap section)
- Bars 70–71 (instrumental passage)
- The fade at the close.

Characteristic rhythmic devices include:

- Prominent syncopation, in accompaniment, sax solos and vocals
- Dotted rhythm in the riff
- Even note lengths in the Gershwin quotation (see below)
- Scotch snap (bar 20)
- Triplets in the rap sections
- The cross-rhythmic effect at bar 80 arising from two consecutive dotted quavers (or equivalent)
- Irregular groupings (e.g. quintuplet at bar 97 and sextuplet at bar 101).

Organisation of pitch: melody and harmony

Bars 1–9

A recurring motif in this track is the two-bar setting of the words 'Inner state of mind'. This pentatonic line rises from E♭ to C, and is harmonised in 3rds on beat 2, broadening out to a triad (beat 3) and a chord of 4ths at the beginning of bar 2 consisting of D–G–C. The whole of the ensuing instrumental is based on two alternating 7th chords on C and D, the A♮ in the Dm⁷ being part of the Dorian mode on C.

The sax melody is fragmentary with component phrases separated by rests. No phrase lasts more than five beats. There are blue notes, that is, chromatically inflected notes, in this case G♭, the diminished 5th of the scale, and ornamentations such as crushed notes and slides.

Bars 10–21

The vocal line starts from a relatively narrow range, but by the close of the section expands to an 11th (G to C). It embraces a reference to Gershwin's song 'Summertime' from *Porgy and Bess*. Here is Gershwin's melody, followed by the line from 'Inner State (of Mind)'

Gershwin: 'Summertime' (transposed)

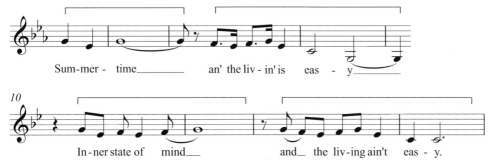

The similarities between the two second phrases are obvious, although the rhythm has been evened out to straight quavers and the low note at the end avoided. The first phrases also share a similar overall outline of G to E♭ and back again.

At this point a two-bar riff is introduced, anchored on C:

Chords now involve Cm and F, with stabbed out punctuations of F to Cm at the end of every other bar. One variation in the harmony occurs at bar 18 ('Knowledge is power'), where the melody contains a brief melisma.

Here there is an acid dissonance with E♮ clashing against the E♭, forming a false relation.

In the rap section at bars 21–35, the harmony reverts to alternating 7th chords, the only melodic interest being two interjections from the sax (bars 31 and 35), the second of which is pentatonic.

The second verse, starting at bar 36, opens with an elaboration of the Gershwin reference. Notice how the melody here is varied by the introduction of higher notes.

The supporting parts are the same as for the first verse, but the motif from bar 1 is woven into the melody, and for the first time 'blue' notes (G♭/F♯) appear in the vocal part (bars 46–47). A second vocal part draws initially on the Gershwin motif, before proceeding to sing scat (nonsense syllables).

This scat passage is supported by a slightly broader range of chords: $C^{7(\sharp 9)}$ (which also occurred in bar 18) followed by a 9th chord on E♭, a half-diminished chord on D and a 7th chord on D♭.

In the course of the second rap section (bars 54–70), the riff reappears with its second bar altered. Besides the saxophone interjections, there is a more lyrical vocal line that is not notated in the score but which draws on the material of the verses. This is in marked contrast to the rapid speech-rhythm delivery of the rap sections.

A two-bar passage of broadly parallel harmony links with the next verse. These two bars (70–71) draw on 4th chords (quartal harmony) – see bar 70^4 – and open 5ths (bar 71, second half of beat 2).

The vocal line of verse three departs still further from the Gershwin-derived material, and at bar 80, the harmony of bar 18 is heard again but now in broken-chord form. A further change is made to the riff at bar 81, where it begins on C rather than F.

Subsequent landmarks include:

- The glissando starting in bar 91 (slightly reminiscent of the opening of Gershwin's *Rhapsody in Blue*)
- More frequent appearances of the motif from bar 1
- Increasingly virtuoso sax solo, with rapid scale (bar 97) and figuration (bar 101)
- Repetitions of short melodic figurations (bar 99)
- Broad chromatic descent in melody at bar 100 (C–B♮–B♭–A)
- Further scat singing (bar 108 for the second time)
- Concluding trill.

Sonority and textures

The track opens with distorted and irrational sounds, and the voices in the first bar of the number proper are also distorted. Other extraneous sounds (e.g. babbling voices) are dubbed on as the number progresses.

Textures are quite varied, and include:

- Homophonic voices (bar 1)
- Melody-dominated homophony (bar 2)
- Melody-dominated homophony involving voices and chordal interjections (from bar 10)
- Homophonic horns and sax at bar 11 and elsewhere
- Rap – chanted voice and accompanying instruments, with saxophone fills
- At bar 45 a second voice enters, with 'descant' line at bar 47
- Broken chord figures (bar 80)
- Free counterpoint develops from bar 101, with voices and sax line
- Monophonic trill at close.

'Lady Day and (John Coltrane)': musical elements

This song is a cover version of a number by Gil Scott-Heron (1949–2011), which appeared in 1971 on the album *Pieces of a Man*.

It was a homage to two major jazz musicians: singer Billie Holiday and saxophonist John Coltrane. Its lyrics concerned alienation, and how best to avoid it, and the album in general could be described as free jazz with influences of modern hip hop. It was described by jazz critic Adam Sweeting as a 'pioneering mix of politics, protest and proto-rap poetry, set to a musical jazz funk hybrid'.

Courtney Pine's version, though faithful to the broad outlines of the original, differs significantly with regard to:

- The shape of the vocal line
- The resources employed (horns, trumpets, sax and bvox)
- The vast expansion of the structure (the links between verses, central instrumental and coda are all much longer)
- The dubbed-on sounds, conversation, and at the close a news report concerning the murder of Stephen Lawrence.

Musical language

The song is notated in staff notation, with a few cross-head symbols (bars 127 and 130) to represent a multiphonic sound and key-clicks. Guitarists are supplied with chord diagrams.

Tempo is given in terms of beats per minute, and the relaxation of pulse near the end is indicated by the term 'Freely'. There are other occasional verbal directions, for example, 'Wide, controlled vibrato between the two notes' at bar 39, and use is made of repeat marks and 'D.S. al Coda' (bar 76).

Structure and tonality

The number is in C minor throughout; rather curiously a one-flat signature is used, but E♭ accidentals are regularly supplied. It is based on 12-bar-blues progressions, albeit treated with considerable freedom (see section on harmony below).

Bars	Section	Details
1–4 (repeated)	Introduction	Background babble, from which emerges the acid, static harmony of $C^{7(\sharp 9)}$
5–32	Verse 1	5–12 $C^{7(\sharp 9)}$ (eight bars) 13–16 $F^{7(\sharp 9)}$ (four bars) 17–20 $C^{7(\sharp 9)}$ (four bars) 21–24 Gm^7–Fm^7–$B\flat^{13}$–$C^{7(\sharp 9)}$ 25–29 Varied repeat of preceding progression with substitutions
33–36	Link	
5–28, then 37–44	Verse 2	
44–76	Instrumental	Variation of blues progression from verse 1
5–26, then 77–86	Verse 1 (repeated, with passage from bar 77 marked as coda)	NB: side-shift from $B\flat^{13}$ to B^{11} in coda
86–118	Coda continued (strict time)	Mainly based on recurring four-bar progression of $C^{7(\sharp 9)}$–F^9–G^9
119–131	Coda continued (free time)	Sustained chords of G augmented–$C^{7(\sharp 9)}$–$B\flat m^{7add4}$

Tempo, metre and rhythm

The number is in fast quadruple time (160 crotchets per minute) until the final section from bar 119, where strict time gives way to slow-moving rubato.

Typical rhythmic devices include:

- Syncopation (bar 7)
- Scotch snaps (bar 31)
- Repetition (including riffs, e.g. bars 29–36)
- Triplets (bar 59) and sextuplet semiquavers (bar 60)
- Long sustained notes in solo part (bars 45–48) gradually 'bent' to produce a glisssando-like effect.

Organisation of pitch: melody

The generally chordal introduction also includes a melismatic vocal flourish, including the 'blue' G♭.

The verse is composed of balanced phrases, dictated by the underlying blues scheme (see section on structure).

Notice the following aspects of the vocal part:

- Syllabic, with melismas at the close of phrases
- Generally conjunct
- Narrow range, though widening in span with the melisma

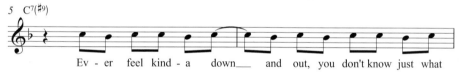

- Ornamentation, for example:
  - Upward-resolving appoggiatura (e.g. bar 26)
  - 'Mordents' (e.g. bar 27)
  - Acciaccaturas (bar 38 in backing vocals)
- Pentatonic elements (e.g. bars 15–16)
- Prominent flat 7th-tonic (B♭–C), as in bar 7 in the above example
- Sequence (e.g. bars 77–80).

The virtuoso sax part is notable for:

- Wide range (three octaves and a minor 3rd – C to E♭)
- Chromatic alterations (e.g. bar 8)
- Chromatic scales (e.g. bar 75)
- Exploitation of contrasting registers (compare bars 85–98 with 119–127)
- Ornamentation:
  - Acciaccaturas (e.g. bar 8)

- Controlled vibrato (e.g. bar 39)
- Bending of notes (e.g. bar 45)
- Fall-offs (e.g. bar 50)
- Sliding up to pitch (e.g. bar 52)
- Glissandos (e.g. bar 55)
- Unpitched notes (e.g. bar 60)
- Multiphonic (e.g. bar 127)
- Key clicks (e.g. bar 130).

> **MULTIPHONIC** refers to the production of two or more sounds on a normally monophonic instrument, that is, a wind or brass instrument.

Organisation of pitch: harmony

The harmonic progressions are blues-derived, although there are some variations on the traditional 12-bar scheme. See the section on structure and tonality above for details of the opening chord progression. The blues cycle consists of:

- Eight bars of an extended chord based on C, with added 7th and 9th. The chord figures indicate a sharp 9th (D♯) rather that the notated minor 10th (E♭), but the stave notation clearly reveals the presence of a false relation (E♮ and E♭) which gives the underlying harmony its characteristic plangent sound
- Four bars on F, extended in the same way
- Four bars on extended C
- The conventional pattern is then abandoned. Gm^7 is as expected, but is heard for only one bar before giving way to Fm^7 (one bar), a 13th chord on B♭ (one bar) and then tonic chord – $C^{7(\sharp9)}$ – as at the start
- The above four-bar pattern is repeated, but with:
  - Passing reference to $F\sharp m^7$ between Gm^7 and Fm^7
  - Insertion of additional chordless bar before closing on tonic.

The instrumental is notable for:

- Continuing use of extended chords
- Avoidance of basic blues progression
  - $C^{7(\sharp9)}$–$E\flat^9$–$A\flat^7$–G^{+7} (repeated)
  - Further repetition of this progression, but with substitution chords (e.g. Bm^7–$B\flat m^7$)
- Chromatic movement of chords (see bass line at bars 53–55 and the parallel chromatically moving 7th chords at bar 65)
- The turnaround at bars 75 and 76, with contrary movement of chromatic descending bass and ascending 'broken' 4ths structures (augmented 4th plus perfect 4th).

The coda is marked by:

- Dramatic semitonal side-shift of chords, from $B\flat^{13}$ to B^{11} before returning to $B\flat^{13}$ and eventually to the tonic harmony
- Several repetitions of a more direct progression, which is broadly subdominant, dominant, tonic from bar 89 (underlining 'It will be alright, baby'), to make the tonality clearer as the end of the piece approaches

■ A final slowing of harmonic rhythm in the section marked 'Freely', with just three long, sustained chords providing additional stability as the end approaches: an augmented chord on G, an extended tonic C and a fade on the unexpected chord of B♭m^{7add4}.

Sonority and texture

The track is a mix of:

■ Voices

■ Backing vocals

■ Keyboard

■ Saxophone

■ Horns

■ Drum program

■ Dubbed voices (a babble of background conversation at the start and a news report at the close).

Mention has already been made of the various extended performance techniques used; for example, multiphonics and key clicks.

There are relatively faint sounds of the drum kit in the introduction, but from bar 5 the drum program comes to the fore, and remains active except for:

■ Bar 28 (verse 1 only)

■ Bars 75–76 (chromatic turnaround)

■ First four bars of the reprised verse after the central instrumental

■ Bar 82

■ Bar 119 to the end.

Texture is essentially melody-dominated homophony with:

■ Riff

■ Vocal and fills

■ Horns providing close harmony e.g. at bar 21

■ Bvox (e.g. from bar 37) with occasional parallel 5ths.

'Love and Affection': musical elements

This number is a cover version of a folk/pop song by Joan Armatrading, recorded in 1974–1975 and released in 1976 as both a single and one of the tracks on the album *Joan Armatrading*. The original ballad was performed by lead voice, backing vocals including a prominent part for baritone singer, guitar, drum kit and alto saxophone.

Courtney Pine's version is faithful to the broad outlines of the song, though there is a more pronounced division between the introduction and the main part of the song, creating an effect reminiscent of the recitative and aria of opera and oratorio. His version also draws on a larger range of instruments, and the final section is much more extended, involving improvisation and the presence of a new counter-melody.

Musical language

The song is notated using staff notation, with chord names and chord diagrams for guitarists. Tempo is indicated in terms of beats per minute.

Structure and tonality

The ballad opens in C♯ minor, but soon settles into the relative major, E major.

The structure is relatively free, with a gradually developing treatment of introductory material being replaced by a refrain-like figure which eventually leads to another contrasting motif.

The main landmarks are laid out in the table below.

Bars	Section	Key	Details
1–12	Introduction	C♯m–E	Voice and guitar
13–14	Link	E	Block chords (E–B–A),
15–32	Development of introductory material	C♯m–E	18–21 derived from 7–12; Riff established at bar 22 while material from bars 20–21 continues
32–45	Further development of introduction	E	'I can really love' derived from bars 20–21, leading to the first appearance of material from the song's refrain ('Oh give me love…')
46–53	Bridge	E	Underpinned by rising bass
54–65	Refrain	E	Eight-bar refrain, extended for four bars over chromatically descending chords from bar 62
66–75	Instrumental	E	Riff continues, but over a tonic pedal of E in the bass
76–83	Refrain	E	Additional tenor saxophone line at bar 80
84–100	Outro	E	Vocals freely based on preceding motifs; a new minor pentatonic line in strings

Tempo, metre and rhythm

The ballad is in a moderately paced quadruple time with 86 crotchets a minute.

The opening 12 bars are sung slightly rubato, after which the number proceeds in strict time to the close.

Note the following devices:

- Offbeat chords (e.g. bars 13–14)
- Syncopations (e.g. bass at bar 15)
- Cross-beat figurations, e.g. 'really move' occupies three quavers and so when repeated immediately falls at a different part of the beat (see music example below)
- The repetition of the word 'love' every three semiquavers at bar 36, producing an ecstatic cross-rhythmic effect
- Triplets (bar 25) and quintuplets (bar 97).

Organisation of pitch: melody

As indicated above, the melody line develops throughout the song.

The opening, rather hesitant figures ('I am not in love, but I'm open to persuasion') are characterised by rising conjunct figures, ornamentation on 'love' and repetition. The succeeding motif is a falling broken chord, after which the rising stepwise figure returns. This pattern returns in the next main section of the song: compare fragment **a** in the example below with bars 16–20. It is followed with another motif which will be developed as the song goes on.

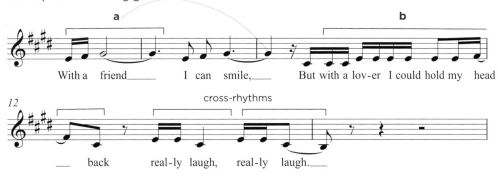

The vocal range in the music example above is relatively narrow – a major 6th (B to G#). It expands to an octave with the pentatonic melisma in bars 14-15, and the lower G# and A are added in bars 20 and 21 at the end of a variant of the above example.

A refrain-like motif first appears in bar 39, and is sung by backing vocals:

At bar 46, an eight-bar bridge section commences, with:

- Repeated notes
- Conjunct movement
- Melisma ('insecure')
- Blue G♮ (bars 47, 50, 52, 53)
- Range of an octave (B–B).

The refrain motif re-enters at bar 54 and overlaps with the 'message' of the song:

This leads to a further new motif:

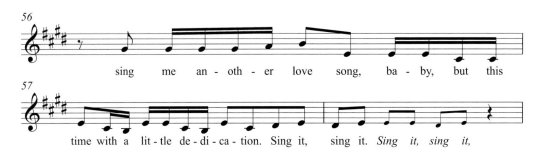

After the instrumental, the two above motifs are heard to the end with the 'refrain', and in the final section counterpointed by a recurring minor pentatonic line in strings.

Instrumental melody writing is marked by devices we have met in the other two numbers.

Note in particular:

- Chromaticism (bass clarinet at bars 14 and 30–31, as well as tenor sax at bar 67)
- Blue notes (G♮ at bar 68 and B♭ at bar 72)
- Slides.

Organisation of pitch: harmony

- In the early stages more minor chords can be heard and there is an avoidance of extended chords and no sense of cadence at bar 12
- From bar 22 the riff dominates much of the song and there are primary major triads (E–A–B^{add4})
- The Bridge is built over rising triads, finishing with G/A and an open-fifths dominant
- Striking chromatic descent from bar 62 (G♮–F♯^{7add4}–F$^{maj\,7(♯4)}$–E)
- False relation, e.g. at bar 72 with B♭ against the B♮ occurring in E minor.

Pine performing in at the Brecon Jazz Festival in 2011

Sonority and texture

The opening section is just for voice with electric guitar and introduces some broken-chord accompaniment figures. The lead vocal varies timbre to allow for an injection of harshness on 'with a lover I can hold my head back'.

Drums are introduced in bar 15, and then continue to the close. The recording is free of extraneous dubbed sound, though at the close a crackle can be heard, recreating the sound heard after a vinyl disc has finished.

The number moves from simple melody-dominated homophony at the opening to a complex polyphonic web of sound at the close as the various strands are woven together.

Dynamics are evident in the move from the generally softer opening to the main part of the song. There is also a particularly effective *crescendo* in the sax part on its entry in bar 66, and an equally telling reduction in sound for the final moment of the song ('Make love').

Set work:
Hounds of Love: 'Cloudbusting', 'And Dream of Sheep' and 'Under Ice'
Kate Bush

Musical context

Composer and performer

Kate Bush (b. 1958) is a British singer, composer and producer whose work draws on a wide range of styles and influences.

Besides the progressive pop aspects of her work, elements of Irish folk music can be heard, stemming from her family connections (her mother came from County Waterford and was a traditional Irish dancer). Bush taught herself to play both piano and violin, and her career effectively began in 1978 with the release of the single 'Wuthering Heights', which remained at the top of the UK singles chart for four weeks. Subsequent singles include 'The Man with the Child in His Eyes',

Kate Bush

'Babooshka', 'Running Up That Hill' and 'King of the Mountain'. Her studio albums include *Never for Ever* (1980) and *Hounds of Love* (1985), the fifth in the series.

Hounds of Love

Hounds of Love **was the first album to be produced in the studio that Bush had built for her own use, releasing her from the time and cost pressures which arose from hiring recording facilities. She drew on a wide range of resources. Besides the vocals and piano provided by Bush herself and the drums, backing vocals, bass and guitar, she also at various points made use of balalaika, didgeridoo, strings (provided by the Medici Sextet), bouzouki played by the leading Irish folk musician Dónal Lunny, uilleann pipes, and the Richard Hickox Singers performing vocal arrangements by the composer Michael Berkeley.**

When issued in vinyl form, the two sides of the album were deliberately designed to form a marked contrast. The first side, entitled Hounds of Love, contained five progressive pop numbers, 'Running Up That Hill', 'Hounds of Love', 'The Big Sky', 'Mother Stands for Comfort' and 'Cloudbusting'. The second – The Ninth Wave – took its title from Tennyson's Poem 'The Holy Grail' from the cycle *Idylls of the King*, which is about King Arthur. Though the poem played no central role in the composition of the songs, a stanza quoted on the sleeve of the CD provides a clue to their content:

> Wave after wave, each mightier than the last
> 'Til last, a ninth one, gathering half the deep
> And full of voices, slowly rose and plunged
> Roaring, and all the wave was in a flame.

There is only the most tenuous narrative connection between the seven songs which make up The Ninth Wave, but Bush herself commented as follows on the underlying idea of a girl drowning at sea:

> The idea is that they've been on a ship and they've been washed over the side so they're alone in this water. And I find that horrific imagery, the thought of being completely alone in all this water. And they've got a life jacket with a little light so that if anyone should be traveling at night they'll see the light and know they're there. And they're absolutely terrified, and they're completely alone at the mercy of their imagination, which again I personally find such a terrifying thing, the power of one's own imagination being let loose on something like that.

The prescribed numbers feature one from the first part of the album – 'Cloudbusting' – and the first two from The Ninth Wave – 'And Dream of Sheep' and 'Under Ice'.

'Cloudbusting': musical elements

This song arose after Bush read *A Book of Dreams* (1973) by Peter Reich. It concerns Reich's memories of his father, the psychologist Wilhelm Reich, and focuses on their life together on the family farm, Orgonon, in Maine.

The title refers to Reich's attempts to make rain by pointing a machine, the cloudbuster, at the sky. The song also touches on Reich's arrest and imprisonment.

Musical language

The number is printed here in the form of a full score, though most of the string sextet parts are condensed on to two staves.

Tempo is indicated by a metronome mark, and chord names are given above each system.

Sonority and texture

The performance forces consist of lead vocal, backing vocals, drums, string sextet, balalaika, Fairlight CMI (Computer Musical Instrument, represented by the three keyboard parts) and whistle effects.

The string sextet is used throughout, giving the number its particular distinguishing quality. The prominent detached chords are reminiscent of the string quartet sonorities of 'Eleanor Rigby' by the Beatles.

The texture is one of melody-dominated homophony, with strings at first providing block chord accompaniment to the lead vocal line.

As the song progresses, various additional layers are added:

- A three-quaver pattern at bar 12 (keyboard 2)
- Quaver figuration in the balalaika at bar 8
- At bar 34 violins provide a counter-melody in octaves
- Treated vocal sample melody at bar 65
- At bar 95 the three lowest string parts, reinforced by keyboard 3, sustain semibreves while the upper parts provide a distinctive rhythm
- Treated vocal sample (keyboard 2) at bar 111.

Rhythm, metre and tempo

The number has a steady moderate pulse of 112 crotchets per minute. The time signature is predominantly quadruple ($\frac{4}{4}$), though there are occasional $\frac{2}{4}$ and $\frac{6}{4}$ bars.

A dominant feature of the accompaniment is the constant crotchet beat (quaver chord, quaver rest) established at the start by the strings. It is also characterised by:

- Steady, reinforcing crotchet drum beats from bar 11
- A backbeat audible at, e.g., bar 18
- Even quavers in the balalaika figure at bar 8
- A recurring mechanical rhythmic figure in the violin (bar 3):

- The sudden brief halt to the crotchet pulse at 'and forget' and 'I won't forget' (bar 17 and bar 50)
- Sustained semibreves in the lower parts (from bar 95) combined with a strong rhythmic figure in the upper string parts:

- The contrasting longer note-values in the violin counter-melody at bar 34
- Longer note values in the additional synthesised line at bar 65
- Syncopation, e.g., keyboard 2 (bars 69–70)
- Offbeat sound effects at close.

The lead vocal line is typified by both the presence of longer note-lengths at the start and the use of speech-rhythm patterns involving much shorter durations.

Organisation of pitch: melody and word-setting

Although the song is in C♯ Aeolian minor, the melody itself could be regarded as being, for the most part, in B mixolydian.

The range of the lead vocal is a minor 10th, from G♯ below middle C to B above. The vocal melody is predominantly syllabic, with very occasional slurred pairs.

Beginning on the dominant of C♯, the melody is initially characterised by leaps of 3rds, 4ths and 5ths, but narrows in range from bar 9.

The remaining melodic content consists of:

- Violin – a narrow-range figure first heard at bar 3 is later expanded, for example from bar 17, where it eventually broadens to span a 5th (B–F♯) at bars 31–2

- A further violin counter-melody in octaves at bar 34, opening with stepwise descent through a 5th, answered then by a conjunct rising line.

- A line on synthesiser, initially drawing on only three pitches – B, C♯ and F♯ – at bar 65, but expanding from bar 73 to include G♯ and E. Overall it spans a 9th. This can be seen in Kbd. 2

- Vocalised Bvox refrain-like material from bar 111, opening with a leap of a minor 7th (C♯–B), then descending through G♯, F♯ to D♯.

Organisation of pitch: harmony

The song is based on the constant rotation of a limited number of dissonant, added-note chords:

- C♯m^7

- B major with added 9th

- A major with added 9th and 6th.

Occasionally another chord appears, including G♯ minor with added 4th (e.g. bar 12) or F♯^{7} with added 4th (e.g. 32).

All chords contain both B and C♯, which are the two gravitational centres of the melody. Variations in harmonic treatment include:

- Bass movement from root to the 4th below, e.g. C♯ to G♯ at bar 18, alternating root and second inversions of the same seventh chord

- Substitution of the expected A chord at 20 with F♯^{7}, with an added 4th (B) in the bass

- Changes in harmonic rhythm, e.g. at the opening the C♯ and B chords each have two beats and the A chord four, whereas from bar 95, chords are allotted four beats.

Tonality and structure

The song is in C♯ minor, and though some melodic lines appear to be based on B, there is no modulation.

Broadly, the song follows a verse and chorus pattern with instrumentals:

Bars 1–8	Verse ('I still dream…')
Bars 9–18	Bridge ('When you and sleep…')
Bars 18–33	Chorus ('But ev'ry time it rains…')
Bars 34–41	Verse ('On top of the world')
Bars 42–51	Bridge ('To be a threat')
Bars 51–68	Chorus ('But ev'ry time it rains…')

Bars 69–81	Instrumental, involving synthesised melody
Bars 81–98	Chorus ('And ev'ry time it rains…')
Bars 99–136	Instrumental and coda, featuring chorus material ('Ooh, just saying it…') and Bvox.

'And Dream of Sheep': musical elements

Musical language

This number uses conventional notation for vocals and piano, with chord names indicated above the system.

Tempo is indicated by a metronome mark, and detailed dynamic markings are provided, as well as pedal indications for piano and articulation marks. As the piece goes on, parts for bouzouki and whistles are notated, as well as dubbed speech.

Sonority and texture

Besides lead vocal accompanied by piano, there are parts for bouzouki, whistles and dubbed voices and effects.

> The Bouzouki is a lute-like instrument used in Greece and, in recent times, Irish traditional music. Here it is played by Dónal Lunny, a leading Irish folk musician.

The texture is essentially melody-dominated homophony, with prominent broken-chord accompaniment and additional figurations from the bouzouki.

Rhythm, metre and tempo

At 80 crotchets per minute, the song moves at a moderately slow pace. It is in quadruple time $\frac{4}{4}$ with occasional variations, for example, a number of $\frac{2}{4}$ bars, as well as a $\frac{3}{4}$ bar at bar 47 and $\frac{5}{4}$ at bar 51, creating an appropriately fluid feel.

The track features rubato, and there is a reduction in speed at the close. Characteristic rhythmic patterns include:

- Dotted rhythms (e.g. 'white' in bar 9 and the bass line at bars 15–17)
- The occasional triplet (e.g. 'heavy with' at bar 49)
- Scotch snaps (e.g. 'stupid' in bar 29).

> Notice how rhythmically relaxed the song sounds in performance, for example, the gentle jazz quavers at 'If they find me…', as compared with the notated syncopations in the Anthology.

Organisation of pitch: melody and word-setting

The overall lead vocal range is a major 9th (B below middle C up to C♯ at 'Every gull'), though for the most part the upper limit is B, and towards the close the vocal line occupies the lower range of B-G♯.

Set in the key of E major, the line is marked by:

- Distinctive leaps, e.g. the perfect 5ths in the opening phrase
- Repeated notes ('My face is all lit up')
- Mainly syllabic word-setting, although there are slurred pairs and brief melismas, particularly at phrase-endings, e.g. 'up' at bar 7
- Repeated 3rds at 'If they find me racing...' (from bar 8)
- Low tessitura at close, with the song finishing on the lower dominant, so underlining the sense of the text ('deeper and deeper').

Organisation of pitch: harmony

The number centres on the key of E major, and mainly revolves around the following chords with functional effect:

- I
- IIb
- V
- VI^7.

A tonic pedal is used in the chorus ('If they find me racing...'), and other striking chords include:

- V with added 9th at bar 21, giving rise to a chord made up of 4ths
- VI with added 9th at bar 22
- The 4ths chord heard on whistles in bar 41.

Tonality and structure

The song is in E major throughout, despite the studied avoidance of chord I until the tonic pedal at bar 8, and is cast in a straightforward verse–chorus structure:

Bars 1–7	Verse ('Little light...')
Bars 8–15	Chorus (If they find me racing...')
Bars 15–19	Link 1
Bars 19–26	Verse ('Oh, I'll wake up to any sound...')
Bars 27–36	Chorus ('I'd tune in...')
Bars 36–40	Link 2
Bars 40–53	Coda ('Ooh, their breath is warm...')

'Under Ice': musical elements

Musical language

This number uses conventional short score notation consisting of three or four staves as required. Tempo is indicated by metronome marks, and chord names are given above each system. Some dynamic markings are provided.

Sonority and texture

Vocals exploit two distinct ranges (low at the start and a higher continuation at bar 53). In addition there are backing vocals, synthesised string sounds, dubbed voices, and synthesised effects at the close.

The texture is lean, producing an appropriately bleak sound throughout. The fragmentary vocal line is underpinned by a bass line and short, two-part string figurations.

Rhythm, metre and tempo

This number is dominated by the insistent bass notes, which occur on the crotchet pulse throughout. The tempo initially increases from 65 beats per minute to 108. There is a slackening of pulse in the final bars.

The number starts and ends in quadruple time but frequently alternates with triple time passages.

A characteristic pattern is the three-quaver figuration heard in the strings at the start:

This pattern is sometimes extended into a two-bar phrase (e.g. bars 3 and 4) and is adopted in the vocal line, for example at 'Everywhere' and 'Not a soul, on the ice'.

A further feature is a two-note pattern ('So white'), with the second note lengthened:

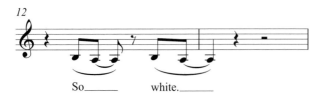

The synth pad introduced in the second bar is sustained throughout the song. Other rhythmic features include:

- Scotch snaps (e.g. bar 27)
- Triplets (e.g. bar 50)
- The longer lengths of such phrases as 'The river has frozen' (bars 14–16).

Organisation of pitch: melody and word-setting

The range of the lead vocal is from A below middle C to C a 10th higher (bar 53), although the tessitura is mainly low.

The lead vocal line is characterised by:

- Nervous, 'staccato', mainly stepwise two-pitch figure
- Short lyrical sections, including: 'The river has frozen over', which spans a 5th and features a prominent leap of a 4th (A–D) followed by a 5th (A–E)
- Mainly syllabic setting, with some slurred pairs
- Long, descending chromatic portamento at close, from the climactic top C in bar 53.

Organisation of pitch: harmony

Conventional chords are avoided. The synthesised violins and the vocals provide passing dissonances.

The bass outlines the bare bones of a functional structure, implying variously tonic (A), submediant (F), mediant (C) and subdominant (D). The dominant (E) is avoided.

The final chord is (A–B–E rather than a straightforward tonic chord, the electronic effects creating even greater ambiguity.

There are many open parallel fifths in the synth strings.

Tonality and structure

The tonality of the main part of the song is A minor, as the bass notes clearly indicate. At the conclusion, less 'rational' electronic sounds take over, undermining the tonality.

Bush here avoids conventional structuring in favour of a through-composed piece involving alternation of fragmentary melodic motifs:

Bars 1–8	Introduction	Synthesised upper strings from bar 3
Bars 8–13	Motif 1	'It's wonderful...'
Bars 14–18	Motif 2	'The river...'
Bars 19–24	Motif 1	'Not a soul...'
Bars 24–29	Motif 2	'I'm speeding...'
Bars 30–39	Motif 1	'In the ice...'
Bars 40–45	Motif 2	'There's something...'
Bars 46–58	Motif 1 and Coda	'Moving under ice...'

Set work:

Revolver: 'Eleanor Rigby', 'Here, There and Everywhere', 'I Want to Tell You' and 'Tomorrow Never Knows'

The Beatles

Musical context

The music of the Beatles embraces a wide range of stylistic elements, notably rock and roll, blues and folk music.

Their work was marked by a striking lyricism and flair for capturing situations through a perfect match of word and song. *Revolver* was their seventh album and, standing more or less at the midpoint of their recording career, marked the start of a distinctive new phase in their development. It was released on August 5, 1966, and at the same time two numbers extracted from it ('Yellow Submarine' and 'Eleanor Rigby') appeared on a single 7-inch disc. Its issue coincided with the group's final concert tour.

Revolver was 34 weeks in the album charts, and continues to enjoy widespread esteem.

The album came third in a Music of the Millennium poll organised by the HMV group, Channel 4, the *Guardian* and Classic FM in 1997 (first place went to *Sgt. Pepper's Lonely Hearts Club Band* and second to *Thriller* by Michael Jackson).

It differs from the preceding albums in that it was more studio-based, thus establishing fundamental, new approaches in the creation and production of popular music. The use of the studio was built into the creative idea behind the album, rather than existing simply as a means of preserving the performance for posterity.

Experimental production aspects included:

■ Automatic double-tracking

> **AUTOMATIC DOUBLE-TRACKING** sometimes known as artificial double-tracking, was developed in 1966 at the Abbey Road Studios. Previously, if double tracking was required to enrich the vocal or instrumental sound, the track had to be recorded twice. With automatic double-tracking, two linked tape-recorders could create a doubled track with just one take, and at the same time delay the second track by a fraction of a second to give the impression that two parts were involved.

■ Variable tape speeds, e.g. recording at a faster tempo than was eventually heard on the disc

■ Use of tape-loops

> **TAPE-LOOPS** arise from the cutting and splicing end to end of a magnetic tape recording. The resulting circle or loop can be played continuously. The technique was developed in the 1940s by Pierre Schaeffer.

■ Playing recorded sounds backwards ('backmasking')

■ Dubbed sound effects.

The album was also notable for other reasons:

■ Use of classical performance forces. Besides the 'doubled' string quartet used in 'Eleanor Rigby', Alan Civil played French horn on 'For No One'

■ Indian influences are evident in the use of sitar and tabla on 'Love You Too' and sitar in 'Tomorrow Never Knows'

■ Avoidance or very free treatment of conventional popular music structures and further distancing of the band from their earlier 'Merseybeat' style

> For examples of earliest Beatles songs, see the band's debut studio album *Please, Please Me*.

■ Presence of 'psychedelic' elements, the result of experimentation with LSD, reflected in increasingly colourful musical timbres

> **PSYCHEDELIC** refers to art and music of the mid-1960s that attempted to capture the mind-altering effects of such hallucinatory drugs as LSD. In the case of the Beatles, this aspect of their work was reflected in unusually colourful timbre and imagery and attempts to recreate meditative experiences. Ringo Starr later commented that drugs were taken, but 'we never did it to a great extent at the session. We were really hard workers.'

- Widening of the range of subjects covered. Of the four numbers under discussion, only 'Here, There and Everywhere' is a conventional love song.

The album was produced by George Martin and recorded and mixed by Geoff Emerick, a process that required 300 hours of studio time. Its rather obscure title seems to have referred both to guns and to revolving gramophone record turntables.

'Eleanor Rigby': musical elements

This strikingly original song has to do with loneliness and futility. In place of the typical line-up of instruments, a string group was used, drawing on eight performers. This was not an octet as such, with eight independent parts, but a doubled string quartet.

Musical language

Staff notation appropriate to the instruments employed is used for this number. Tempo indications are given in terms of numbers of beats per minute.

Structure

The song is in modified strophic form, consisting of:

- Introduction
- Verse and Refrain (twice)
- Bridge (based on the Introduction)
- Verse and Refrain
- Coda.

Each verse consists of two five-bar lines, with a sometimes loose rhyme-scheme:

Verse 1	been	dream
	door	for
Verse 2	hear	near
	there	care
Verse 3	name	came
	grave	saved

Its intriguing metrical scheme is evident in the musical setting of the first verse:

Bars	Section	Details
1–8	Introduction	Two four-bar phrases, subdivided into two and a quarter bars vocal ('Ah, look at all the lonely people') and instrumental fill
9–18	Verse	Two five-bar statements, each phrased 1 + 3 + 1, the vocal statements at odds with the accompaniment and harmonic scheme
19–26	Refrain	Two four-bar phrases, subdivided into three bars vocal and one bar instrumental fill

Tonality

The song is anchored firmly to E minor, with some striking modal inflections (see Melody).

Organisation of pitch: melody

One immediately striking feature of the melodic writing is its modal ambiguity.

The introduction is composed of a repeated rising and falling melody. Initially there is a stepwise line rising from E to A, and over the first chord of C major, the presence of an F♯ implies Lydian mode. This initially bright sound is negated by the plunge down to a G, a 9th below the highest note, harmonised by an E minor chord.

There are several interesting melodic features in the vocal line during the verses:

- The mode seems to be E minor Dorian, evident in the C♯, but this is replaced by a C♮ (Aeolian) in the final bar of the phrase

- The first bar of the vocal line, with its triadic descent, highlights the names of the characters (Eleanor Rigby and Father McKenzie)

- Besides the Dorian inflection, the next bars of each line of the verse are marked by a descending sequence and syncopation

- The final single bar of the verse highlights the situation or the message (e.g. 'Lives in a dream', 'Who is it for?' 'No one comes near', 'No one was saved').

Note that the first note of the song as given here (A) is as it sounds on the recording. In the course of the number (e.g. on 'Father McKenzie') it sometimes appears to be a G, as has been printed in some other editions.

The first bar of the refrain's melody is similar in outline to that of the verse. In contrast, however, the remainder of the melody avoids the sixth and seventh degrees of the scale altogether, involving only the first, third, fourth and fifth notes of the scale. The line effectively highlights the despair of the situation, first by an upwards octave leap (followed by a rapid descent to the tonic), and then in the second phrase with a leap of a minor 10th, before closing on the mediant.

Organisation of pitch: harmony

The song is built on two chords, E minor and C major, but notice that at bar 61, in place of C major, the chord is A minor with minor 7th. This chord extends into bar 62.

Overall, the harmonic rhythm is slow, in marked contrast to the song's brisk pace:

- Introduction: the chords alternate every two bars, starting with C major
- The verse opens with E minor for three bars, followed by two bars of C
- The refrain is built on E minor throughout, with sustained E in cellos, and a chromatic counter-melody in violas featuring D♭ (whose *alter ego* is the 'Dorian' C♯).

The relentless, closed-in harmonic scheme contributes strongly to the overpowering pessimism of the number.

Tempo, metre and rhythm

The tempo is a fast quadruple, with 136 crotchet beats a minute. Apart from a slight unmarked *ritenuto* at the close, the tempo is maintained throughout.

The song is built on insistent repeated crotchets, enlivened by quaver figures (see bars 3–4). Sustained notes appear in the cellos in the refrains.

Syncopation occurs frequently in the vocal parts (e.g. bars 2, 9–11, 20–21).

Sonority and texture

The string parts were arranged by the band's producer George Martin, who stated that he had been influenced in part by Bernard Herrmann's score for *Psycho*. Certainly the writing is often aggressively staccato with mechanical-sounding figurations.

The string parts were deliberately performed non-vibrato, and recorded with the microphones close to the instruments to produce a raw, intense sound. Vocal harmonies, with the line doubled a 3rd below at the opening, were provided by Lennon and Harrison supporting McCartney, who sang the verses.

The texture is predominantly homophonic, with the repeated staccato chords frequently off-set by sustained notes in other parts – for example at the opening, and also from bar 19 (with the descending chromatic line in the viola and the pedal in the cello).

There are a number of significant variations in subsequent stanzas:

- Bar 30, additional rising scale in quavers in cello
- Bar 33, sustained, syncopated viola line, broadly a 6th below vocal line
- Bar 40, crotchets rising by step in violin I
- Bar 54, sustained, syncopated violin II line, broadly a 3rd below vocal line
- Bar 59, cello doubles vocal line
- Bar 63, contrapuntal combination of upper backing vocals line from Introduction with refrain.

'Here, There and Everywhere': musical elements

This exquisite romantic ballad was a favourite of both Lennon and its composer, McCartney, as well as George Martin. According to McCartney, it was inspired by Brian Wilson's number 'God Only Knows' which appeared on the Beach Boys' album *Pet Sounds*, the same year as *Revolver*.

Musical language

Staff notation is used for piano and vocals. Chord names are given for guitars, and though the tempo is given in terms of beats per minute, there are traditional Italian 'rubato' and 'a tempo' directions.

Sonority

It is sung by McCartney, using automatic double-tracking, and supported by lead guitar, bass guitar, acoustic guitar, drums and vocals.

In spite of the apparent simplicity of the sound, the multiple role played by McCartney (vocal, bass and acoustic guitars) and the three-part backing vocals would have required blending of several takes.

Texture

The ballad is almost entirely melody-dominated homophony, the guitar part alternating between block chords and a broken-chord figuration.

Throughout the verse, three-part vocals ('Oo-') are heard, and in the final verse, another vocal line is added at bars 21–22. A chromatic fill can be heard in bar 15.

Structure and tonality

Bars	Section	Key	Details
1–3	Introduction	G – B♭ – V of G	The shift to B♭ anticipates the shift of key in the bridge
4–11	Verse 1	G	Touches briefly on E minor

4–12	Verse 2	G	Finishes with the dominant of B♭
13–16	Bridge 1	B♭–G minor	B♭ really only lasts for one chord, the rest of the bridge being in G minor
17–24	Verse 3	G	
13–16	Bridge 1	B♭–G minor	
17–25	Verse 4	G	Additional vocal part at bars 21 and 22
25–30	Coda	G	Based on verse chords

The above analysis uses the terminology of popular music, though interestingly, the number is a perfect example of binary form with introduction and coda.

Organisation of pitch: melody and harmony

The vocal line is mainly syllabic throughout.

In the introduction it outlines broken triads, closing on the dominant in preparation for the verse. There is frequent parallel movement in the harmony here and at other points in the song.

Verse

The underlying harmony is 'phrased' regularly: 2 + 2 + 1 + 1 + 1 + 1 bars. The melody is counter-phrased against this background (1 + 2 + 2 + 3), and is characterised by its relatively wide range (a 9th) and the free movement between monotone passages, conjunct movement and graceful, expressive arching leaps.

The chords, moving in parallel, are I–ii–iii–IV, followed by a sudden shift to an F#m chord, paving the way for a hint of E minor. The return to the tonic is via supertonic and dominant 7ths.

Notice the following features:

- An appoggiatura at bar 5 (on 'each')
- The dissonant E in bar 7 resolved by the upward movement of the harmony
- The dissonant vocal line in the first part of bar 8
- The brief false relation in bar 9 (C♮ in vocal and C# in harmony)
- Harmonic sequence (bar 9–10).

Bridge

Counter-phrasing is evident here as well: notice how the final phrase, starting in bar 16, overlaps the start of the third verse in bar 17.

The key of G minor is clearly defined by the iv–V^7–I progression in bars 14 and 16.

Coda

Notice the rising line in bars 28–29, and the plagal cadence at the close.

Tempo, metre and rhythm

The tempo is very moderate at 84 crotchets per minute. It is in quadruple time, though the introduction is disturbed by a bar of $\frac{7}{8}$. The introductory bars are also performed rubato, before the steady pulse of the main part of the song is established in bar 4.

The word-setting has an almost conversational quality, and this is reflected in the flexible rhythmic schemes with notes carried over the starts of beats, Scotch snaps and gentle syncopations.

'I Want to Tell You': musical elements

This number is by George Harrison, and according to Harrison himself, concerned 'the avalanche of thoughts that are so hard to write down or say or transmit'. The song's sense of frustration is evident in the markedly dissonant harmony.

Musical language

Staff notation is used for piano and vocals, and chord names are given for guitars.
The tempo is given in terms of beats per minute with an additional direction to applying jazz quavers. In this arrangement, structural indications are also given (e.g. D.S. al Coda).

Sonority and texture

The number involved Harrison's double-tracked vocals and lead guitar, while McCartney provided bass guitar and piano.

A particular feature of the song is the three-part vocal harmonisation (e.g. 'My head is filled with things to say'), with Lennon and McCartney supporting Harrison. Besides the drum kit, we hear tambourine, maracas and handclaps.

The texture is melody-dominated homophony throughout.

Structure and tonality

There is scarcely any deviation from the key of A major.

Bars	Section	Key	Details
1–4 (repeated)	Introduction	A major with prominent flattened sevenths	Fade in (guitar riff)
5–15	Verse 1	A	
16–26	Verse 2	A	
27–34	Bridge 1	(B minor)–A	
16–26	Verse 3	A	
27–34	Bridge 2	(B minor)–A	
16–25	Verse 3 repeated	A	
36–45	Coda	A	Fade-out, involving guitar riff and three-part vocals

Organisation of pitch: melody and harmony

The song is built on a limited amount of material. It fades in with a guitar riff in which a flattened 7th is prominent, leading to an alternation between chords I and IV.

The desperation of the lyrics is conveyed in the fragmentary nature of the melodic setting, with dislocated phrases of varying lengths, some as short as a bar, but extending to three and a half bars at the end of each verse. The lead vocal has a range of a major 7th (E–D♯), but the harmonising voices rise higher at the end of each statement (A and B at bar 8).

The harmony hints at the difficulty of transmitting thoughts in:

- Its limited number of chords
- Acciaccaturas, for example D♮ on D♯ at bar 8
- The jolting effect of the sudden shift to the B^7 in bar 8 (and elsewhere)
- The jarringly dissonant E minor 9th (F♮ over E), regarded as one of the most remarkable effects in the Beatles' repertoire, at bars 10–14 (and elsewhere).

In the bridge, the range of the vocal line becomes more limited, moving from the persistent monotone B ('But if I seem to act unkind'), to F♯ at bar 31, before closing on A. The chords convey a similarly claustrophobic feel, moving from B minor to B diminished and then A, before repeating the process.

Notice the use of melisma in the coda.

Tempo, metre and rhythm

At 124 crotchets a minute, this is a brisk number in quadruple time.

Jazz quavers are present in the guitar riff which also features triplet crotchets.

> **JAZZ QUAVERS** are the replacement of straight quavers with unevenly performed pairs, giving a triplet feel, i.e. as crotchet–quaver, sometimes referred to as a swung rhythm.

Triplet quavers appear in the closing bar of the bridge, propelling the music on to the next verse.

Verses are typified by insistent crotchets on piano, while vocal parts are heavily syncopated.

'Tomorrow Never Knows': musical elements

This song was the first on the album to be recorded. Its text was assembled by Lennon and was based on *The Psychedelic Experience: A Manual Based on the Tibetan Book of the Dead* by Timothy Leary, Richard Alpert and Ralph Metzner.

Harrison later remarked that though the text was obscure, it was to do with meditation, which went beyond waking, sleeping and dreaming in the quest for pure consciousness, freed from the clutter of the physical world.

Musical language

The score is a combination of staff notation (including sitar and bass guitar) with bass guitar also given in tab form, the typical drum kit form of notation and a series of verbal cues and commands (e.g. entries of loops, continuation of sitar, bass and drums parts, as well as e.g. organ and tack piano).

Conventional structural devices are also used (e.g. repeats and D.S. al Coda).

Sonority

The number has a unique sound quality resulting from complex studio engineering. Some typical devices include:

- Treatment of Lennon's vocal part. The opening stanzas were recorded with automatic double-tracking

- The verses after the instrumental were distorted by being run through a revolving Leslie speaker (found in Hammond organs) as Lennon wished his voice to sound like chanting Tibetan monks

- Use of tape-loops, of which the following are audible in the course of the song:
  - The 'seagull' effect which was actually a speeded up tape of McCartney (first heard at c. 0.08)
  - An orchestral chord of B♭ major (0:19)
  - An electric guitar phrase, reversed and played at double speed (0:22)
  - Sitar-like sound, reversed and played at double speed (0:56).

You may be able to hear others, as George Martin said that 16 loops were used in all. Only one take was made, as the assembly of this material was inevitably 'aleatoric'.

> In **ALEATORIC** music chance plays a role, very often through the rhythmic freedom allowed the performers. Its use became widespread in the 1960s, notably in the work of the Polish composer Witold Lutosławski.

Texture

The solo voice is supported by a drone C throughout, along with a bass guitar riff from bar 3. Drums also play throughout. The use of sitar and tambura hint at Eastern meditation.

The web of tape loops produces an electronic polyphony with occasional homophony (the chords of B♭ and C).

Structure and tonality

The key is C, with prominent flattened 7th, as in the Mixolydian mode.

The song is strophic and its basic structure is as follows:

- Faded-in introduction
- 3 verses (eight bars each)
- Instrumental (16 bars)
- Four verses (eight bars each)
- Coda, focused on repetitions of the final bars of the verse
- Outro (fade).

Organisation of pitch: melody and harmony

The opening bars of the verse (bars 6–9) outline the tonic broken chord of C with powerfully direct effect. The two last phrases move from the fifth degree up to the flattened 7th and then the tonic.

The melodic material of the tape loops is much wider in range and also more random. Besides the flattened seventh, flattened thirds (bar 23) can be heard.

Besides the drone, the only other harmonic element is the presence of two chords: B♭ moving to C.

Tempo, metre and rhythm

Tempo in the vocal part is moderate and contrasts markedly with the feverish activity in the other parts. Devices include:

- Syncopation
- Triplet crotchets
- Triplet quavers in the guitar solo loop
- Dotted rhythms and Scotch snaps can also be heard in this solo.

Test yourself

Below are five short questions on each set work. These are not 'exam questions' but are intended to help you get to know each work better.

Most questions use the command words listed in Appendix 5 of each specification (with which you will need to be familiar when preparing for exams). For each set work there is also a sample essay question for each level. These correspond to Question 6 in Pearson's Sample Assessment Materials. Essays at the two levels are marked from different assessment grids, as may again be seen from the Sample Assessment Materials. The allocation of marks is different, with fewer marks at AS implying the need for less information. At A Level there is greater emphasis on saying how and why particular things happen in the music, and relatively less on just saying what happens. When answering the questions below, you should refer to the printed score of the relevant work or movement.

In your exam you will have a special booklet containing the scores you need. You will not be allowed to take a copy of the anthology or other printed music into the exam room.

Tracks from *Back in the Day* (Courtney Pine)

Short questions:

a. Name the extended techniques used by Pine in 'Lady Day and (John Coltrane)'.

b. List the musical borrowings in the three prescribed pieces.

c. Describe the harmony of 'Inner state (of mind)'.

d. Explain the extent to which blues is important in these numbers.

e. Discuss Pine's use of dubbed sound.

Essay questions:

AS

Evaluate Pine's use of instrumental and vocal resources and texture in 'Lady Day and (John Coltrane)'. Relate your discussion to other relevant works. These may include set works, wider listening or other music.

A Level

Evaluate Pine's use of instrumental and vocal resources, texture and harmony in *Lady Day and (John Coltrane)* and *Love and Affection*, with particular reference to his treatment of the blues idiom. Relate your discussion to other relevant works. These may include set works, wider listening or other music.

Tracks from *Hounds of Love* (Kate Bush)

Short questions:

a. List the instruments used in each of the three prescribed songs.

b. Give the ranges of the lead vocal in each song.

c. Discuss the word-setting in each song.

d. Explain how the texture of 'Under Ice' differs from that of 'And Dream of Sheep'.

e. Describe the rhythm and metre of 'Cloudbusting'.

Essay questions:

AS

Evaluate melody, word-setting and tonality in 'Cloudbusting'. Relate your discussion to other relevant works. These may include set works, wider listening or other music.

A Level

Evaluate melody, word-setting, structure and tonality in 'And Dream of Sheep' and 'Under Ice', with particular reference to the way the narrative content of each song is conveyed. Relate your discussion to other relevant works. These may include set works, wider listening or other music.

Tracks from *Revolver* (The Beatles)

Short questions:

a. List precisely the instrumental forces used in 'Eleanor Rigby'.

b. Describe the structure of 'Here, There and Everywhere'.

c. Discuss melody and harmony in 'Tomorrow Never Knows'.

d. Discuss rhythm in 'I want to Tell You'.

e. Explain why 'Tomorrow Never Knows' would not be suitable for live performance.

Essay questions:

A Level only

Evaluate rhythm, harmony and tonality in 'Eleanor Rigby' and 'Here, There and Everywhere', with particular reference to the way different experiences are portrayed. Relate your discussion to other relevant works. These may include set works, wider listening or other music.

Fusions

OVERVIEW

The works in this Area of Study are all examples of the blending together of diverse cultures and traditions.

AS **A** *Estampes,* Nos. 1 and 2 (Debussy)

AS **A** Tracks from *Caña quema* (Familia Valera Miranda)

A Tracks from *Breathing Under Water* (Anoushka Shankar)

Introduction

Musical 'fusion' is a relatively modern term. But there are examples in works from earlier eras in which the existence of musical cultures outside the mainstream tradition is at least acknowledged – although in such cases there was often little impact on the underlying style and content.

Examples of this approach can be found at least as early as the Renaissance, as in *La Mourisque*, a courtly French *basse danse* published in Antwerp in 1551 by Susato, seemingly devised to accompany the dance of a Moor. In the classical era, the Viennese fear of – and fascination with – Turkish culture was expressed through such works as the last movement of Mozart's Sonata in A (K. 331) with its 'Rondo alla Turca', and was also reflected in the composer's singspiel *Die Entführung aus dem Serail* (*The Abduction from the Seraglio*).

Don't forget that as late as 1683 Vienna was besieged by Turkish forces, as a consequence of which the Ottoman Empire was for decades viewed with considerable suspicion in the more easterly parts of Europe.

Initially, so-called Turkish percussion (triangle, bass drum and cymbal) was employed to produce a comic effect, or else a quasi-military sound (Haydn's Symphony No. 100). Gradually it became a regular part of the orchestra, and by the time of Beethoven's Ninth Symphony was used to thrilling effect to underline the message of Schiller's *Ode to Joy*.

Later in the 19th century an ever more sympathetic attitude to non-European music can be detected, especially in the work of Russian composers, such as Balakirev's *Islamey*, *Tamara* and *Song of Selim*, and Rimsky-Korsakov's *Sheherazade*, *Zuleika's Song* and *The Barber of Baghdad*. Here motifs associated with 'oriental' or Arabic music (notably the use of melodic lines made up of augmented 2nds and semitones, as found in the three highest notes of the harmonic minor scale) were sometimes introduced to create an appropriate atmosphere. The trend continued into the 20th century with Ravel's song-cycle *Shéhérazade* and some works by Bartók (e.g. Piano Suite Op. 14), Holst (*Beni Mora*) and Szymanowski (*Songs of the Infatuated Muezzin*). The introduction of elements from other musical traditions also extended to Latin American, in the case of Copland (*El Salón México* and *Danzón Cubano*), and in the case of Debussy's *Estampes* we encounter fine examples of an accommodation of Indonesian gamelan influences ('Pagodes') and Spanish styles ('La Soirée dans Grenade').

Opposite: Gongs from a Javanese Gamelan

Set work:

Estampes, Nos. 1 and 2 (Pagodes and La soirée dans Grenade)

Claude Debussy

Musical context

Estampes (literally 'prints' or 'engravings') dates from 1903 and marks a significant departure for Debussy in his approach to writing for piano. It involved the development of a more Impressionistic style for the instrument (he had already developed such an approach in the orchestral works *Prélude à l'après-midi d'un faune* (1894) and *Nocturnes* (1899)), and in this respect he may have been influenced by Ravel, whose *Jeux d'eau* had appeared early in 1902.

Ravel in fact expressed some irritation at the way his own work had been overlooked, and wrote to complain in these terms to the critic Pierre Laloy: 'You propound at length on a rather special kind of piano writing, the invention of which you ascribe to Debussy. But *Jeux d'eau* appeared at the beginning of 1902, when the only known works of Debussy were the three pieces [...] *Pour le piano* which [...] I deeply admire, but which from a purely pianistic view point conveyed nothing really new.'

Claude Debussy

Debussy's adoption of this form of pianistic Impressionism is seen in a particularly extreme form in the first of the three pieces of *Estampes*, 'Pagodes', with its delicate evocation of an oriental scene (pagodas) through pentatonicism, its harmonic stasis or at most very slow-moving harmonic changes, and use of pedal to create a vibrant, richly textured wash of sound.

The term 'Impressionism' has been applied to both painting and music. It was first used, pejoratively, in connection with Monet's *Impression: Sunrise*, painted in 1872 and exhibited in 1874 at the first of a series of eight Impressionist exhibitions.

By 1887 we also find it used in connection with Debussy's *Printemps*, a work for female voices and orchestra that he composed after receiving the Prix de Rome. In the secretary's report of the Académie des Beaux-Arts, mention is made of Debussy's tendency to cultivate the strange and the unusual, as well as the composer's feeling for colour. At the same time, however, he was condemned for overlooking the importance of clarity in design and structure, leading to that vague Impressionism 'which is one of the most dangerous enemies of truth in any work of art'.

In fact a direct comparison with art is not helpful: the painters associated with this movement represented scenes from nature, necessarily fleeting impressions since light and atmosphere are subject to constant change. In contrast Debussy believed that, though music is the art that is nearest nature, it should not be 'confined to reproducing, more or less exactly, Nature, but the mysterious correspondences which link Nature with Imagination'. In this respect, he allied himself more closely to symbolism, primarily a literary phenomenon, and sought to create works of art that were symbols of concepts rather than direct evocations of the real world.

Debussy's first acquaintance with the Javanese gamelan dated back to the Paris World Exhibition of 1889. At the 1900 Exhibition, he also heard a Balinese gamelan, which was apparently more delicate in texture. Debussy seems to have regarded the gamelan as a means of breaking free of the constraints of European music, commenting on one occasion on its ability to express every shade of meaning and at the same time to 'make our tonic and dominant seem like ghosts'. Much later he wrote: 'There still are, despite the evils of civilization, some delightful native peoples for whom music is as natural as breathing. [...] Their traditions reside in old songs, combined with dances, built up through the centuries. Yet Javanese music is based on a type of counterpoint by comparison with which that of Palestrina is child's play.'

'Pagodes': musical elements

Sonority, texture and dynamics

For this piece, Debussy uses almost the full range of the piano from B just over three octaves below middle C to A♯, over three octaves above.

Pedal is required throughout, although indications are sporadic, and indeed at the start of the piece somewhat ambiguous. Here Debussy requires both sustaining and una corda pedals to be applied, but does not indicate any changes. The next indication comes at bar 11, where he again asks for both pedals to be used but this time only up to bar 14. A final indication occurs at bars 27–31, again for both pedals, although note bars 61–64, which are a repeat of bars 11–14. For the rest of the piece, use of pedal is clearly at the pianist's discretion, though it is clear enough from the few indications there are that the composer expected a deliberately hazy effect with the piano made to sound, as the composer once put it, as though it had no hammers.

> **UNA CORDA** is the indication showing that the pianist should use the left foot pedal, which moves the hammers sideways. The hammers strike fewer strings, or in the case of the low single strings, are 'off-centre', so producing a softer sound with a different, almost muted, timbre.

Textures vary considerably in density and type, with changes in sound quality enhanced by exploitation of the piano's full dynamic range, from *délicatement et presque sans nuances* (perhaps best explained as 'delicately and almost without dynamic variation') to full *ff*.

Bars	Dynamic	Textural detail
1–2	*pp* (una corda)	Layered in low to middle range.
3–6	*pp*	Melody with chordal accompaniment and supporting pedal (drone)
7–10	*pp*	Melody with supporting pedal (drone), internal counter-melody and chords
11–14	*p* (una corda)	Pedal supporting two-part counterpoint, each part in octaves
15–18	*p* with *cresc.* and *dim.*	Melody with two- or three-note chords, supported by triplet figure of two alternating notes
19–20	*p*	Layered: octave melody, octave triplets in inner part; longer low octaves
20–22	*cresc.* and *dim.*	Triplets in higher part creating bell-like sounds; octave melody in inner part; longer low octaves
23–26	*pp*	Two-part figure, which is briefly imitative; pedal notes
27–30	*pp* (una corda)	LH melody, sometimes in octaves, in middle to lower range; ornamented by two-part passage of 4ths and 5ths in RH
31–36	*p*	Texture reduces to just a major 2nd chord, which then provides support to melody from bar 33

37–40	*p* – latterly *cresc.*	LH melody and chords overlaid with rapidly moving bell-like sounds
41–44	*ff*	Chords doubled two octaves apart, supported by single gong-like bass notes
45–49	*pp* – later *cresc.* And *dim.*	Texture reduces to major 2nd with ornamental semiquavers an octave higher, under which the melody from bar 33 reappears
50–53	*p*	Repeat of melody in LH octaves with single notes below and trills above
53–72		Reprise of bars 3–22 (with some modification in bar 72)
73–77		Reprise of bars 41–44, modified to incorporate triplets and with the last bar repeated
78–98	*ff* to 'aussi *pp* que possible'	Rapid filigree work starting high in RH and developing into figuration that spans two octaves. The melody, heard in single notes, then octaves and with a light supporting harmonisation, is heard in the middle ranges (LH), the whole supported by long bass notes.

Tempo, metre and rhythm

Debussy directed this piece to be performed *modérément animé* (moderately quickly), with the pulse clearly subject to rubato as seen from the numerous *ritenutos*

The time signature is simple quadruple ($\frac{4}{4}$), the only departures occurring at bars 92 and 94, where bars of $\frac{2}{4}$ are inserted to underline the temporary six-beat structures at this point.

The rhythms in this piece are hugely diverse with many technical features associated with Debussy's Impressionist approach:

- Syncopation (e.g. bar 1), even before a clear beat is established
- Tied notes carried over bar lines, weakening the 'on-beat' feel (e.g. bars 3–4)
- Steady quavers in motif at bar 7
- Triplets (e.g. bar 11)
- Quintuplets (from bar 80)
- Heterorhythms, or cross-rhythms, e.g. twos against threes (bar 23) and eight demi-semiquavers against three quavers (bar 78)
- Shorter note lengths, perhaps reproducing the effect of the higher-pitch instruments in the gamelan (e.g. demisemiquavers at bar 37)
- Long gong-like sounds in bass.

Organisation of pitch: melody

Much of the melody is built on two-bar phrases drawing on pentatonic structures. Its first melodic line is actually constructed from only four pitches: G#–C#–D#–F#, with the fifth note of the pentatonic scale – the B – being supplied in the accompanying harmonic structure.

Skeleton score (as are many of the subsequent examples)

At bar 11, the same four-note figure is presented in a triplet variation as part of a passage of two-part counterpoint, the B now supplied in the lower part.

A similar approach is employed as part of an imitative treatment at bar 23:

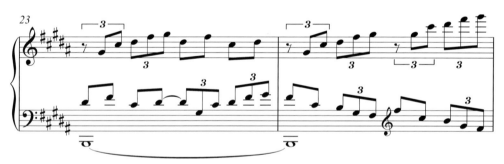

In contrast, the melody in the four-bar section from bar 15 uses a contrasting note range G#–A#–C#–D#–F#, now with a chromatic harmonisation, while at bar 19, a different distribution of the original occurs, the melody consisting of B–G#–F#–D#, with the remaining note of this pentatonic fragment – the C# – appearing in the triplets.

The central passage of the movement, commencing at bar 33, strikes a new, more acid note with the chromatic E♯, though the set of pitches also involves just five notes.

A final pentatonic motif can be heard at bar 37, drawing on the original set of pitches.

In connection with pentatonicism, it should be noted that the filigree ornamentation that runs from bar 78 to the close also uses pentatonic patterns based on the notes that appeared at bar 15.

In broad contrast is the five-note LH countermelody first heard in bar 7, which moves by step and so does not follow the gapped outlines of the pentatonic scale as such.

Organisation of pitch: harmony

The harmony of this piece is non-functional and draws heavily, but not exclusively, on pentatonic material. As a consequence it has a largely static quality. The harmonic rhythm is slow, often with only slight changes as part of the 'changing background' approach.

CHANGING BACKGROUND refers to the accompanying of similar or the same melodic material with different harmonies (sometimes hinting at contrasting keys) and textures. It is associated in the first instance with Russian composers of the 19th century, a fine early example being Glinka's *Kamarinskaya*. It can also be heard in 'Mercury' from *The Planets* by Holst.

The opening chord, gradually built up, is an open 5th plus major 2nd (B–F♯–G♯). It expands at bar 3 to become a B major added 6th chord (B–D♯–F♯–G♯).

Other prominent landmarks include:

- B major with added 6th and flattened 7th (bar 5)
- B major[13] (bars 7–10)
- Diminished triad (bar 16, beat 2)
- Interval of a major 2nd (F♯ and G♯) used in isolation (colouristic rather than functional) at bar 32 and then as part of a chord at bar 37 (C♯–B–C♯)
- Pentatonic harmonisation from bar 37, involving some approximate parallelism and open 5ths chords

■ The final section of the piece, with its pentatonic wash underpinned by slowly descending bass line, eventually settling on the tonic, B. Within this scheme, the A natural at bar 82 is 'chromatic'.

Structure and tonality

'Pagodes' is in ternary form with coda. Because of its pentatonic content, the tonal scheme rarely departs from the region of B major, though there is some ambiguity.

Bars	Key	Section
1–2	B major	Introduction
3–32	B major–G♯ minor (bar 11)–B major (bar 23)	Section A
33–53	F♯–D♯ minor	Section B
53–77	B major–G♯ minor–D♯ minor	Section A with reference to material from Section B
78–98	B major	Coda, based on material from Section A

'La soirée dans Grenade': musical elements

It has often been remarked in jest that the best Spanish music has been composed by French composers, notably Bizet, Ravel and Debussy.

Indeed Debussy's intuitive feeling for Spanish music, and especially that of the southernmost region of Andalusia, is all the more striking as he only once entered the country, spending just six hours in San Sebastián at a bull fight. The title translates as 'Evening in Granada', the city of Granada being a major cultural centre in Andalusia.

The authenticity of his Spanish work, which besides 'La soirée dans Grenade', included *Ibéria*, 'La sérénade interrompue' (Préludes, Book 1), *Lindaraja* for two pianos, and *La puerta del Vino* (Préludes Book 2) impressed the Spanish composer Manuel de Falla, who described 'La soirée dans Grenade' as an 'evocation of reflections of moonlit images in the lakes of the Alhambra', which was 'nothing less than miraculous'. He further remarked that though there are no direct quotations from Spanish folklore, 'the entire piece down to the smallest detail makes one feel the character of Spain.' That character is evident mainly through the habanera rhythm that runs through most of the piece, the plaintive 'Moorish' melody heard at the opening and the guitar-like effects that occur as the piece proceeds.

> **MOORISH** is a term sometimes applied to music of the Andalusia region on account of its links with North African and Arab culture. The whole of the southern region of Spain was under Islamic rule until 1492, and there is considerable evidence of Islamic influence in this part of the country.

Sonority, texture and dynamics

Debussy here employs a six-octave range from C♯ three octaves below middle C to C♯ three octaves above.

He draws on well-sustained sound, as at the opening with pedal points and, though not marked, application of the sustaining pedal. In other parts of the piece, he uses staccato articulation (e.g. bar 38) and also distant, almost 'off-stage' effects, such as the sudden interjection of *Léger et lointain* ('light and distant') staccato articulated guitar-like strumming sounds (bar 109).

There are no specific requests for una corda pedal.

Textures draw on various types of homophony, often layered, and dynamics cover a wide range from *ppp* to *ff*.

Bar	Dynamics	Texture
1–6	*ppp*	Dominant pedal in bass, reinforced by treble rising by octaves, habanera rhythm in the middle part of the texture
7–14	*pp*	Melody in LH with very high inverted C♯ pedal in RH
15–16	*ppp*	Two single lines
17–20	*pp*	Block chords with single sustained bass note
21–22	*pp*	Widely spaced open octaves (C♯ pedal)
23–28	*p/pp*	Chords over habanera-rhythm pedal
29–32	*pp* and *cresc.*	As in bar 17
33–37	*mf-p*	Chords over habanera-rhythm pedal
38–50	*mf-ff*	Homophonic, latterly with melody in octaves
51–59	*dim.*	Melody moves into middle part, supported by habanera figure in LH and chords above in RH
60	*pp*	Widely spaced open octaves (C♯ pedal), as in bar 22

61–91	*p/pp*	Chords over habanera-rhythm pedal, some more densely textured than before (e.g. bar 78)
92–95	*pp*	Block chords with single sustained bass note
96–106	*pp*	Expands by bar 98 to three-part texture consisting of octave melody in the middle plane, with single bass note per bar and chordal habanera rhythm in uppermost plane
107–108	*pp –dim.*	Single bass note
109–112	*pp (cresc.– dim.)*	Figuration using alternating hands; single notes in LH and chords in RH
113–114	*p*	Chords over habanera-rhythm pedal
115–118	*pp (cresc.– dim.)*	Figuration using alternating hands, single notes in LH and chords in RH; RH in bar 118 an octave higher than in bar 117
119–121	*p*	Chords over habanera-rhythm pedal
122–129	*pp*	Three-layer texture: melody in middle plane, with broken-chord support in bass and octave habanera rhythm in uppermost plane. Notice how the material has to be distributed between the hands, with LH *(m.g.)* crossing over to take part of the melody.
130–136	*pp*	Texture gradually simplified to chords in middle plane with isolated notes in bass and fragmentary octave habanera rhythm in top plane. Notice that this is the only part of the piece in which Debussy indicated how he wished the sustaining pedal to be used.

The term 'pedal' has been used in comments on the first part of the piece for convenience, though technically it is not a 'textbook' example as there is no harmonic movement involved.

Tempo, metre and rhythm

Debussy indicates that the piece is to be played as a habanera (*Mouvement de habanera*), and that the pianist should begin slowly in a nonchalantly graceful rhythm (*Commencer lentement dans un rhythme nonchalamment gracieux*).

It is in duple time ($\frac{2}{4}$) with sudden switches to triple time ($\frac{3}{4}$) at bars 109 and 115 for the two 'distant' interjections. There are indications that the performer should alternate between rubato and *tempo giusto* (strict time). Notice also that the passage starting at bar 38 should be performed 'very rhythmically' and that at bar 67 'with more abandon'.

The piece is dominated by the habanera rhythm with its characteristic dotted notes clearly announced in the first bar.

Other rhythmic features include:

- Triplets (bars 9 and 15)
- Syncopation (e.g. bars 11, 33–36, 67)
- Hetero-rhythm, e.g. two against three in bars 33–34
- Scotch snaps (e.g. bars 33–36)
- Long drawn-out sounds at the beginning and end.

Organisation of pitch: melody

'La soirée dans Grenade' is built on a limited number of melodic motifs. The first is the rather orientalised line at bar 7:

Its plaintive 'Moorish' qualities derive from the juxtaposition of semitone and augmented 2nd intervals (some of which are bracketed above).

Other features include:

- Delicate ornamentation
- Limited range – it spans only an octave, and much of it is concentrated in the upper half
- Internal one-bar repetitions
- Overall descent
- Avoidance of balanced phrasing.

The second motif, at bar 17, with its balanced two-bar phrases, ascends by step and also contains repeated notes and is marked by harmonic parallelism.

The whole-tone scale is introduced in the motif which commences at bar 23, its line characterised by a stepwise rising third and immediate fall back to the starting note.

A sequence of falling 3rds, can be seen in the line at bar 33.

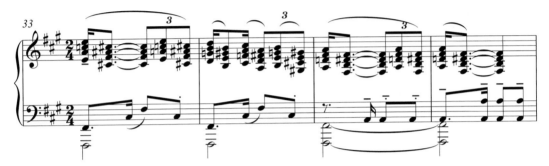

The new melody at bar 41 is also characterised by its lengthy descent. It could almost be heard as a diatonicised major-mode version of the very opening line.

Organisation of pitch: harmony

The harmonic vocabulary is much more varied than is the case in 'Pagodes', and typical devices include:

- Pedal points
- Parallel 7th chords (see bar 17 example)
- Whole-tone harmonies (see bar 23 example)
- False relations between adjacent chords (see bar 33 example)
- Open 5ths chords (bar 38)
- Chords of 5ths and 4ths (bar 38, last quaver)
- Simultaneous false relation (bar 52)
- Parallel triads (bars 109–110).

Structure and tonality

The piece consists of an alternation of a series of motifs in various, not always easily definable keys, mostly related to the F♯ minor tonic. It is framed at the beginning and end by statements of the 'Moorish' theme. Notice how the 'interruption' identified below is accentuated by the extreme tonal contrast.

Bars	Section	Key	Details
1	A	Around F♯ minor	Dominant pedal, eventually heard with 'Moorish' theme, tending towards dominant of the dominant at bar 15
17	B1	C♯ pedal	Parallel 7th chords
21		C♯ pedal	
23	B2	C♯ pedal	Whole-tone chords
29	B1	F♯ pedal	Parallel 7th chords
33	B3	F♯ pedal	Extension, with prominent falling 3rds
38	C	A major	Notice the surface energy within a mainly static harmonic and tonal context
61	B2	C♯ pedal	Whole-tone (as previously)
67	B3	F♯ major	Varied and extended
78	B2	C♯ pedal	Whole-tone structures replaced with common chords
92	B1	C♯ pedal	Extended from bar 96
98	C	A major	Supported by dominant pedal
109	'Interruption'	C Mixolydian	*Léger et lointain*
113	B3	F♯ major	
115	'Interruption'	A Mixolydian	*Léger et lointain*
119	B3	V of F♯ major	
122	A–B1	F♯ minor– F♯ major	Closes with falling 2nds idea (possibly an augmentation of opening of both A and C)

If you would like to hear Debussy's own performance of 'La Soirée dans Grenade', preserved on a piano roll recording from 1913, go to: www.youtube.com/watch?v=PekrB_luGlc

Set work:

Caña Quema: 'Se quema la chumbambá' and 'Allá va candela'

Familia Valera Miranda

Familia Valera Miranda

Musical context

The fusion of styles and cultures in these two Cuban pieces involves the combination of an essentially European model, introduced to the island by Spanish settlers, with Latin American music, especially that of Haiti and Puerto Rico, which in some respects had strong links with African culture.

The prescribed songs both date from the early years of the 20th century and are the work of previous generations of the Valera Miranda family. This group is one of the most celebrated of the bands working in east Cuba, the Oriente region, which embraces San Luis, the Sierra Maestra, Guantánamo and its main city, Santiago de Cuba, where Familia Valera Miranda are based.

The performers can trace their origins back to two main branches: the Durañona/Román-Valera line and the Cutiño/Basulto-Mirandas.

> The group is led by Félix Valera Miranda (lead vocal and guitar), the other performers being his wife, Carmen Rosa Alarcón Ganboa (maracas, backing vocals), his sons Enrique (cuatro, clave, vocals), Raúl Félix (double bass and vocals) and Ernesto (bongo and vocals), and family friend Rádames González Brugal (cuatro, clave and vocals).

In the 19th century these families were subsistence farmers, cultivating crops and trees for use as timber. Some of them were also ardent nationalists who involved themselves in the fight for freedom against Spanish colonialists, a struggle which led to the founding of the independent Republic of Cuba in 1902.

The Spanish element in their music is immediately obvious in the use of guitars, the cuatro (a sort of guitar with four double courses, used in Cuba) and the double bass. The Afro-Cuban influence is evident in the use of maracas, bongos and claves.

> Other typical instruments used by the band, but not in these numbers, include the bandurria (a sort of lute) and the tres (a guitar-like instrument with three double courses specifically mentioned in the texts of both songs).

Cuban music

In the early years of the 19th century, the island's capital city – Havana – was the largest seaport in the Americas, far exceeding in size those of Boston and New York. It also enjoyed a thriving, cosmopolitan cultural life, with a respected university and a number of theatres.

Unsurprisingly, its musical scene at that time was markedly European in orientation, the Spanish influence being evident in the prevalence of such dance-types as the pasodoble, while other 'old world' dance styles included the waltz, minuet and mazurka. The more sophisticated art-music repertoire included Italian opera and German Lieder.

The more specifically Cuban styles included a sensuous, vocal genre, the habanera (which of course we have already encountered in Debussy's La soirée dans Grenade). It was derived from the Cuban contradanza, and was characterised by use of that dotted rhythm, which Debussy exploited to great effect. A romantic song repertoire also developed in the course of the 19th century. These songs were known as trova, and were performed by the so-called trovadores who took their name from the troubadours, the secular minstrels of Medieval Europe. Other types of Cuban music, popular from the late 19th century onwards, include canción, son and bolero.

There is in fact considerable mixing of styles and types, often with no very clear differentiation between the various categories. For example, the term 'canción', derived from the French word chanson, simply meant song, and became associated with the trovadores and latterly other forms of Cuban music, such as the bolero. It was usually a lyrical outpouring of the singer's feelings, and as it lacked a strongly percussive accompaniment has come to be applied to any number which is not primarily designed for dance.

Other types of vocal music – notably the son, a forerunner of salsa – were provided with texts which were more political, topical or nationalist in nature – a trend which continued into the 20th century.

The title of the CD from which these two numbers are taken, *Caña Quema*, means 'Burnt Cane', and refers to a number by Lorenzo Hierrezuelo (1907–95) concerning the sugar export quotas imposed on Cuba by the USA. This action led to the collapse of the sugar market, resulting in turn in the burning of crops and hardship among the farmers.

'Se quema la chumbambá'

This humorous song originated following a fire which broke out on a plot of land (chumbambá) belonging to the Valeras.

When informed of this disaster, the matriarch of the household replied that she was not in the least interested as she was busy with the household chores: 'En no quemándome yo, que se queme el mundo entero' ('As long as I'm not burning, the whole world can be on fire').

Its 'son' characteristics are evident in:

- Use of call and response (verse and chorus, or pregón and coro, described as 'Lead Vocal' and 'Backing Vocals' in the Anthology)
- Duple metre
- A 2–3 son clave pattern, i.e. a repeating two-bar pattern from bar 6 with two notes in the first bar and three in the second
- Restricted harmonic vocabulary of basically tonic and dominant chords
- Instrumental passage breaking up the strophic structure
- Verse scheme based on Spanish metrical patterns.

Notice the terminology at this point: clave (singular) refers to the rhythmic pattern, while claves (plural) applies to the instrument.

Musical language

The Anthology score is a staff notation of a piece that was originally improvised. Maracas and claves rhythms are notated on separate single lines, while a two-line stave is used to allow for the contrasting pitches of the bongos.

A full score is used at the start, but the constantly repeating double bass, bongo and clave pattern parts are omitted between bars 14 and 182. The vocal parts are given in full as well as the cuatro solo.

Sonority and texture

The performing forces are:

- Solo male voice ('lead vocal' or 'pregón') and male-voice chorus (coro)
- Cuatro, the four-course guitar-like instrument
- Guitar
- Pizzicato double bass
- Maracas
- Bongos
- Claves.

The texture is essentially melody-dominated homophony, although there is rhythmic polyphony arising from the interaction between cuatro, vocal parts and percussion section.

The vocal parts of the Coro section are homophonic, the two parts singing in intervals of 3rds, 6ths, diminished 5ths (as in '-ma' in bar 23) and perfect 4ths.

'Se quema' opens with monophony in the cuatro (apart from a two-note chord in bars 3–4). The cuatro part also embraces multi-stopped chords in its extended solo section (e.g. in bars 83 and 144–145).

The guitar provides a chordal accompaniment, the chords consisting variously of four and six notes.

Rhythm, metre and tempo

As expected in a son, the piece is in a brisk duple time (notated as two minims in a bar). A prominent feature is the 2–3 son clave rhythm, heard here on claves. Notice, however, how it underlies the vocal lines of the Coro section, where it reverses to become a 3–2 pattern:

Other notable features include:

- Almost constant quaver pulse on the bongos
- Syncopation (e.g. cuatro solo, bar 83)
- Vocal phrases beginning off the beat on the second quaver of the bar
- Every fourth bar being marked by a three-crotchet rhythm in the vocal lines
- Triplet crotchets in the cuatro solo (e.g. bars 95–96)
- Cross-rhythmic effect produced by use of a repeating three-quaver pattern in bars 91–94 of the cuatro solo.

Organisation of pitch: melody

The number is characterised by:

- Paired two-bar phrases
- Solo vocal line built from the first six notes of the G minor scale
- There are two main vocal elements in the solo part:
  - The lead vocal's 'Candela', refrain which opens on the dominant. This recurring motif, which is immediately repeated, consists of 11 syllables (4 + 7) and finishes with three emphatic tonic notes
  - The contrasting, more elaborate 'narrative' phrases (e.g. 'Mamá que me estoy quemando...') also begin on the dominant but have a more speech-like (*parlando*) quality as they accommodate additional syllables in the same performing time of two two-bar phrases
- Notice how the backing vocals' phrases commence on the mediant or supertonic

A double bassist performing in a street in Santiago de Cuba

- The cuatro's opening material consists of balanced rising and falling phrases in which 3rds play a prominent part and indeed form a broken diminished 7th chord in the second bar
- The cuatro's extended solo features an altogether broader range, incorporating:
  - Additional chromatic notes (C♯, E♮, F♮)
  - Broken dominant 7th patterns (bars 97–98)
  - Leaps of minor 9th (bars 91–94).

Organisation of pitch: harmony

In the vocal sections of the song, the chord choice involves only tonic and dominant 7th chords of G minor, enriched by the occasional E♭ from the cuatro, creating a brief dominant 9th overall, and resulting in the outlining of diminished 7th chords.

Notice the C and E♮ notes in bars 89–90 of the cuatro solo, the E effectively adding a major 9th to the dominant 7th chord. Notice also the simultaneous false relation in bar 107.

Structure and tonality

The number is in G minor throughout, without any hint of modulation.

It is based on the alternation of pregón (lead vocal) and coro (backing vocals) phrases, but the pregón material involves both the main refrain ('Candela') and the additional narrative elaborations. The resulting overall structure is as follows:

Bars	Performing forces	Description
1–12	Instrumental	Introduction
13–21	Pregón	'Candela' refrain (repeated four-bar phrase)
21–28	Coro	Refrain
29–37	Pregón	Verse 1 ('Mamá que me estoy quemando...')
37–44	Coro	Refrain
13–21 (repeat)	Pregón	Refrain
21–28	Coro	Refrain
29–37	Pregón	Verse 2 ('Que se quema la sabana...')
37–44	Coro	Refrain
45–53	Pregón	Verse 3 ('Que se quema esta familia')
53–60	Coro	Refrain
60–69	Pregón	Refrain
69–76	Coro	Refrain
76–177	Cuatro	Solo
177–181	Pregón and Coro	Refrain
182–DS bars 14–21	Pregón	Refrain
21–28	Coro	Refrain
29–37	Pregón	Verse 4, labelled verse 3 in Anthology ('Mamá que se queme Emilia...')
37–44	Coro	Refrain
183–186	Coro	Coda: refrain

'Allá va candela'

Translated roughly as 'There goes Mr Fire', this song concerns the agitation of one of the members of the band on falling deliriously in love.

It is described as a bolero-son, the bolero being used mainly for romantic subjects. The Cuban bolero is in moderate quadruple or duple time, unlike the European dance of the same name which has three beats to the bar. Closely linked to the trova tradition, it originated in the final years of the 19th century, and in its earliest form was composed of two 16-bar sections, separated by a guitar instrumental. The bolero-son became a particularly popular dance in Cuba, its underlying dance rhythm becoming associated with the rumba.

Musical language

The anthology score is a staff notation of a piece that was originally improvised. Maracas and claves rhythms are notated on separate single lines, while a two-line stave is used to allow for the contrasting pitches of the bongos.

Instrumental parts are given in their entirety at the start of the bolero. From bar 17, only the cuatro and vocal line are given. From bar 39, a new double bass line and maracas rhythm are notated, after which only the solo parts are given until the final three bars.

Sonority and texture

The performing forces are:

- Solo male voice (labelled 'vocals' in the anthology score) and male-voice chorus (first heard in bar 40).
- Cuatro
- Guitar
- Pizzicato double bass
- Maracas
- Bongos
- Claves.

The texture is essentially melody-dominated homophony, with a very brief passage of monophony for the cuatro at the opening. The vocal parts of the chorus are confined to two-note octave interjections on 'Mama'. The cuatro part includes multi-stopped chords in its extended solo section in the middle. Some of these chords are spread.

Rhythm, metre and tempo

'Allá va candela' is in the moderate quadruple time of the bolero-son at the start. At bar 39, there is an *accelerando* into the second section of the song (a 'son' section), which moves at 96 minims per minute.

Other notable features include:

- Flowing quavers on cuatro at the start
- Syncopation (cuatro, bar 5, and see also bars 139–141)
- Vocal phrases begin with anacrusis
- Crotchet triplets in cuatro (e.g. bar 68)
- Dotted rhythms in bass at bars 7–8 and also at bar 39 where a 3+3+2 pattern develops.

Organisation of pitch: melody

The number is characterised by:

- Balanced phrasing
- Vocal lines built entirely from the notes of the E major scale
- The solo vocalist's line covers a range of a 12th (B–F♯)
- The opening melody lines are notably more flexible and lyrical than those of 'Se quema'
- Prominent falling 5ths at the close of phrases, e.g. bar 42:

The rapidly repeated note in bar 30 represents the beating heart:

- The cuatro's introductory material is built first on a broken-chord tonic triad and then anticipates fragments from the subsequent vocal line
- The cuatro's extended solo in the central passage introduces variety by incorporating:
  - Chromatic notes (e.g. bars 75–76)
  - A chromatic scale (bars 82–83)
  - Repetitions, e.g. bars 120–121 and 122–123
  - Ornamentation (acciaccatura and glissando).

Organisation of pitch: harmony

The piece draws mainly on the tonic chord (sometimes incorporating an added 6th in the melodic lines) and dominant 7th (with occasional 9th).

There is a very occasional use of the subdominant (see bars 29 and 141) and the dominant of the dominant (see bar 18). The cuatro solo leads to a wider harmonic range in passing (e.g. the parallel 4ths at bar 75 and the dominant 11th with minor 9th at bar 79).

A member of Familia Valera Miranda playing the cuatro

Structure and tonality

'Allá va candela' remains in the key of E major throughout.

A striking feature of the structure is the avoidance of a repeat of the opening lyrical bolero material as the song proceeds:

Bars	Forces	Description
1–15	Instrumental introduction	Cuatro, anticipating opening of vocal part (see bar 5)
15–24	Solo vocal	Theme A: Ten-go la bo-ca__ co-mo lin-ter - na,
25–31	Solo vocal	Theme B: Co - ra - zón_____
32–38	Solo vocal	Theme C: Des - de los pi - es____
39–61	Solo vocal and coro	Chorus – 'Allá va candela' – (see above under melody) is built on a broken chord of E major, a falling 5th and includes also the two-note response ('Mama') in octaves. This two-bar phrase is frequently repeated, sometimes with slight variations. The song settles into the duple-time son at bar 43.
33–66	Solo vocal and coro	Varied repeat of Theme C ('Desde los...') and 'Allá va candela'
66–123	Cuatro solo	
124–138	Solo vocal and coro	Repeat of the Chorus at bars 43–50, with modifications to the text.
138–145	Solo vocal	Theme C ('Desde los...')
145–163	Solo vocal and coro	Repeat of chorus ('Allá va candela'), with solo vocal improvisation

Set work:

Breathing Under Water: 'Burn', 'Breathing Under Water' and 'Easy'

Anoushka Shankar

Musical context

Anoushka Shankar (born 1981) is a sitar player and composer. She is the daughter and former pupil of Ravi Shankar (1920–2012), who did much to make the sitar, an instrument from the Indian classical music tradition, known in the West. She has been active in promoting her father's work, including performing his sitar concertos with orchestras such as the London Symphony Orchestra and the London Philharmonic.

As a composer, Anoushka Shankar has explored fusions between Indian music and various genres including flamenco, jazz, electronica and Western classical music.

Among albums other than *Breathing Under Water*, Shankar has produced *Traveller* (a fusion of Indian Classical music and Spanish flamenco). *Home* (in which she returns to her roots in Indian Classical music) and *Land of Gold* (a response to the sufferings of refugees and others caught up in war).

Anoushka Shankar

Breathing Under Water

Breathing Under Water was released in 2007. 'Burn' was track 1, 'Breathing Under Water' track 3, and 'Easy' track 7.

The album is a collaboration between Anoushka Shankar and Utkarsha (Karsh) Kale (pronounced 'Kah-lay'). Salim Merchant, an Indian composer of film music, was responsible for the string composition and arrangement of 'Burn' and 'Breathing Under Water' and Norah Jones was one of the composers of 'Easy'.

The lyrics

The verses of 'Burn' concern different aspects of being in love – being 'lost' and being 'at home'. Most of the imagery is connected with the sun, moon and stars, the word 'burn' appearing only in the line 'Falling pieces of a broken moon burn the sun'.

In 'Easy' the singer is disillusioned with love now that she is no longer young. 'Feeling is easy' but she has been 'shown the other side' and now 'know[s] better'. 'Breathing Under Water' has no lyrics.

Fusion

All three songs bring together musical traditions from India and the West.

The main strands are as follows:

- The Indian classical tradition, with Shankar's sitar playing. In 'Burn' we hear the sarangi, a fretless bowed string instrument. Small cymbals (manjira) are used in 'Burn' and in 'Easy'
- The Indian 'Bollywood' film music tradition, with the use of the Bombay Cinematic Orchestra Strings in 'Burn' and 'Breathing Under Water'
- Western pop and rock music, notably with:
    - Use of electric guitar, synthesiser, drum kit and drum program
    - Aspects of form in 'Burn' and 'Easy'
    - The harmonic structure, most clearly in 'Easy'.

Musical language

The specially commissioned anthology scores use conventional staff notation.

Much would have been improvised in performance, but the string players at least would have required fully notated parts.

Musical elements

Sonority

The three tracks show considerable diversity in terms of sonority.

'Burn'

'Burn' is the most lavishly scored. Sitar and strings are heard together first – other instruments being added later in the introduction (see bars 14 and 22 for details). Listen carefully for the *pianissimo* and very high 'Ethereal Synth Pad' in verse 1. At bar 37, the 'Fat Lead Synth[esiser]' helps to launch the first chorus.

A 'synth pad' is a special background effect created by a synthesiser.

A new touch of 'Eastern' colour is provided by the sarangi in bars 46–53. Although the album credits do not mention Western orchestral instruments other than strings, listen for the brass at bar 94, harp and flute (entering in bars 102–104) and the concluding solo cello.

> The cellist on this track is V. R. Shekhar. Anoushka Shankar is credited with piano as well as sitar, but any piano sound is hard to detect. Noah Lembersky is the vocalist.

'Breathing Under Water'

'Breathing Under Water' is essentially a sitar solo with strings, but there are occasional wordless vocal phrases (sung by Sunidhi Chauhan), the first of which covers an isolated long rest in the sitar part. Cues on the score signal the addition of woodwind and horns at bar 18. Notice also the brief addition of flute near the end and the little chromatic solo for cello. Karsh Kale is credited in the album sleeve note with 'keyboards' (not prominent in the recording) but not with tabla (for which see bar 27).

'Easy'

'Easy' is the most Western of the three set songs, with a prominent role for electric guitar and piano, the latter played by Norah Jones (Shankar's half-sister) who is also the vocalist.

Texture

'Breathing Under Water'

The simplest textures are to be found here. Section 1 is entirely melody-dominated homophony, with slow-moving string chords accompanying the sitar melody.

Later, to help expand the sound, the texture is a little more complex, with traces of melody in the strings (independent of the sitar melody and subordinate to it) and occasional wordless vocal counter-melodies.

'Burn'

In the introduction, the slow-moving string tune (from bar 3 – see music example below) is the primary melodic interest, with some octave doubling for additional emphasis. The sitar provides a counter-melody: this contrasts strongly with the main melody because of its different timbre and lower pitch range, and because it is less continuous and more diverse and vigorous in rhythm.

Norah Jones, co-composer of 'Easy'

Elsewhere homophonic textures are sometimes more complex (e.g. with at least three sources of melodic interest in bars 70–73).

'Easy'

In verses 1 and 2 the singer is the centre of attention, but with an accompaniment that has distinct character on account of its very active bass line. Elsewhere there is some interplay between voice and sitar, the latter providing short fills as in bar 45. The sitar is the principal focus when the voice is silent – note the intricacy of its melodic line in the introduction.

Dynamics

'Breathing Under Water' and 'Easy' are mainly quiet with few dynamic markings. Notice, in the former, the chilling effect of the A minor chord (with the *diminuendo* in bars 34–35) and the *pianissimo* vocal phrase that follows.

'Burn' has more variety. Listen for example to:

- The opening attack on sitar (f) over low strings (p)
- Some magical quiet moments (such as the pp Ethereal Synth Pad at bar 30 and the *diminuendo* to p at bars 104–106 after the $f\!f$ at bar 98)
- *Crescendo*s into new sections – notably at bar 37 (for Chorus 1) and at bar 97 (for Chorus 2).

Structure

'Burn'

'Burn' is based on the verse–chorus form common in Western pop music. Changes of sonority play an important part in marking out the structure.

Bars	Section	Detail
1–29	Introduction	■ 1–2: Introductory gesture for sitar and string basses, with C♯ (tonic) bass ■ 3–21: Extended theme for strings (with sitar) ■ 22–29: More forceful and more fully scored eight-bar passage leading into verse 1
30–37	Verse 1 'Dancing…'	Eight-bar verse (two similar four-bar phrases, each with two similar two-bar phrases)
38–45	Chorus 1 'Dance with me…'	Eight-bar chorus (two similar four-bar phrases, with a linking phrase 'Search with me')
46–53	Bridge	Featuring sarangi. Independent of verse and chorus but again eight bars with two similar and rather repetitive four-bar phrases
54–77	Verse 2 'Falling…'	■ 54–61: Corresponds with 30–37, but is differently scored. Bars 62–65 ('Your eyes…') are a four-bar extension ■ 55–73: uses the string melody from bar 3 (with different harmonies) ■ 70–73: repeat of the vocal melody from 62–65 (ending 'I am home' rather than 'I am lost') NB: 66–73 can be regarded as a second Bridge. However, the reuse of the melody from 62–65 at 70–73, continuation of the string melody, and similar scoring throughout suggest that 54–77 form a single unit – unless we consider 74–77 as a separate link into Verse 3
78–97	Verse 3 'Dancing…'	■ 78–85: Same vocal melody (and words) as in 30–37, differently scored ■ 86–93 An eight-bar instrumental 'interruption' for sitar and strings (providing harmonic and tonal contrast) ■ 94–97 The vocal melody from 62–65 ('Your eyes…') slightly varied, with a brief appearance of the chorus idea 'Dance with me' in 96. These four bars are a kind of 'pre-chorus'
98–104	Chorus 2	With first- and second-time endings. The first time there is another (partial) repeat of the 'Your eyes' phrase. With the six-fold repetition of a new string motif (including 'modal' B♮), the song seems to be drawing to a conclusion, but the chord in bar 104 keeps things 'open' for the coda
105–110	Coda	Ends away from C♯ minor, in an ambiguous tonality whose final (open 5ths) chord is rooted on D (see 'Tonality' and 'Harmony' below)

'Breathing Under Water'

The structure as a whole is original; it is best heard as a gradual unfolding, unified by varied repetitions of several important ideas.

Bars	Section	Detail
1–18	1	Four phrases in an A Aᵛ B Bᵛ pattern (similar – perhaps by chance – to classical binary form): ■ 1–4 (idea A): An undulating four-bar theme for sitar, ending on chord V of the home key, D♭ ■ 5–10 (A): An extended variation of 1–4 (melody ending halfway through the chord of A♭ heard in 10–11) ■ 11–14 (idea B): Another four-bar theme for sitar (with distinctive quintuplet at the end), ending on chord I ■ 15–18 (B): Variation of 11–14. The ending of the melody and the start of a new accompaniment idea (Section 2) do not co-incide
18–35	2	This section provides tonal and thematic contrast. Notice again how phrases in the sitar part and in the accompaniment do not co-incide, contributing to a pleasing sense of structural freedom. ■ 18–21: (New) 4-bar phrase in orchestra ■ 19–22: New theme for sitar ■ 22–25: Variation of 18–21 with additional (higher) parts in accompaniment ■ 23–26: Variation of 19–22 (very free towards end) ■ 27–35: New material (but similar in style and texture)
35–53	3	■ 35: First entry of wordless female voice ■ 36–40: Sitar repeats bars 1–4 (A) from Section 1 ■ 42–52: Sitar: compare 6–16 (A, B) ■ 38: Strings have new material, but the opening three-note ascent (D♭, E♭, F) may echo bars 18–19
53–70	4	There is a new repeat of A, the sitar part of bars 1–4, (an octave lower) in 53–56. Note also the three-note ascent in the strings at 54 heard at the start of Section 2 and at 38 ■ 57–66: New material, with some repetition of the string melody (58–61 = 62–65) ■ 67–70: Repeat of sitar part from 15–18 (B)
71–77	Coda	There is a new four-bar phrase for sitar, a final wordless phrase for voice, and a lingering plagal cadence (IV♭m⁶–I)

'Easy'

'Easy' uses the AABA song form that was so popular in the first half of the 20th century, with three verses (A) and a middle eight (B). Typically sections are eight bars in length, but a couple of extensions provide some additional interest.

Bars	Section	Detail
1–8	Introduction (instrumental)	Two four-bar phrases, the second with the three-chord progression that dominates much of the song (see 'Harmony')
8^3–20^2	Verse 1	'It's only love…'. Eight bars but with an extension on the last syllable, and a passage without voice acting as link to verse 2)
	Verse 2 (with second-time ending)	'When I was young…'
21–33	Extension of verse 2 (Or could be thought of as a link)	The words 'I know' from the end of verse 1 are slowly sung three times, leading to the concluding 'better'
34–41	Instrumental	The three-chord progression continues
42–49^2	Middle eight	'Now I've been shown…'. As customary in a middle eight, the harmonic structure is different (so the three-chord progression is rested)
49^3–57^2	Verse 3	'It's only love…'
57^3–63	Coda	'feeling is easy…'

Tonality

'Burn'

'Burn' is in C♯ minor except at the very end.

In fact, the note C♯ is present most of the time – either notated in the score or indicated by chord symbols. It is sometimes present as an added or 'sus' (dissonant suspended) note – for instance in bar 21 where the chord is G♯ (G♯–B♯–D♯) but with C♯ as a sus(pended) 4th.

The music is almost entirely diatonic. Frequently we hear the note B♯ (the leading note of the C♯ minor scale familiar from so much Western 'classical' music), but elsewhere the unraised seventh scale degree, B♮, suggests the Aeolian mode:

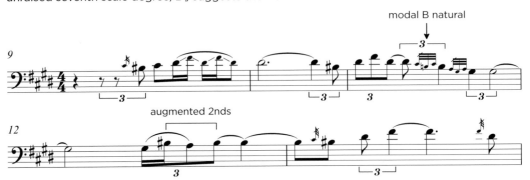

The only change of key comes when we may be least expecting it, in the coda. There is a kind of interrupted cadence in bars 103–104, and the A minor chord in bar 105 takes us into a rather ambiguous tonality whose final chord is rooted on D. This final chord lacks a third, and so is neither major nor minor – thus heightening the ambiguity.

'Breathing Under Water'

'Breathing Under Water' clearly ends in D♭ major, with what is described in the table above as a 'lingering plagal cadence'.

Section 1 alternates chords of B♭ minor and A♭ – which could represent I and VII in an Aeolian B♭ minor, but are more likely to be VI and V in D♭ major. D♭ major is eventually suggested by a somewhat disguised plagal cadence in bars 14–17.

> Bar 16 has the first D♭ (tonic) chord, but even this is partly 'disguised' by a 'sus 4'.

Section 2 is more ambiguous tonally. It has a key signature of four sharps and no accidentals, but is not really in E major or C♯ minor (there are no E major or C♯ minor chords). The chord that occurs most frequently is A major, the D♯s perhaps hinting at a Lydian (see box) version of A major – although the final chord is A minor.

> The 'Lydian' mode is like a major scale but with the fourth degree (subdominant) raised by a semitone.

Sections 3 and 4 are almost entirely diatonic and are tonally ambiguous in much the same way as Section 1, until the clear ending in D♭ major.

'Easy'

The key signature of 'Easy' is six flats and there are no accidentals, but the concluding chord is neither the tonic of G♭ major nor of E♭ minor.

The song ends (as it begins) with a chord of D♭^(sus4) (D♭–F–A♭ plus G♭).

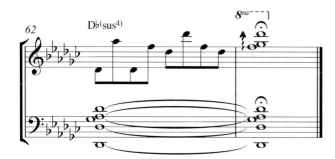

Are we therefore listening to a piece whose tonic is D♭ and whose scale is that of the Mixolydian mode on D♭ (D♭, E♭, F, G♭, A♭, B♭, C♭, D♭)? Almost certainly not. Inclusion of the G♭ in the opening and closing D♭ chords (see music example above) gives an 'open', unfinished effect. These D♭ chords are probably modified dominants (V) not tonics (I). The almost constant repetition of the two-bar chord progression G♭$^{(sus\,4)}$/B♭, C♭$^{(sus\,2)}$, D♭$^{(sus\,4)}$ is surely an embellished version of the progression Ib–IV–V in G♭ major.

So, in short, the song is in G♭ major throughout, but ending on the dominant. The note D♭ (the dominant of G♭) is a member of every chord in the piece.

Organisation of pitch: harmony

Some ordinary root position triads are used (as in bars 1–2 of 'Burn').

There are also some 'slash chords'. In bar 10 of 'Breathing Under Water', for instance, the chord symbol is A♭/B♭, which means that the basic chord is A♭, but with B♭ in the bass. Some slash chords are inversions, such as the D♭/A♭ in bar 64 of 'Breathing Under Water' (second inversion of a D♭ chord).

There are numerous 'sus (or 'suspended') chords'. Normally in a 'sus chord' the third of the chord is omitted and replaced with a neighbouring note, a 4th or a 2nd above the root.

> The 'sus' note is often (but not always) sounded in the previous chord – a kind of 'preparation' that has something in common with the stricter preparation of suspensions in traditional Western harmony.

Sometimes the third is heard together with the 'sus' note. For example, in bar 21 of 'Burn', the G♯$^{(sus4)}$ chord symbol accounts for the strings' C♯, but not for the sitar's B♯. Third-plus-sus4 combinations sometimes occur with D♭$^{(sus4)}$ chords in 'Easy'.

With 'add' (or 'added note') chords an extra note is added to a triad or 7th chord. In bar 3 of 'Burn' the C♯m/G♯ chord has an 'add 4' (= F♯): the notes heard at the beginning of the bar are G♯–C♯–E, plus F♯ (see box). The E^6/B in bar 16 is an E chord (with B in the bass) and an 'added sixth' (C♯). Other non-chord notes are also heard in 'Burn' – D♯ and B in strings and sitar respectively.

Under 'Tonality' we noticed the more or less continuous presence of C♯ (the tonic) in the chord scheme for 'Burn' and of D♭ (the dominant) in 'Easy'. These notes principally underpin the tonality – rather than serving as Western-style pedal points or Eastern-style drones.

Organisation of pitch: melody

Vocal melodies

In 'Burn' the singer uses a small and fairly low range (almost entirely within the minor 6th C♯ to A). Much movement is conjunct and intervals larger than a 3rd are exceptional. A motif made up of a rising 2nd and falling 3rd (as in bars 30–31) is prominent (see box). The hypnotic narrowness and repetitiveness of the melodic line accord well with the generally static harmony of the vocal sections.

> The rising 2nd-falling 3rd motif in the vocal line is perhaps derived from the string melody of bars 19–20. See also the sarangi's C♯–D♯–B♯ pattern (from bar 46).

In the verses of 'Easy' (the song where the influence of Western popular music is strongest) the vocal range is wider – a 9th from A♭ to B♭. There are some intervals of a 4th and even a rising octave (bar 44) to highlight the crucial words 'the other side'.

The wordless vocal melodies in 'Breathing Under Water' are quite varied – compare the three separate phrases in bars 55–67. Eastern influence is apparent in, for example, the microtonal glissandi of bar 64.

String melodies

The long and slow-moving violin melody in 'Burn' (first heard at bar 3) uses the same notes (C♯ to A) as the vocal melody, but is freer in its use of small leaps and has some doubling at the upper octave.

In 'Breathing Under Water' the string parts provide mainly a chordal accompaniment, but there is some sense of melody from bar 54. A long succession of minims covers a perfect 12th from (middle) D♭, rising strongly at first but later within a 4th with stepwise movement and minor 3rds.

Sitar melodies

The range of the sitar is greater – after all, one of the aims of the album was to 'showcase' Anoushka Shankar's playing.

In 'Burn', higher pitches occur more frequently as the song continues, but still with some marked contrasts of range in bars 66–77. The tessitura is generally higher in 'Breathing Under Water' so that the sitar can sing out above the string accompaniment. Where the strings have most melodic interest (parts of Section 4), the sitar is at its lowest.

In all three numbers the sitar part is elaborate with much ornamentation, some of it shown in the transcription by mordents or (as in bars 9–14 of 'Burn') by single or groups of acciaccaturas. In 'Burn' and 'Easy', phrases are often fairly short and well separated by rests – for example, where the sitar has 'fills' in the middle eight of 'Easy'.

In 'Breathing Under Water', where the role of the sitar is more obviously melodic, the phrasing is more continuous. Here there is considerable repetition and close variation in the sitar part, whereas elsewhere there is more of an improvisatory feel.

Microtonal intervals (so characteristic of the sitar and of much Eastern music generally) are heard in all three numbers. These cannot be precisely notated (unlike the quarter-tones in Saariaho's *Petals*) but occur in glissandi between notes a 2nd or 3rd apart.

It is unclear how far systems of organising pitch in Indian classical music underlie Shankar's sitar playing. For example, intervals of the augmented 2nd are prominent in some Indian music, as in *Rag Bhairav* from the previous Edexcel anthology – but in 'Burn' these intervals (as in bars 12 and 19) can be explained as belonging to the Western harmonic minor scale. In fact, throughout the sitar (and sarangi) parts very few notes appear in the score that are outside C♯ harmonic minor (the exceptions being a few 'modal' B♮s).

In 'Breathing Under Water' the occasional F♭s and C♭s (in D♭ major) seem to invite comparison with the lowered third and seventh scale-degree 'blue' notes from the jazz tradition.

Tempo, metre and rhythm

'Burn'

The tempo (♩=80) and $\frac{4}{4}$ (simple quadruple) metre are maintained throughout, but the rhythmic activity varies a great deal.

Initially the string parts have long notes (the bass chiefly in semibreves) which gently define the quadruple metre. The sitar is much freer and more rhythmically diverse with various triplet groupings, syncopated rhythms, and a mixture of long and very short notes – it has a free improvisatory character perhaps suggestive of the introductory *alap* section of a raga. In the last part of the introduction, percussion (live and electronic) and synth bass inject more movement into the music, with a clear and insistent 'beat' (perhaps a reference to the *jhala* section of a raga).

There is much syncopation in the vocal part, sarangi and lead synth. parts (as well as in the sitar).

'Breathing Under Water'

The tempo is ♩=120 throughout, but with a *rit.* for the lingering final vocal phrase. The metre is again $\frac{4}{4}$, but with a single $\frac{2}{4}$ bar at bar 37 as the sitar re-enters and overlaps with the vocal phrase. Notice also the opening three-beat 'pick-up' bar.

The sitar part is mostly rapid and rhythmically diverse with fairly frequent syncopation, and some triplets and quintuplets. It is complemented by the string parts, which lack syncopation and whose chords often last for one or two whole bars.

'Easy'

The tempo is ♩=84, and the metre again $\frac{4}{4}$ (with a five-quaver 'pick-up' bar and an isolated $\frac{3}{4}$ bar (bar 31) whose function is to press forward rather than repeat the 'full' $\frac{4}{4}$ rhythm of bar 29). The sitar part is sometimes (as in bars 6–7) more rhythmically ornate than in 'Burn' and 'Breathing Under Water'.

The most striking feature in 'Easy' is the syncopated guitar rhythm first heard in bar 2.

Test yourself

Below are five short questions on each set work. These are not 'exam questions' but are intended to help you get to know each work better.

Most questions use the command words listed in Appendix 5 of each specification (with which you will need to be familiar when preparing for exams). For each set work there is also a sample essay question for each level. These correspond to Question 6 in Pearson's Sample Assessment Materials. Essays at the two levels are marked from different assessment grids, as may again be seen from the Sample Assessment Materials. The allocation of marks is different, with fewer marks at AS implying the need for less information. At A Level there is greater emphasis on saying how and why particular things happen in the music, and relatively less on just saying what happens. When answering the questions below, you should refer to the printed score of the relevant work or movement.

> In your exam you will have a special booklet containing the scores you need. You will not be allowed to take a copy of the anthology or other printed music into the exam room.

Estampes: Nos. 1 and 2 (Debussy)

Short questions:

a. Name the type of scale used in 'Pagodes'.

b. Give three harmonic devices used in 'La Soirée dans Grenade'.

c. Explain why 'La Soirée dans Grenade' is a habanera.

d. Describe the harmonic rhythm in bars 1–30 of 'Pagodes'.

e. Describe the textures of 'Pagodes' at bars 3 and 23.

Essay questions:

AS

Evaluate dynamics and sonorities in 'Pagodes'. Relate your discussion to other relevant works. These may include set works, wider listening or other music.

A Level

Evaluate sonorities, textures and melody in 'Pagodes', showing how Debussy varies his basic material. Relate your discussion to other relevant works. These may include set works, wider listening or other music.

Tracks from *Caña Quema* (Familia Valera Miranda)

Short questions:

a. Name the characteristic musical features of 'Se quema la chumbambá'.

b. Explain why 'Allá va candela' is a bolero.

c. Describe the cuatro.

d. Compare the vocal ranges of the two prescribed numbers.

e. Explain what a 3–2 rhythm is.

Essay questions:

AS

Evaluate melody and structure in 'Se quema la chumbambá' and 'Alla vá candela'. Relate your discussion to other relevant works. These may include set works, wider listening or other music.

A Level

Evaluate melody, rhythm and structure in 'Se quema la chumbambá' and 'Allá va candela', showing how the son differed from the bolero in Cuban music. Relate your discussion to other relevant works. These may include set works, wider listening or other music.

Tracks from *Breathing Under Water* (Anoushka Shankar)

Short questions:

a. Describe the melody for strings in bars 3–21 of 'Burn'.

b. Explain the chord symbols in bars 1–4 of 'Burn'.

c. Describe the harmony and tonality of 'Breathing Under Water'.

d. Compare the writing for sitar in 'Breathing Under Water' and in 'Easy'.

e. Analyse the structure of 'Easy'.

Essay questions:

A Level only

Evaluate the sonority, melody and structure of 'Burn' and 'Breathing Under Water' with reference to the fusion of Indian and Western styles. Relate your discussion to other relevant works. These may include set works, wider listening or other music.

New directions

OVERVIEW

The three set works in this Area of Study show a few of the 'new directions' in music taken since 1910.

AS **A** **Three Dances for Two Prepared Pianos, Dance No. 1 (John Cage)**

AS **A** *Petals* **(Kaija Saariaho)**

A **Movements from *Le sacre du printemps* (*The Rite Of Spring*) (Igor Stravinsky)**

Introduction

The pace and extent of change in music was greater in the 20th century than in previous centuries. This should not surprise us: there have been equally rapid and diverse developments and experiments in politics, society and technology.

Igor Stravinsky's *The Rite of Spring*, a work for massive orchestral forces, was strikingly original in sonority and rhythm particularly – although, as the notes below reveal, this work did not come entirely 'out of the blue'.

Kaija Saariaho's *Petals* effectively demonstrates some of the new sounds available from a single instrument – the cello – especially when enhanced by electronics.

> The wider listening works suggested in the specifications are designed to broaden your knowledge and experience of 'new directions'. They include pieces by three leading figures in 20th-century music: Karlheinz Stockhausen, Pierre Boulez and Olivier Messiaen.

Opposite: A John Cage prepared piano

Set work:
Three Dances for Two Prepared Pianos, Dance No. 1

John Cage

Musical context

Composer

> See Cage's own account of his musical career up to 1948, 'A Composer's Confession', at www.nws.edu/ JohnCage/AComposersConfession. html. It is a 'must-read'.

John Cage (1912–1992) was one of several highly original 20th-century American composers – and one of the most important figures of the avant-garde.

> 'Avant-garde' is a French expression widely used to describe people or works that deliberately – and often provocatively – break new ground, pushing previously accepted boundaries.

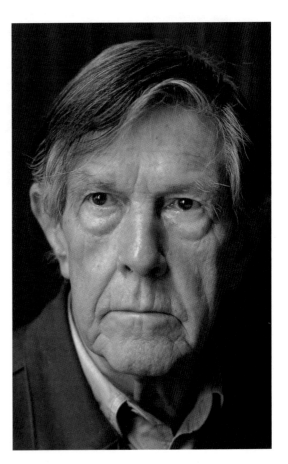

John Cage

Cage was a pupil of Henry Cowell (1897–1965), who had a powerful influence on him. Cowell was open to all kinds of musical influences, including some from outside the Western Classical tradition. Cowell sometimes went to extremes of chromaticism and rhythmic complexity and adopted striking new approaches to structure. He even explored forms of graphic notation as early as the 1920s and the use of improvisation. He wrote for some of the forerunners of electronic instruments, as well as employing some novel 'extended' piano techniques (as in *The Banshee* of 1925).

In the late 1930s, Cage worked as a dance accompanist, at which time he met the dancer Merce Cunningham, his future partner in work and life. He began to concentrate on music for percussion, which, in its limited use for precisely pitched sounds, he considered a pathway to the 'all sound music of the future' (see box).

> Cage's phrase is quoted by David W. Bernstein in *The Cambridge Companion to John Cage*, ed. David Nicholls (Cambridge University Press, 2002), page 69. Other composers based in America had already moved in the same direction as Cage, including, as well as Cowell, the French-born Edgard Varèse (1883–1965).

Providing a percussion ensemble for dance can be difficult in terms of space and expense. Cage soon found a clever solution: the 'prepared piano' – a piano in which items such as bolts and screws are inserted between some of the strings to produce various types of percussive sounds (rather than the normal precise pitches).

> For more information about the 'preparation' of the pianos in the set work, see 'Sonority' below.

Cage wrote a number of works for prepared piano in the 1940s and 1950s. Although the most important are the Sonatas and Interludes (1946–1948), the Three Dances have a special appeal with their remarkably 'extroverted virtuosity' and 'impressive percussive effects' (*Cambridge Companion*, page 80).

> The Sonatas and Interludes were among the first works to show Cage's interest in Eastern philosophy and religion. This interest also revealed itself in a fascination with silence, most famously in his *4'33"* for any instrument(s) (1952) where the musician(s) do not play a single note. It also led to the widespread use of what Cage termed 'chance operations', as in *Music of Changes* (1951).

Three Dances for two Prepared Pianos, Dance No. 1

Cage's 'Three Dances', written for two amplified prepared pianos were composed in 1944 (revised 1945). They were commissioned by the piano duo Arthur Gold and Robert Fizdale and premiered by them in New York in 1945. In 1947, the dances were choreographed as *Dromenon* by Merce Cunningham.

Musical language

The work is presented in a full score consisting of the two piano parts, the first printed above the second.

Ordinary traditional staff notation is used, but accidentals are applied differently. Every note that is a natural is written without a natural sign, and every note that needs a sharp or flat sign has its own accidental – as in the following passage (Piano 1, RH):

Cage's preface lists the instruments as 'First piano' and 'Second piano'. Here for brevity we say 'Piano 1' and 'Piano 2'. 'RH' and 'LH' are abbreviations for 'right hand' and 'left hand'.

A comprehensive list of the 'preparations' to be made to the piano, reproduced from the original, hand-written edition of the work, can be found on pages 384 and 385 of the Anthology.

Cage did not provide bar numbers, but a numeral in a box shows where each new phrase begins. For example, there is a '2' in bar 3 and a '3' in bar 8. We will refer to these numerals as 'No. 2', 'No. 3', and so on. A '1' is implied but not stated at the very beginning.

Use of the *una corda* (soft pedal) is shown by the words '*una corda*', for example at Nos. 26 and 46, with '*tre corde*' telling the player when to lift the pedal. The sustaining pedal is indicated with the standard 'Ped.' marking and broken line, for example at Nos. 70 and 79.

Musical elements

Structure

From 1939 until the mid-1950s, Cage employed a highly original approach to structure, based on mathematical proportions. The same proportions operate on a small scale (at the 'microcosmic' or 'microstructural' level) and also control the large-scale structure (the 'macrocosmic' or 'macrostructural' level).

Cage referred to this principle of large structure replicating small structure as 'micro-macrocosmic'. Today we would recognise it as a 'fractal' structure, seen in many features of the natural world, in which each sub-division is a miniature version of the whole. Such structures can be found, for example, as the basis of a snowflake or a fern leaf.

Cage's 'mathematical' approach to structure has several precedents, although we cannot be sure how much he knew or was influenced by, for example, medieval isorhythmic motets, or some of the music of J. S. Bach or Webern. Probably some contemporary American avant-garde composers (including Ruth Crawford Seeger, with her use of 'verse form') were more influential. Cage's work with dancers certainly had an impact: he sometimes had to compose music for dances whose structure 'was determined by numbers of counts' (*Cambridge Companion*, page 70).

Cage himself describes how he developed his structural approach in 'A Composer's Confession' (see online reference on page 268).

Numbers – parts and phrases

The starting point for our study of Dance No. 1 is the following sequence of nine numbers, which together add up to 30:

2   5   2   2   6   2   2   7   2

Each set of 30 bars (a 'part') is divided into nine 'phrases', the lengths of which in bars correspond to the numbers above. The first part works like this:

Number of bars	Numeral in score
2	none, but 1 is implied
5	2
2	3
2	4
6	5
2	6
2	7
7	8
2	9

The terms 'part' and 'phrase' are Cage's own (see his description of *First Construction in Metal* in 'A Composer's Confession').

The rest of the movement has eight more 30-bar parts, each subdivided into phrases in the same way (with boxed numbers on the score to indicate the beginning of each phrase). The final part, for example, has the phrase Nos. 73 to 81 (= repeat of bars 211–240).

In this chapter we will refer to the boxed number that appears in the Anthology score at the beginning of a phrase when talking about the whole phrase up to the next number. Instead of actual boxed numbers , we use the abbreviation 'No.' or 'Nos.' plus the relevant numeral(s) – 'No. 2', 'No. 3', and so on.

The tempo of the work is ♩=88, with a time signature of $\frac{2}{2}$. (Please note, the time signature is incorrectly notated as ♩=88 in the Anthology and the time signature is changed in error to $\frac{4}{4}$ part way through No. 25). So each 30-bar part takes about 40 seconds to perform.

Dance No. 2 has the metronome mark ♩=114 (time signature $\frac{2}{2}$). In order to make each part last for about 40 seconds at this higher speed, Cage has increased the length of each of the nine phrases by one, so that a 'part' now lasts for 39 bars.

| 3 | 6 | 3 | | 3 | 7 | 3 | | 3 | 8 | 3 |

> Only Dance No. 1 is set for study, but, to see and hear it in context, we must spend a few moments on the structure of the other dances.

In other words, a part now has more bars, but still takes the same time to perform (because of the increase in tempo).

Dance No. 3 takes the process further with an even faster tempo (♩=168, time signature $\frac{2}{2}$) and phrases with the following numbers of bars:

| 5 | 8 | 5 | | 5 | 9 | 5 | | 5 | 10 | 5 |

Again, each part takes about 40 seconds to perform.

There are 30 parts in the Three Dances all together, as follows:
- In Dance No. 1 there are 9 parts, each of 30 bars
- In Dance No. 2 there are 10 parts, each of 39 bars
- In Dance No. 3 there are 11 parts, each of 57 bars.

The numbers 9, 10 and 11 therefore
- Occur as above on the grand scale (at the 'macrocosmic' level)
- Occur on a small scale (at the 'microcosmic' level) within each 30-bar part of Dance No. 1 (2, 5, 2 = 9; 2, 6, 2 = 10; 2, 7, 2 = 11).

Structure from the listener's point of view

It is impossible as a listener to follow consistently the numerical sequence that makes up each part of the movement (2 5 2 – 2 6 2 – 2 7 2). The music often flows across phrases, or changes character abruptly where there is no phrase division.

In Part 1, for example, there is no clear division between the first two-bar phrase and the following five-bar phrase (from No. 2) – whereas there *are* complete breaks before the six-bar and seven-bar phrases (Nos. 5 and 8). There *is* on the other hand a change of texture and musical content part way through the 6-bar phrase (No. 5).

Occasionally even the division between one part and the next is not clearly audible, as at the beginning of No. 28, where Part 4 begins.

Repetition

Dance No. 1 does not use large-scale form-building repetitions of musical material in the manner of 'classical' forms such as rondo, sonata form or ternary.

However, Part 8 of the movement is repeated note-for-note as Part 9. This sectional repetition gives additional weight towards the end and a sense of closure, and the effect is strengthened by the many restatements of the distinctive two-bar idea in Piano 1, RH (see the music example under 'Melody' below).

There is repetition on a much smaller scale – involving motifs and rhythmic patterns, not complete textures – within the first two parts (up to and including No. 18) to help build unity and coherence:

- Piano 2, both hands – compare Nos. 5, 11 and 17
- Piano 1, LH and Piano 2, both hands – No. 13 refers back to the start of the movement
- Rhythmic patterns with a group of three quavers preceding groups of two quavers occur in Piano 1 in No. 8 and Piano 2 in No. 14.

Parts 8 and 9 re-introduce a few motifs from Parts 1 and 2, including the following:

- In No. 64, the rising three-quaver figures from Nos. 5, 11 and 17
- In No. 69, the motif originally in Piano 2 at No. 3.

Are there vestiges of ternary structure (A B A) here? That is, Parts 1–2 (A) use motifs absent from the middle five parts (B) but which re-appear in Parts 8–9 (A).

Sonority

Cage described how to 'prepare' the pianos in his original introductory 'Table of the Preparations':

> 'Mutes of various materials are placed between the strings of the keys used, thus effecting transformations of the piano sounds with respect to all of their characteristics.'

Traditionally a 'mute' restricts vibrations of a string (in the case of string instruments) or a column of air (with brass instruments).

In Three Dances for Two Prepared Pianos, each muting device stops the normal resonance of the piano's sound – leaving a percussive sound which, depending on the material used, can, for instance, sound rather 'dead' or may strike you as a kind of piano equivalent of pizzicato. Precise pitches are largely neutralised, but in a few longer passages notated as rising scales (e.g. in Piano 2, LH in No. 62) there is still some impression of rising pitch.

The mutes include bolts, screws, pieces of weather strip, rubber and plastic, and 'pennies' (US cent coins). Pianos 1 and 2 are to be set up differently as shown in the 'Table of the Preparations'.

On both pianos the players have to 'prepare' almost all notes between the C two octaves above middle C and the E below middle C, plus a few notes just above this range and several up to a 12th below it (see box). Only prepared notes are used – so 'ordinary' piano tone is never heard.

The notes left unprepared differ slightly for each piano.

It is unclear exactly how Cage decided on the particular type of 'mute' to be used with each note, but his intention was to create considerable variety (rather than, for example, the use of bolts for high notes or rubber for low ones).

> The preparations used with one pair of pianos must be difficult to reproduce *exactly* in another pair, despite Cage's very precise instructions about the positioning and nature of each mute. So in terms of sonority there is likely to be some variation between one performance and another (and in any case different types and makes of pianos will have built-in timbral differences).

Dynamics

Much of Dance No. 1 is quiet, and an important feature is the 'gradual diminuendo through the repeat to the end' (direction in score for Nos. 73–81).

At times there is little or no dynamic change (for instance in much of the opening 30-bar part or No. 17) – which gives a certain almost machine-like quality to the music.

But there are strong dynamic contrasts elsewhere, notably between the very quiet beginning to No. 36 and the *ff* passage with repeated accents very soon afterwards.

There is considerable variety in Nos. 20–23, with different dynamic levels in different parts of the texture (for instance, accompanying patterns with quavers and quaver rests are marked at *p*, while more important features are *mf* and *f* with sometimes plentiful accents).

Texture

The two piano parts are independent – that is, one never doubles the other, and generally the patterns and ideas used in each are different.

For much of the time there is two-part writing for each piano – with one note in each hand – as for example at the beginning of No. 5. Exceptions include the 'octaves' in Piano 2, RH at the beginning, and the 'perfect 5ths' in the LH here and from time to time elsewhere.

> References to intervals are in inverted commas to remind us that this is just how they *look* in the score.

The texture is usually contrapuntal (see box), with two or more largely independent layers, as at the beginning (see for instance the music example under 'Tempo, metre and rhythm'). Here the first pianist's hands, widely separated, repeat a three-quaver motif in similar motion until a repeated-note pattern with crotchets emerges at the beginning of No. 2. Piano 2 has an offbeat quaver pattern in 'octaves' in the RH and an on-the-beat crotchet pattern in the LH.

> Contrapuntal devices such as canon and imitation are not used.

Briefly there is homorhythmic writing (all parts having the same rhythm, in this case constant quavers) in Nos. 7 and 9 – which helps to clarify the $\frac{2}{2}$ metre. Occasionally there is something more like 'ordinary' homophony, as in Nos. 38–40, with the *ff* and heavily accented 'melody' in Piano 1, RH standing out from a two-note accompaniment pattern in LH and the pattern in Piano 2, LH (which is at first a 6½-beat rhythmic ostinato).

Cage achieves contrast by varying the texture from four parts (or more, as in No. 17) to monophonic writing, two-part texture (as at the end) and three-part writing (as in Nos. 38–40).

Tempo, metre and rhythm

The (fast) tempo is indicated solely by the metronome mark, which should be ♩=88 (rather than the ♩=88 marked in the Anthology). There is no verbal instruction such as 'Allegro', and no changes of tempo are required.

The metre throughout is simple duple with a minim beat (time signature $\frac{2}{2}$).

Occasionally simple duple metre is very clear – as in Nos. 7 and 9, where every part has three groups of four quavers (plus a concluding minim in No. 9).

Usually, however, the metre is obscured (often very considerably) by simultaneous use of 'contradictory' rhythmic groupings or 'cross rhythms'. There is never rhythmic chaos, though: at least one part will normally follow, or stay close to, simple duple $\frac{2}{2}$ metre.

Such rhythmic obscurity may seem strange in a piece entitled 'dance', but remember:

- This is modern dance, not a 'conventional' classical dance type such as minuet or gigue
- The music was choreographed by Merce Cunningham and performed by a group of dancers including himself.

We can see in detail how the mixture of metrical obscurity and clarity works if we study the beginning of the movement:

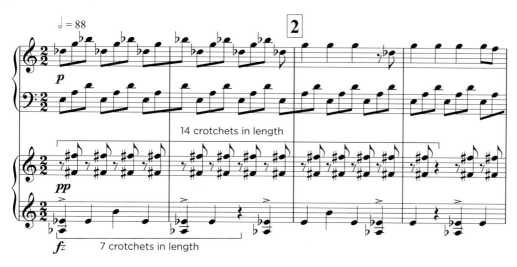

- Piano 1 begins with groups of three quavers characteristic of a compound time such as $\frac{6}{8}$
- These groups, which continue in LH as far as No. 4, cut across bar lines and do nothing to establish $\frac{2}{2}$ metre
- Piano 2, LH has accents at the beginnings of bars 1 and 2, as if to establish the metre, but its pattern is effectively part of a *seven-crotchet* unit (counting the rest) heard four times – see bracket on music example
- Piano 1, RH 'comes to the rescue' in bars 3 and 4 with patterns that reinforce the metre, but at No. 3 contradicts it with three-quaver groups beginning on the off-beat
- Piano 2, RH has offbeat quavers, which play some part in reinforcing the metre. However, these come in two cycles, each lasting 14 crotchets (counting the rest), that coincide with the four seven-crotchet figures in Piano 2, LH – see music example.

Almost all notes in the movement are quavers or crotchets – so that the most complex of cross-rhythmic effects are achieved by simple means. There are no triplets or other tuplets, and no dotted notes.

The widespread use of rhythmic ostinato (see box) helps to ensure coherence – even though these patterns often work against the underlying $\frac{2}{2}$ metre.

John Cage with Merce Cunningham in 1986

In this piece the term 'rhythmic ostinato' refers both to repeated motifs (such as the three-quaver figures in the music example above) and to longer repeated phrases such as the seven-crotchet pattern at the beginning of Piano 2, LH. Rhythmic ostinati repeat the same 'pitches' – and to that extent are also melodic.

For an example of an important rhythmic ostinato that occurs outside the music example quoted above, refer to No. 20:

- Piano 1, LH has a pattern with five quavers (each followed by a quaver rest except for the last which is followed by two quaver rests)

- The uneven distribution of rests means that the pattern starts alternately on and off the crotchet beat.

Follow the progress of this pattern from the beginning of No. 20 to the end of No. 34 (except where there are long rests or other ideas). Notice how the pattern is occasionally varied – notably by extension (there is an additional quaver at the beginning of No. 30, with the pattern now always starting on the beat).

For some very subtle uses of repeating patterns, see:

- Nos. 14 and 15, all parts:
  - Piano 1, RH – a pattern lasting for five crotchets is both extended (second statement) and abbreviated (last two statements)
  - Piano 1, LH – five statements of a motif that lasts for three crotchets (four quavers and a crotchet) are separated by rests of different lengths

- Piano 2 (shared between RH and LH) – there are two complete statements of a 13½-crotchet pattern (with some internal repeats), and then a petering-out
- Nos. 46–62, in Piano 2 (shared between RH and LH, but with a few free bars before the beginning of No. 50). Notice the similarity to the Piano 2 part in No. 14. A pattern of 7½ crotchets' duration (starting with a group of three quavers) is made progressively shorter: 6½ crotchets for No. 50; 5½ from the fourth bar of No. 53 (third crotchet); and so on through 4½, 3½ and 2½ crotchets.

Organisation of pitch

Remember that the score provides the performers with full rhythmic information, but beyond that it merely tells them which keys to strike. It does not indicate the actual (often very imprecise) pitches that will be heard as a result of the 'preparations'.

Harmony

We *hear* nothing that corresponds to any recognised form of harmony, functional or non-functional.

> Occasional triad shapes do not sound like triads (e.g. the 'D minor' chords in Piano 1, LH at the beginning of No. 41).

We might be tempted to speak of 'pedal points' in some passages, notably between Nos. 46 and 62 with the repeated A in Piano 1, LH and (for even longer) the repeated C in Piano 2, LH – but these sounds have no harmonic or tonal significance. In other words, their undefined pitch makes them quite different from, for example, the long bass A near the end of movement 2 in our Vivaldi set work (so clearly a dominant pedal in D minor).

Melody

Frequently, patterns of notes recur, but these are perceived much more in rhythmic terms than as having real melodic identity.

Of a few possible exceptions, the most striking is the two-bar pattern in Piano 1, RH that is heard altogether 16 times in Parts 8 and 9 (from Nos. 64 and 73), and a pitch profile does emerge.

Tonality

There is no sense of tonality, because tonality can exist only where there are clearly defined pitches and an obvious hierarchy of pitches.

In fact, because of the preparations and the effect that these have on the pitch of the piano strings, this music is essentially *atonal*. The notated notes indicate only the *piano keys* that have to be played. The sounds that result bear little relation to the nominal pitch of the notated note (in other words, an A on the keyboard probably will not sound as an A).

Set work:
Petals for Violoncello and Live Electronics

An alternative title (in the edition published by Wilhelm Hansen Helsinki AB) is: '*Petals* for cello solo with optional electronics'.

Kaija Saariaho

Musical context

Composer

Kaija Saariaho, a major figure in contemporary classical music, was born in Helsinki, Finland in 1952. In the 1980s and 1990s she combined electronics and acoustic instruments in a number of works, and computerised analysis of sounds helped her extend her range of sounds and timbres.

Saariaho was influenced by the French composers Gérard Grisey and Tristan Murail, whose music is sometimes referred to as 'spectralist' because it uses 'the acoustic properties of sound itself (or sound spectra) as the basis of its compositional material' (*The New Grove* (2001), 'Spectral music').

More recently, Saariaho has composed operas and other major vocal and instrumental works, and her musical style has become more accessible, with more clearly defined melodic and rhythmic content.

Kaija Saariaho

Among sources of information about Saariaho are the following:

- http://saariaho.org/
- www.youtube.com/watch?v=E0csfEHX_io ('2013 Official Announcement Kaija Saariaho')
- 'A Guide to Kaija Saariaho's Music' by Tom Service (2013) at www.theguardian.com/music/tomserviceblog/2012/jul/09/ kaija-saariaho-contemporary-music-guide.

Petals

In *Petals* Saariaho has used both an acoustic instrument – (violon)cello – and *live* electronics. The live electronics are used to modify the sounds made by the cello. Saariaho was not the first composer to compose in this way, and *Petals* was not her first venture into this area.

The live electronics are 'optional', but they are heard on the anthology recording and are referred to below.

Petals was dedicated to the Finnish cellist Anssi Karttunen, for whom Saariaho has written several works. It was first performed at a festival of new music in Bremen in 1988.

The title refers to 'the petal of the waterlily' (see box). The name of a previous and related work *Nymphéa* (1987) means 'waterlily'. Both works are a response in music to the celebrated paintings of waterlilies (*Nymphéas*) by Claude Monet (1840–1926).

See Pirkko Moisala in *Kaija Saariaho* (University of Illinois Press, 2009), page 34.

Kaija Saariaho herself tells us that:

'The material [of *Petals*] stems directly from Nymphéa *for string quartet and electronics. The name of the piece is derived from this relationship. The opposite elements here are fragile coloristic passages which give birth to more energetic events with clear rhythmic and melodic character. These more sharply focused figures pass through different transformations, and finally merge back to less dynamic but not the less intensive filigration. In bringing together these very opposite modes of expressions I aimed to force the interpreter to stretch his sensibility.'

http://saariaho.org/works/petals/.

Musical language

In *Petals*, Saariaho has adapted ordinary staff notation, or added to it, in order to indicate various special effects. Frequently the notation is 'indeterminate' – in other words, it does not specify every aspect of melody and rhythm as staff notation usually does.

Some details of special notational devices are given in a preface to the score, which must be consulted. For example, a long horizontal arrow pointing to the right means that the player must 'change very gradually from one sound or one way of playing (etc.) to another' (see staves 2 and 3, for example).

Some extensions to ordinary staff notation are not indicated – probably because Saariaho considered them to be familiar from other similar scores; for example, expanding feathered beams in stave 24 to indicate acceleration.

Some indications on the score refer to the manipulation of the live electronics: see 'Sonority' below.

Musical elements

Structure

The title page of the Hansen edition says: '*Petals* is one continuous movement lasting 'approx[imately] 9 min[utes]'. In both the Anthology and Hansen editions, there is a note from the composer that staves marked 'Lento' should always take '*at least* 20"!' (i.e. at least 20 seconds – the italics and exclamation mark are the composer's own). Different performances can thus vary enormously in length.

Not surprisingly for an avant-garde composer, Saariaho does not employ any specific traditional classical form such as binary, and there is no repetition of entire sections as so frequently happens in classical and popular genres.

For much of the piece there is an alternation of very slow (Lento) passages and continuously active and rapid ones (Saariaho described these two types of passage as 'coloristic' and 'more energetic'). However, to some extent the section that begins at stave 17 combines the two styles.

The score does not use bars and barlines, but each stave is numbered. A superscript 1 is just a convenient way of referring to the first part only of the stave; superscript 2 refers to the second part. Where the stave is clearly split into three with dotted barlines, the superscript refers to the relevant third of the stave. If you use this form of reference in an examination, you will need to explain what you mean by it.

Staves	Section type	Tempo	Important features
1–3	'Colouristic'	Lento (very slowly...)	Harmonics, glissando, trills, crescendo
4–7	'Energetic'	♩ = ca. 60 (i.e. about 60)	Decuplet (groups of 10) demisemiquavers, microtonal and chromatic runs, long glissando. Rapid changes of dynamics
8–9	'Colouristic'	Lento	Trills, harmonics, *ppp* or *pp*
10–13¹	'Energetic'	■ ♩ = c. 54 *espressivo* ■ Ends with *rit.* and new tempo ♩ = c. 40	Much more varied melodically (leaps and repeated notes) and rhythmically than staves 4–7. Several short motifs identifiable
13²–16	'Colouristic'	Lento (*as before, senza tempo*) *sempre legatissimo*	Double-stopping and harmonics. Bottom C♯ sustained for a time, then G♯, followed by bottom C♮
17–27¹	(begins 'energetically')	■ ♩ = ca. 60 *poco impetuoso* ■ *Calando* ('gradually slowing and getting quieter') markings towards the end	Bottom C 'pedal' throughout. Rising figures, with increasing use of glissandi and tremolo. Strong dynamic contrasts.
27²–30	'Colouristic'	■ Marked 'Lento' in the original edition, but not in the Anthology ■ *dolcissimo* ■ *Very* slow at end	C pedal used extensively. This section follows on seamlessly from the previous one. Glissandi, tremolos, and trills at the end. Mostly *mp*.

Sonority

Many composers in the 20th and 21st centuries have exploited existing instruments in novel ways as well as creating entirely new sounds, notably through use of electronics.

Saariaho's highly developed aural imagination was apparent even in early childhood when she was convinced that sounds that she could hear in her head at night were coming from her pillow. She experiences synaesthesia, whereby a stimulus to one sense (e.g. sight) sets off experiences in another sense (e.g. hearing). She has said that 'the visual and the musical world are one to [her]... Different senses, shades of colour, or textures and tones of light, even fragrances and sounds blend in [her] mind' (Moisala 2009, page 55).

The cello

> Saariaho is not alone in extending the potential of the cello. To put this work into context, see *The New Grove* (2001): article 'Violoncello', section III, 2: 'The 20th century: Repertory'.

A few parts of *Petals* (notably stave 10) do not involve any instrumental techniques that a capable 19th-century or early 20th-century cellist would not have encountered.

Much of the piece, however, relies heavily on devices and techniques that came into use (or widespread use) only as the 20th century progressed.

The more 'unusual' or adventurous techniques are these:

- Long or very long trills. These are used in several contexts: on single bowed notes; together with an untrilled note (see staves 15^2–16); on harmonics; and during a glissando

- Harmonics. These are mostly of the 'artificial' or 'stopped' type (see box below). Occasionally they occur simultaneously with ordinary notes (as in the middle of stave 14). In the Anthology recording, the two harmonics at the end of stave 13 are heard together for a time. The player is presumably meant to continue playing the first note for a time while playing second note (as well as the reverb carrying over the sound), hence the markings 'sul G' ('on the G string') and 'sul D' ('on the D string')

- Glissandi. These may cover a large or a small interval (compare staves 26 and 27^2). Usually the starting and finishing notes are indicated, but in stave 27^1 the glissando is to finish on the highest note possible. Further on glissandi, see the explanatory notes that Saariaho wrote to accompany the score (Anthology, page 404)

- Microintervals (intervals smaller than a semitone): see Saariaho's explanatory notes and 'Organisation of pitch: melody' below

- Unusual bow pressure. Full black wedge-shaped patterns indicate where bow pressure is added 'to produce a scratching sound, in which the audible pitch is totally replaced by the noise' and where it is reduced to 'move back from noise to tone again'.

> If you are not a cellist yourself, ask someone who is (or who plays another type of orchestral string instrument) to explain and demonstrate how harmonics are created. Alternatively, there is plenty of information at *www.moderncellotechniques.com/left-hand-techniques/harmonics/harmonics-overview/*.
>
> Many harmonics in *Petals* are of the 'touch-fourth' type (e.g. those at the start of the third Lento, stave 13^2): a note of normal shape has a diamond-shaped note a perfect 4th above it, and the harmonic that sounds is *two octaves* above the normal-shaped note.

It may seem surprising that Saariaho wanted scratching sounds and the total replacement of audible pitch by noise in a piece entitled *Petals*. Possibly these sounds were suggested by thinking of a 'water lily feeding *from the underwater mud*' (our italics).

See the programme note about *Nymphéa* on Sarriaho's website.

Live electronics

Saariaho's requirements for the (optional) live electronics (a digital reverb unit and a harmoniser) are set out in her notes to the score, and there is a diagram to show how everything might be set up.

A digital reverb[eration] unit is required with variable reverb time, although the *amount* of reverb is never shown as more than 50% and sometimes as little as 20% (but bear in mind that 'the percentages marked are guidelines only', as are those for the harmoniser). For much of the piece, the reverb time is set at about 2.5 seconds. This is increased later, first to about 15 seconds at the end of stave 21. Glissandi are increasingly employed from here onwards, so that any blurring effects merely add to the sense of pitch indeterminacy. In the extremely slow-moving ending (stave 30$^{2-3}$) reverb time is gradually doubled to about 30 seconds.

Reverb[eration] is the continuation of a sound after it has been produced. Natural reverb time can be increased or decreased artificially (e.g. to improve the rather 'dead' ambience of a small room in which much sound is absorbed by carpets and soft furnishings).

A harmoniser (see box below) does *not* harmonise a melody by adding chords to it! It is used (at times, not constantly) to enrich sounds by shifting their pitch (usually microtonally) and then combining the pitch-shifted version(s) with the original. Saariaho wants, if possible (see her explanatory notes) pitch-shifted versions about half a semitone higher *and* about half a semitone lower to be combined with the original, but is prepared to accept the higher transposition only.

Saariaho's preference was for a Yamaha SPX90 (a type now discontinued) with a pitch change program.

The use of the harmoniser centres on passages where increased bow pressure leads to precise pitches being replaced by noise. It is usually activated a little in advance of these passages, and de-activated shortly afterwards (as in staves 2–3 and 8–9).

Dynamics

Massive variations in dynamic markings occur, most of all in the long section beginning at stave 17: markings in staves 25–26 range from *ffff* to *pppp*. Some 'fragile coloristic passages' are at times dynamically robust, especially when noise replaces 'tone'.

Texture

Most of the music is monophonic – not surprising in a work for solo cello. Although there is some double-stopping (as in the pp passage in stave 13 just before the Lento), nothing justifies use of any such terms as homophony or melody-dominated homophony.

Tonality

There is no tonality in the sense understood in most Baroque, Classical and Romantic music, because there is no functional harmony to establish major and/or minor key(s).

Neither is there the kind of 'atonality' encountered in many serial works – for such works regularly recycle a pre-ordered 12-note row without showing preference for any particular note.

Saariaho *is* prepared to repeat notes, however, and there may be vestiges of tonal thinking.

The cello's lowest note (C on two leger lines below the bass stave) is heard most of the time from stave 15^2 to the end. In fact it is so prominent that it might be said to emerge as a 'tonal centre', even as a (tonic) pedal. However, a number of ascending figures from stave 17 onwards rise to F♯ and contradict any sense of C major or minor. And the note C may well be emphasised so much chiefly because of its characteristic timbre as the instrument's lowest note (and the product of an open string).

> Nevertheless, is it just accident that notes from the C major scale are quite prominent in staves 1–3, 8–9 and arguably even in staves 4–7?

Perhaps in staves 10–13[1] we may be able to detect some kind of tonal contrast in Saariaho's preference for (the open-string) D and its 'dominant' and neighbouring open string, A.

There is additional tonal contrast in the early part of the third Lento (from stave 13^2) through emphasis of C♯ and G♯.

Organisation of pitch: harmony

Harmony occurs wherever two or more distinct sounds are heard simultaneously. It is not limited to the kinds of chords that dominated music from late medieval times to the beginning of the 20th century.

> Sometimes in *Petals* we hear just a single pitch, so that there is no harmony. Frequently elsewhere, trills and glissandi produce blurring of two or more pitches, especially when reverb is applied, but without any traditional harmonic implications.

There are certainly no such 'traditional' chords in *Petals* and no successions of intervals that clearly suggest traditional chord progressions.

> Harmony can be *implied* even in monophonic writing, because notes that sound in close succession may imply intervals or chords.

The third Lento (from stave 13²) contains several intervals made up of an ordinary bowed or open-string note plus an artificial harmonic (or of two simultaneous artificial harmonics). The intervals in this section, as the music example below shows, are mixed in terms of size and tension, some being more dissonant than others. They do not form any obvious 'progression', although many contain the note G♯.

The following example shows the first five chords heard in the Anthology recording of the third Lento (from 3:00 to 4:00), arising from the discernible overlap of notes that are notated 'one after the other' in the Anthology score (from stave 13² to 14¹). The overlap of notes in this section results from the reverb, which is at 50%, and also, possibly, the cellist actually performing the last note of stave 14 while continuing to play the note before it for a time (the layout of the original edition of the score seems to suggest this, and the indications in the Anthology score to play the two harmonics on different strings, 'sul G', then 'sul D', would seem to back this up). The example below omits prolongations of single notes, and (for ease of reading) uses the treble clef instead of the tenor clef.

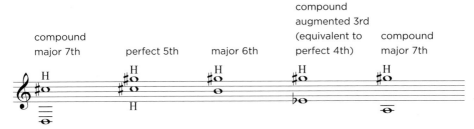

H = artificial harmonic

In the following section, successive passages (stave 17¹, 17², 17³, etc.) have plenty of dissonance, beginning usually with B and A♯ against C (major 7th and augmented 6th).

> In her programme note on *Nymphéa* at ⟨http://saariaho.org/works/nymphea/⟩, the composer states that 'the basis of the entire harmonic structure is provided by complex cello sounds that I have analysed with the computer'. Exactly what this entailed is not indicated, and in any case it is beyond the scope of this syllabus. If, nevertheless, you would like to know a little more, see Saariaho's notes on *Lichtbogen* on the same website.

Organisation of pitch: melody

The first energetic section (from stave 4) features:

- Quarter-tone (half-semitone) microintervals (throughout stave 4 but in some parts only of staves 5 and 6). Remember that the special notation involved is shown at the head of the score
- Glissandi (stave 7) which on the cello involve the tiniest possible microtonal intervals

- Ascending figures – whose ranges gradually expand up to and including the glissandi in stave 7. The brackets in the music example below indicate the first six ascending figures stave 4.

[Reverb at 40%]

* G flat in score, but presumably should be G lowered a 1/4 tone

The second 'energetic' section (stave 10, marked 'espressivo') is more clearly melodic, with greater diversity of interval sizes (although these are relatively narrow in terms of the cello's total range and capabilities). There is no microtonal movement except in three short glissandi. Descending figures predominate towards the end, and they become more wide-ranging up to the climactic (but **pp**) figure in stave 13.

Beginning at stave 17, there are predominantly rising figures, each over a bottom C, and often beginning with a short rest followed by B–A♯ (as mentioned above under 'Organisation of pitch: harmony').

The Lento sections have little melodic content.

Tempo, metre and rhythm

The music alternates between Lento (without metronome mark) and faster tempi indicated by approximate metronome marks and Italian terms expressing character, such as '*poco impetuoso*'. Remember that Saariaho adds the following direction to the first Lento section: '*very* **slowly: the duration of every stave in this tempo should always be** *at least* 20"!'

> This slowness is surpassed in the last stave of *Petals*, which takes 55 seconds or more to perform. But this is rapid compared with Saariaho's *Vers le blanc* of 1982 (for computer), a minimalistic work that consists of the transformation of one chord into another over a period of 15 minutes.

In the Lento sections many, even most, notes are semibreves simply to indicate extreme slowness. In other words, these semibreves are just long notes of imprecise length: they are not thought of as divisible into four crotchets and two minims, in the usual way, although there are shorter notes from time to time, such as the *furioso* quavers in stave 26. Generally however there is no sense of metre, and therefore no barlines or time signatures.

> What appear to be dotted bar lines (e.g. in staves 17 and 30) have no metrical meaning – they show where particular events begin and end.

In the first of the more energetic sections there are repeated groups of ten demisemiquavers (decuplets), each a crotchet in length. Although each of staves 4–6 has four groups, there is no sense of quadruple metre. The rhythm becomes completely free with the glissandi and tremolo of stave 7.

Kaija Saariaho with cellist Anssi Karttunen, for whom she wrote *Petals*

The second quicker section (from stave 10) is again notated precisely with short notes beamed together into groups, each of which lasts for a crotchet. However, the number of tuplets (see box below), ties and ornament signs prevents any sense of metre or regularity except briefly in the middle of stave 11. And without a clear sense of metre it is pointless to speak of syncopations.

> In a tuplet, a note is divided equally into an irregular number of smaller notes. In stave 10, the second quaver is a triplet (three triplet semiquavers lasting for a quaver), and later on in the stave there are two sep*tuplets* (marked '7', each with seven semiquavers lasting for a crotchet), a sex*tuplet* ('6') and two quin*tuplets* ('5'). Italics are not normally used in these names – but we have used them here to show the derivation of the term 'tuplet'.

To begin with, the third more active section (from stave 17) is mostly notated exactly, but again there is no sense of metre. There are successive 'bursts' of sound, each beginning with a bottom C. These 'bursts' are of varying length. Increasingly timing is imprecise (with pauses, non-notated glissandi and some indeterminacy of pitch) – until the final three staves, which proceed in 'free' semibreves (some with pauses) and a few less extended notes which are notated as minims.

> Some groups of notes have single beams (as if they were quavers), with a slash through the first stem of the group and the first part of the beam. This slash apparently signifies inexact duration and is probably comparable with the slash through the tail of an acciaccatura.

Set work:

Le sacre du printemps: Introduction, 'Les augures printaniers' ('The Augurs of Spring') and 'Jeu du rapt' ('Ritual of Abduction')

Igor Stravinsky

A LEVEL

Musical context

Le sacre du printemps (The Rite of Spring) **is regarded as one of the most significant works in the history of early 20th-century music.**

It was the third of a series of ballet scores composed by the Russian composer Igor Stravinsky (1882–1971) for Diaghilev's Ballets Russes. Here he continued to pursue the development of the Russian nationalist style he had adopted in his preceding works, *The Firebird* (1910) and *Petrouchka* (1911), both of which draw extensively on folk music.

Igor Stravinsky

Sergei Diaghilev (1872–1929) was a Russian impresario who made Russian opera and ballet better known in the West through his Ballets Russes company. He was an enormously influential figure who commissioned work not just from Stravinsky but also from Debussy (*Jeux*), Ravel (*Daphnis et Chloé*) and Richard Strauss (*Josephslegende*). He also engaged such artists as Bakst and Picasso to design stage sets and costumes, and his choreographers included Fokine, Nijinsky, Massine and Balanchine.

Stravinsky was born into a musical family – his father was a principal baritone with the Mariinsky Theatre in St Petersburg – and he soon gave up his law studies to become a pupil of Nikolai Rimsky-Korsakov (1844–1908), the leading Russian nationalist composer of the time. While training with Rimsky-Korsakov, Stravinsky completed a number of orchestral works, notably the Symphony in E♭ (1907), *Scherzo fantastique* (1908) and *Feu d'artifice* (1908), the last of which caught the attention of Diaghilev, leading to the composer's long-lasting collaboration with the impresario.

Nineteenth-century Russian composers showed a particular interest in the use of folk song in their work. One of the earliest was Glinka (1804–1857), the composer of the operas *A Life for the Tsar* (1836) and *Russlan and Ludmilla* (1842). The most prominent nationalist composers of the next generation were based in St Petersburg and formed a group known variously as 'The Five' or the 'Mighty Handful'. These were Mily Balakirev, Aleksander Borodin, César Cui, Modest Mussorgsky and Nikolai Rimsky-Korsakov. Some of their most celebrated works included the operas *Prince Igor* (Borodin), *Boris Godunov* and *Khovanschina* (Mussorgsky) and *Shéhérazade* and *The Golden Cockerel* (Rimsky-Korsakov). Though the Moscow-based Tchaikovsky was not a member of this group, his work too has a markedly nationalistic character.

In general terms, the Russian national style differs from that of German composers of the time in a tendency to use varied repetition rather than motivic development, the use of structures composed of contrasting blocks of sound, a stress on the use of changing backgrounds (harmonic and orchestral) and a liking for colouristic effects in general. Debussy, who spent some time in Russia in his early years, was strongly influenced by Russian nationalist approaches in his own work.

According to Stravinsky, *The Rite* had its origins in a dream or 'fleeting vision' he had while finishing the orchestration of *The Firebird* in spring 1910. It centred on a 'young maiden dancing to the point of exhaustion before a group of men of fabulous age'. The artist and designer Nikolai Roerich (1874–1947) also played a major role in the development of the concept. Diaghilev had previously used Roerich's designs for a staging of the Polovtsian Dances from Borodin's *Prince Igor*, and by this time, he was regarded as Russia's leading specialist on pagan antiquity. Over the years he had produced an impressive series of paintings of prehistoric scenes, notably *The Elders Gather* (1898), *Idols* (1901), *Ancient Life* (1904), *Ritual Dance* (1904) and *Yarilo's Gully* (1908) – Yarilo being the Slavonic sun god to whom the sacrifice is made at the end of *The Rite*.

Nikolai Roerich's *The Great Sacrifice*, one of his scene designs for *The Rite of Spring*

Roerich and Stravinsky expanded the action backwards from the final scene (Stravinsky's original dream), and the ballet came to comprise a series of 'pictures from Pagan Russia'. The prescribed extracts come from the opening of the first of the work's two parts, the section initially entitled 'The Adoration of the Earth'. As Roerich said, it 'transports us to the foot of a sacred hill, amid green fields where Slavonic tribes have gathered for their vernal games'. An early synopsis by the composer refers to a series of ancient Slavonic rituals reflecting the joy of spring: 'The orchestral introduction is a swarm of spring pipes (dudki); later the curtain goes up, there are auguries, khorovod rituals, a game of abduction'.

DUDKI is both Polish and Russian for wind pipes; **KHOROVOD** is a type of dance, sometimes described as a 'round' dance, although the choreography is often more involved than is implied by this definition.

Another synopsis, given below, was sent to the conductor Sergei Koussevitsky ahead of a performance of *The Rite* in Moscow, in February 1914.

[*The Rite of Spring*] represents pagan Russia and is unified by a single idea: the mystery and great surge of the creative power of Spring. The piece has no plot, but the choreographic succession is as follows:

Part 1: THE [ADORATION] OF THE EARTH

The spring celebration. It takes place in the hills. The pipers pipe and the young men tell fortunes. The old woman enters. She knows the mystery of nature and how to predict the future. Young girls with painted faces come in from the river in single file. They dance the spring dance. Games start. The Spring Khorovod follows. The people divide into two groups, opposing each other. There is the holy procession of the wise old man. The oldest and wisest interrupts the spring games, which come to a stop. The people pause trembling in the presence of the great ritual. The old men bless the earth. *The Kiss of the Earth.* The people dance passionately on the earth, sanctifying it and becoming one with it.

Part 2: THE GREAT SACRIFICE

At night the virgins hold mysterious games, walking in circles. One of the virgins is appointed by fate, being caught twice in the perpetual circle. The virgins honour her, the chosen one. They invoke the ancestors and entrust the chosen one to the old wise men. She sacrifices herself in the presence of the old men in her great holy dance, the great sacrifice.

The *Rite of Spring* was first performed on May 29, 1913 at the Théâtre des Champs-Elysées in Paris, and as is well known, precipitated a riot and fist fights between different factions in the audience. The open dress rehearsal the preceding day, attended mainly by artists and musicians, had passed off without incident, but the fashionable audience at the official first night was provoked by both the music and Nijinsky's choreography. The performance was conducted by Pierre Monteux and the role of the Chosen One was danced by Maria Piltz.

Musical elements

Sonority

Stravinsky scored *The Rite of Spring* for an exceptionally large orchestra, with many transposing instruments.

The 'Introduction' and 'Jeu du rapt' sections do not have a key signature, and this is a conscious choice, not an indication necessarily that we are in C major. The transposing instruments are still written at transposing pitch in these movements, not concert pitch, despite sharing the blank key signature.

The transposing instruments used here are:
- Piccolo (sounding an octave higher than written)
- Alto flute in G (sounding a perfect 4th lower than written)
- Cor anglais and horn in F (sounding a perfect 5th lower than written)
- Clarinet in B♭ (sounding a tone lower than written)
- Clarinet in A (sounding a minor 3rd lower than written)
- Piccolo clarinet in D (sounding a tone higher than written)
- Piccolo clarinet in E♭ (sounding a minor 3rd higher than written)
- Bass clarinet in B♭ (sounding a major 9th lower than written)
- Trumpet in D (sounding a tone higher than written)
- Bass trumpet in E♭ (sounding a major 6th lower than written)
- Tenor tuba in B♭ (sounding a tone lower than written)
- Contrabassoon and double bass (sounding an octave lower than written).

The instrumentation ranges from use of a limited number of instruments to tutti. In a score as rich and diverse as this, it is only possible to indicate some landmark moments.

Introduction

As might be expected, the 'dudki' section is scored mainly for wind instruments. This provides us with a striking anticipation of Stravinsky's subsequent liking for bands lacking 'emotional' string sounds, as in *Symphonies for Wind Instruments*, *Concerto for Piano and Winds* and *Symphony of Psalms* (the latter requiring only cellos and double basses in the string section). One of the work's most arresting features is the high unaccompanied solo for bassoon at the start which baffled early audiences.

The critic Georges Pioch, who was present at the open rehearsal, recalled thinking that it must have been an oboe, while those around him believed it was either a muted trumpet or clarinet. It was only on asking Monteux, the conductor, that they learned the truth.

Other woodwind effects include tremolandi in flutes (Fig. 7) and flutter-tonguing (marked 'Flttz.' in the score) in flute, oboes and clarinet (Fig. 10).

Strings do not play any melodic material. Their involvement is limited to:

- Pizzicato violin and viola (the latter incorrectly marked 'Vc' in the Anthology) (Fig. 4)
- Violin trill (Fig. 6)
- Pizzicato solo cello (Fig. 7)
- Single sustained bass note on solo double bass (Fig. 8)
- Divisi double basses, four playing harmonics, one muted, one playing pizzicato with two muted cellos (Fig. 10)
- Glissandi harmonics effect on violas (Fig. 11).

In this chapter, 'Fig. 4', 'Fig. 6' and so on refer to the sections beginning with the boxed numbers above the stave.

'Les augures printaniers' (Figures 13–37)

One of the most famous effects in *The Rite* comes at Fig. 13 with the eight-part string chords formed by four sets of double-stopping (i.e. violin II, viola, cello and bass). Each chord is heavily accented through the use of a down bow, and reinforced by intermittent doubling by eight horns. In marked contrast is the passage at Fig. 14, lightly scored for cor anglais, bassoons and pizzicato cellos.

Other notable and novel effects in this section include:

- Muted trumpet chords followed by flutter-tonguing in flutes and clarinets (Figures 16–17)
- *Col legno* (with the wood of the bow) at Fig. 24 combined with tremolandi in bassoons and violins, all supporting a melody in the horn
- The highly variegated background texture at Figures 28–29, involving trills in clarinets and bassoons, ostinato in the trombone, flute melody, string scales, triangle and antique cymbals, overlaid by trumpets in parallel chords
- Tremolo harmonics in violin I at Figures 33–34
- Horn glissando effects at Fig. 36.

'Jeu du rapt' (Figures 13–37)

At Fig. 39, Stravinsky calls on four solo violins to play what he has described as a 'detached glissando'. As this is doubled by flutes, it is probably near inaudible. Horns are asked to play *bouché* (hand-stopped) accented notes at Fig. 40.

Texture

The opening of the work is monophonic for one bar, followed by a passage for two parts at bars 2–3. At Fig. 1, the texture expands to three parts in a passage best described as melody and accompaniment.

A 'layered' texture is employed at Fig. 4, four-part (legato) homorhythms at the fifth bar after Figure 6, and from Fig. 7 a free, rather than imitative, contrapuntal scheme is apparent.

'Les augures printaniers' proceeds through a variety of textures:

- Homorhythmic chords (Fig. 13)
- Ostinato with broken-chord support (Fig. 14)
- Melody-dominated homophony with melodic fragments heard over repeated chords (Fig. 15)
- Hetero-rhythmic layers (Fig. 16) of ostinato in straight quavers with triplet quavers in violas, overlaid with chordal blasts and brief melodic snatches
- Brief canonic entries (Figures 20–21), a very rare use of this type of writing in this work
- Melody-dominated homophony, with richly layered accompaniment (Fig. 25).

'Jeu du rapt' similarly features a variety of textures, but notice the almost full homophonic tutti at Fig. 43.

Dynamics

The dynamic range of the first three sections of *The Rite of Spring* covers the full range *pp–ff* (the first *fff* does not occur until the climactic bars of the 'Spring rounds' (Khorovod) one bar before Fig. 54 (outside the Anthology excerpt), and *ppp* is reserved for the Introduction to the Second Part of the ballet).

Interestingly, Stravinsky did not indicate a dynamic level for the bassoon solo, either at the opening or on its return at Fig. 12, evidently leaving this aspect to the discretion of the instrumentalist and conductor.

Tempo, metre and rhythm

Such was the rhythmic complexity of *The Rite* that at first Stravinsky was unable to work out a way of notating the final dance from Part 2, with its constantly shifting metres and asymmetric schemes. In fact, the original version of the final scene was written down in even shorter rhythmic values than those of the present revised version. Though the opening sections of the ballet are not as rhythmically involved, there are still numerous changes of metre and tempo.

The Introduction is to be played *Lento tempo rubato* at the start, and its quasi-improvisatory quality is conveyed through frequently changing time signatures and gradations of tempo (e.g. *poco accelerando, più mosso*).

The stamping chords at the start of 'Les augures printaniers' (Fig. 13) are in duple time, with frequent asymmetric stresses. This section of the work is to be played *tempo giusto* (strict time), its relentless pulse only interrupted by the presence of a pause before Fig. 22. There are two triple-time bars before Fig. 28, but thereafter the signature remains in $\frac{2}{4}$.

'Jeu du rapt' is marked *Presto*, and in contrast to the preceding section is notably less regular metrically. It opens in $\frac{9}{8}$, sometimes subdivided into $\frac{4}{8}$ + $\frac{5}{8}$ (see Figures 39 and 41). Notice the rapidly changing signatures from Fig. 42 and the way that the melodic material at Fig. 47 is variously stressed in terms of either $\frac{6}{8}$ or $\frac{3}{4}$.

Rhythms range from apparent simplicity (e.g. the quavers and semiquavers at Figures 14 and 25) to much more complex patterns, involving:

- Subdivisions of the beat into triplets (e.g. Fig. 3), sextuplets (e.g. Fig. 4), septuplets (e.g. Fig. 10) and groups of 10 (e.g Fig. 9)

- Hetero-rhythms, e.g. eight demi-semiquavers against six semiquavers (Fig. 5), four semiquavers against three quavers (Fig. 7) and threes against twos (Fig. 16)

- Offbeat stress, e.g. 'straight' offbeat quavers at third bar of Fig. 31, and the asymmetric accents at Fig. 13

- Regular displaced stress in first violins at Fig. 40, with every fourth quaver in $\frac{9}{8}$ accented

- Syncopation, e.g. Fig. 32, bass line.

Organisation of pitch: melody

Stravinsky's earliest works draw extensively on folk music. Latterly, he tried to downplay the use of ethnic material in *The Rite*, claiming that the opening bassoon melody was the only folk melody in the score. Pressed further on the issue, he remarked that if any of his Russian period pieces sound like folk music, 'it may be because my powers of fabrication were able to tap some unconscious "folk" memory'. In reality, it is probably the case that Stravinsky drew heavily on a collection of 1,785 Lithuanian folk songs, edited by Anton Juszkiewicz and published in Kraków in 1900 as *Litauische Volks-Weisen*. This in itself seems surprising as Lithuania is in no way 'Russian', and if anything had enjoyed closer links with Poland for centuries.

It is possible that in choosing this material, Stravinsky and Roerich were mindful of the fact that paganism persisted longer in Lithuania (as late as the 15th century) than in Russia itself. Not only that, the folk material which has been identified in *The Rite* was drawn from ceremonial songs, and also calendar or seasonal songs that were considered to have a particularly pure pedigree. Stravinsky's teacher, Rimsky-Korsakov, had earlier remarked that 'the whole cycle of ceremonial songs rests on ancient pagan sun-worship which lives unconsciously in the people'.

The opening theme of *The Rite* was derived from the following melody in the Juszkiewicz collection (No. 157), here transposed to aid comparison:

Example 1

Stravinsky's adaptation in the bassoon line retains the broad pitch outlines of the original four three-bar phrases, but presents them with grace notes, changing time signatures and a degree of rubato (again, to aid comparison, the melody is here notated in treble rather than tenor clef):

Example 2

Phrase 1   Phrase 2   Phrase 3 shortened   Phrase 4

Commentators have also observed a link between the opening theme and the 'Dumka parobka' bassoon solo from Mussorgsky's *Sorochintsi Fair*.

Example 3

Typically, Stravinsky's melody draws on only a limited number of notes, its rather modal quality deriving from the use of a hexatonic (six-note) scale, which feels rather like an extension of a pentatonic scale. Latterly, Stravinsky also introduced two chromatic notes, B♭ and G♭.

Another firm link between the Juszkiewicz collection and the prescribed sections of *The Rite* occurs in 'Jeu du rapt' three bars after Fig. 37. Here is the Lithuanian melody, which has been transposed down a semitone for the sake of comparison:

Example 4a

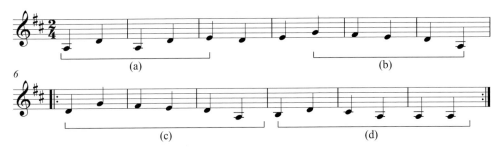

Here is Stravinsky's melody:

Example 4b

In this case the pitch outline has been preserved almost intact, but while Stravinsky's reworking has kept to regular note lengths, the time signature has been radically altered and the last two phrases separated by a rest.

It is very unlikely that all the borrowings will ever be identified, but it is true that many melodic fragments bear such hallmarks of folk music as grace-note ornamentation, modality and relatively limited ranges. The cor anglais melody at Fig. 2, for example, (shown here at concert pitch) draws initially on just four pitches (C♯–D♯–F♯–G♯), and only much later (in the fifth bar of Fig. 3) incorporates an E (notated as a B in the transposing score). Notice also the extensive use of ornamentation, a common feature in all woodwind parts.

Example 5

Other characteristic features, not all of them so obviously folk-like, include:

- Chromatic lines, e.g. Fig. 4 in the piccolo clarinet

Example 6

- Wide leaps, e.g. third bar of Fig. 8 in the flute
- Angular lines, involving 4ths and 5ths, e.g. Fig. 9 in both oboe...

Example 7a

Ex. 7

... and piccolo clarinet

Example 7b

- Ostinato figures, notably the four-note pattern which runs throughout 'Les augures printaniers' after first appearing in the fourth bar of Fig. 12 in the violins

Example 8

- Repeated note figures and conjunct lines, e.g. the trumpet from the second bar of Fig. 15...

Example 9a

... and the following musical material from the fifth bar of Fig. 28 (a motif which returns in the 'Spring Rounds' at Fig. 50):

Example 9b

■ Breaking down and reconstituting of melodic lines. A particularly good example of Stravinsky's approach can be found in his treatment of the folk-like melody beginning at Fig. 25 (below). Notice how elements of the first four-bar phrase are reworked in the second four-bar phrase, and then how cells from these melodies are fragmented and repeated throughout the passage from Fig. 28–37. A similar process occurs towards the end of 'Jeu du rapt'.

Example 10

■ Whooping hunting calls (perfect 5ths) at Fig. 40 in 'Jeu du rapt'.

Example 11

Organisation of pitch: harmony

Stravinsky combines his non-functional and dissonant harmonic language with such folk elements as drones, pedals and ostinato as well as forms of parallelism. Some typical devices are indicated below:

■ Parallel 4ths (Fig. 1 in clarinets)

■ Parallel 4ths and 7ths (Fig. 3 in bassoons)

■ Whole-tone structures, e.g. the chord of Bb–D–E–G♯, albeit clouded by chromatic movement, at Fig. 8

■ Bitonal structures, e.g. Fig. 13 with its combination of Fb major (enharmonic E major) in the bass and dominant 7th of Ab in the treble.

Example 12

This chord forms the basis for a lengthy, harmonically static passage.

- Polytonal structures, e.g. Fig. 14 with chords of E major, E minor, C major and V⁷ of A♭
- Superimposed 5ths chord (E♭–B♭–F–C–G–D), combined with C major broken chord (from bar 4 of Fig. 16)
- Superimposed 4ths chord (one beat before Fig. 18)
- Parallel second inversion 7th chords in the trumpets, embedded in the middle of an opulent orchestral texture (Fig. 28 – see example 9b)
- Dissonances involving 9th chords (Fig. 37)
- Dissonance arising from the free movement of lines
- Chords involving both major and minor elements, e.g. Fig. 47, where the F minor second inversion is laced with an A♮ and a G♭.

Structure and tonality

The music proceeds in 'blocks' of sound, sometimes internally organised as a sort of mosaic made up of short contrasting fragments, or else is through-composed. By this time, Stravinsky had moved away from any use of functional tonality, but there are vestigial tonal references, perceptible mainly in the melodic content.

Reference point	Tonality	Content	Musical example
		Introduction	
Bars 1–3	Hexatonic on A - major–minor ambiguity	Lithuanian folk song (a) – chromatic continuation – Lithuanian folk song reprised	Ex. 2
Figs 2–4	C♯	Cor anglais melody (b)-(a)-(b)	Ex. 5
Figs 4–6	E major background	Chromatic line (c)	Ex. 6
Figs 6–8	Moving to region of B♭	(b) varied with continuation – (c)-(b)-(c)-(b)-(c)	

Fig. 9	F Mixolydian in oboe and piccolo clarinet	Angular woodwind melodies: (d¹) and (d²)	Ex. 7 and 7b
Fig. 10	E maj/min⁷ background to polytonal winds	(c) + (b) + (d²) + (d¹)	
Fig. 12	A♭ minor	(a) reprised a semitone lower than at the opening; first appearance of the four-note ostinato	Ex. 8
		'Les augures printaniers'	
Figs 13–14	Bitonal (F♭ major + V⁷ of A♭) – polytonal – bitonal	Chords	Ex. 12
Fig. 15	Bitonal	Chords plus conjunct melodic fragment (e)	Ex. 9a
Figs 16–17	Bitonal – E♭ + C + V⁷ of A♭	Ostinato with (e) varied	
Figs 18–22	Bitonal	Chords plus a melody involving repeated notes and conjunct movement (f), eventually treated canonically	
Figs 22–24	Moving to modal C	Ostinato	
Fig. 25	C Mixolydian	New folk-like melody (g) plus C pedal and ostinato with (e) at Fig. 26	Ex. 10
Fig. 27	E♭ Mixolydian	(g) varied on alto flute	
Figs 28–30	E♭ Mixolydian expanded through addition of G♭s in strings	(g) varied and continued + (h) ['Spring Rounds' theme]	Ex. 9b
Fig. 31	Expanded D	(g) fragmented	

Fig. 32	Expanded C – with bass syncopated ostinato gravitating to dominant	(g) fragmented	
Figs 37–47		**'Jeu du rapt'**	
Figs 37–40	Melody on A Mixolydian, with bitonal support (V^7 of A♭ + C)	Second Lithuanian folk song (i)	Ex. 4
Figs 40–41	Horn 5ths (A–D) alternating with melody in B♭	Horn call (j); (i)	Ex. 11
Fig. 42	Polytonal, involving E♭, F♯⁷, C and a diminished 7th		
Fig. 43	Expanded F♯, down-shifted to expanded F	Contrasting material (k); mainly stepwise movement harmonised in block chords	
Fig. 44	V^7 of B♭, with horns on D		
Fig. 46	On F	(i) fragmented	
Fig. 47	F major/minor; concludes with E♭ trill linking with 'Spring Rounds' section	(i) fragmented and punctuated by chords	

Further study

You may like to hear a performance of *The Rite of Spring* conducted by Stravinsky himself dating from 1960, available under the Sony BMG Music Entertainment label. If you regard yourself as a competent pianist you could find someone to join you in trying the piano duet version of the work, arranged by the composer.

Test yourself

Below are five short questions on each set work. These are not 'exam questions' but are intended to help you get to know each work better.

Most questions use the command words listed in Appendix 5 of each specification (with which you will need to be familiar when preparing for exams). For each set work there is also a sample essay question for each level. These correspond to Question 6 in Pearson's Sample Assessment Materials. Essays at the two levels are marked from different assessment grids, as may again be seen from the Sample Assessment Materials. The allocation of marks is different, with fewer marks at AS implying the need for less information. At A Level there is greater emphasis on saying how and why particular things happen in the music, and relatively less on just saying what happens. When answering the questions below, you should refer to the printed score of the relevant work or movement.

In your exam you will have a special booklet containing the scores you need. You will not be allowed to take a copy of the anthology or other printed music into the exam room.

Three Dances for Two Prepared Pianos: Dance No. 1 (John Cage)

Short questions:

a. Define 'prepared piano'.

b. Describe the use and effect of contrasting dynamics at the beginning of the sixth part of the movement at No. 46.

c. Explain the importance of the numbers 2 5 2 2 6 2 2 7 2 in the structure of this movement.

d. Explain how repetition is used in this movement.

e. Discuss how appropriate the title 'dance' is to this music.

Essay questions:

AS

Evaluate the sonority and rhythm in the first of John Cage's Three Dances for Two Prepared Pianos.

Relate your discussion to other relevant works. These may include set works, wider listening or other music.

A Level

Evaluate the sonority, texture and rhythm in the first of John Cage's Three Dances for Two Prepared Pianos, with reference to how novel their treatment was in the mid-1940s.

Relate your discussion to other relevant works. These may include set works, wider listening or other music.

Petals (Kaija Saariaho)

Short questions:

a. Describe the structure of *Petals*.

b. Explain the following string-playing techniques: double-stopping; glissando; artificial harmonics.

c. Explain how the music develops from the beginning of stave 17 to the middle of stave 21 (*mp*).

d. Compare the first and second 'energetic' sections (staves 4–7 and 10–13¹).

e. Discuss the importance or otherwise of including the 'optional' electronics.

Essay questions:

AS

Evaluate Saariaho's use of sonority and dynamics in *Petals*. Relate your discussion to other relevant works. These may include set works, wider listening or other music.

A Level

Evaluate Saariaho's use of sonority, dynamics and tempo as means of exploiting the expressive and technical potential of the cello. Relate your discussion to other relevant works. These may include set works, wider listening or other music.

Movements from *Le sacre du printemps* (Igor Stravinsky)

Short questions:

a. Name the instrument used, and the clef used, at the start of the work.

b. Identify motifs that originated in folk music.

c. Explain why Stravinsky drew on Lithuanian folk music.

d. Identify the longest passage without a change of time signature.

e. Describe the chord that is heard at the start of 'Les augures printaniers'.

Essay questions:

A Level only

Evaluate rhythm, metre and melody in the Introduction and in 'Les augures printaniers', with particular reference to the ways the two sections are contrasted. Relate your discussion to other relevant works. These may include set works, wider listening or other music.

Answers

The answers given below are *not* exam-style mark schemes, but are designed to provide guidance.

For the answers to the short questions, in some cases we simply refer you to particular sections and sub-sections of the notes on the set work in question. Re-reading these notes will provide you with appropriate information, although you may not always need to use all the information in the section or sub-section referred to.

When you have answered an AS essay question, you should check what you have written against the relevant section of the relevant chapter from this book (e.g. structure and tonality).

Each essay question begins with the word 'Evaluate', and you are expected to make judgements and draw conclusions rather than just state facts (see Appendix 5 in Edexcel's specifications).

Therefore say, whenever you can, *how* and *why* things happen, rather than just *what* happens. Wherever possible, also give examples to illustrate points that you have made.

At A Level each essay question has a special 'angle' – for example how certain elements contribute to certain effects. This will probably mean that you need to be more selective than at AS and more precise in the detail that you provide. The information below is for the A Level questions only.

For each question you must refer to 'other relevant works'. These will depend on suggestions from your teacher and your own independent listening, and may well include the 'wider listening' work(s) listed in the specifications (Appendix 4).

Area of Study: Vocal music

Cantata 'Ein feste Burg ist unser Gott' BWV 80, Movements 1, 2 and 8 (Bach)

a. See the article on Bach, section 'Cantata 'Ein feste Burg ist unser Gott': original purpose', beginning on page 76.

b. Alto part (a fugal-style answer to the tenor's subject) is a 5th higher, with some modifications so that the tonic-dominant D–A can be answered by dominant-tonic A–D.

c. The strings double the voices, but with some elaboration (heterophony). Before the vocal basses enter, there is an independent instrumental bass (violoncello). Oboes and violone (who present the chorale in canon) are independent of the voices.

d. See section 'Treatment of the chorale melody' (especially remarks on Movement 2) beginning on page 77.

e. See section 'Cantata 'Ein feste Burg ist unser Gott': the text', on page 77.

Question 6

For the A Level question your comments should demonstrate how all *three* elements concern the treatment of the chorale melody.

You may refer to the considerable melodic change and ornamentation of the chorale in the voice-parts of Movement 1 (compare the basic form heard in Movement 8).

This is characteristic of the fugal/imitative writing in these parts. The oboe and violone parts generally keep closer to the basic form, to help make the identity of the chorale as clear as possible.

The basic rhythm of the chorale is often enlivened in the voice-parts. Changes in the oboe and violone parts are generally limited to what is necessary to make the canon work, and to permit the canon to fit with the rest of the texture.

Structurally, each phrase of the melody is introduced fugally/imitatively, and then stated more clearly in the two canonic parts, so that the structure of the melody (including the initial repeat) dominates and shapes the whole structure of the movement.

The Magic Flute, **excerpts from Act 1 (Mozart)**

a. See the article on Mozart, sections on 'Opera' and 'The Magic Flute' (pages 86 and 87).

b. The recitative has vocal phrases supported by detached chords in the orchestra, and some instrumental phrases (incorporating the type of syncopation heard in the introduction). The aria has more continuous melody-dominated homophony (and includes features such as the countermelody at bar 36). See also remarks under 'Texture' (page 94) and 'Tempo, metre and rhythm' (page 95).

c. Just listing dynamics is not helpful – as anyone can see what these are from the score! Try to say why certain dynamics are used. See the section on 'Dynamics' (page 95).

d. See the second part of the section on 'Structure and Tonality' (from page 89).

e. See the first part of the section 'Organisation of pitch: Melody' (from page 91), and the second paragraph of 'Texture' (page 94). Sometimes all voices are heard simultaneously (notably at bar 54); note also, for example, the dialogue between Papageno and Tamino, followed by their singing together in agreement.

Question 6

In the A Level question your comments on the *three* elements should demonstrate how they underline the dramatic situation in 'O zittre nicht'.

Concerning structure, you may refer to the contrasting functions of the various sections: introduction (announcing the Queen, urgent and powerful), recitative (her initial approach to Tamino – reassurance and flattery), the slow Largo (with apparent self-pity, rage against her adversary and a cry for help). The faster Allegro moderato features an extravagant display to suggest power and a degree of threat.

Minor tonality is used for the end of the recitative, and for most of the Largo, where the darkest emotions are expressed. (G minor specifically was Mozart's favourite key for sad or tragic music.) Major tonality suits the regal nature of the opening and the implied or anticipated triumph of the Allegro moderato.

Fundamental to the harmony are chords I and V, but more 'colourful' chords help to underline important moments in the text (e.g the Neapolitan sixth in G minor for 'tiefbetrübte Mutterherz' in the recitative).

On Wenlock Edge, Nos. 1, 3 and 5 (Vaughan Williams)

a. For 'Dorian mode', see section on 'Tonality', sub-section 'Is my team ploughing?' (page 105). The Mixolydian mode is similar to a major scale, but with the seventh degree naturalised or flattened (e.g. GABCDEFG): see also, under 'Tonality', the note on 'Bredon Hill' (page 105).

b. A stormy atmosphere is created principally through sonority (e.g. trills and tremolos) and dynamics (including frequent crescendos and diminuendos). Note also rapid (semiquaver) movement in the piano part, and parallel harmonic movement that often involves false relations.

c. See sections on 'Tonality' and 'Organisation of pitch: Melody' (pages 104–106). 'Bredon Hill' has greater use of brief melismas.

d. You might mention that the piano plays almost continuously in the latter, but in the former is largely restricted to passages featuring the friend's replies. Here the piano is prominent (with cello) – compare its use alone in stanza 3 from 'Bredon Hill'. Compare also the density of textures – greater in 'Bredon Hill', to create atmosphere.

e. Main points include the following. Clear enunciation of text, often with long and relatively high notes on stressed syllables. Clear musical response to the stormy character of the lyrics (compare question (b)). Change of melody for stanza 3 matches the shift in time ('Then, 'twas before my time').

Question 6

Much of the effectiveness of the song lies in the *contrasts* between the music for the dead man and the music for the living friend.

For example: the dead man's melodic line is generally stepwise with a narrow range, while the friend's melody is more active and wide-ranging. Under melody, note also the repetition of bars 5–6 a 4th *higher* at 39–40 as the emotional temperature rises, and the 'dying-away' in bars 55–58 as the instrumental idea falls through four octaves.

The initial disembodied mood is created partly by the free rhythm of the introductory instrumental idea, with its mixture of triplet and non-triplet patterns, ties, and syncopation (bars 4–5). The rhythm of the friend's music is more varied than the dead man's – notably with more long notes.

In terms of texture, the introductory idea is entirely homorhythmic – the parallel movement almost suggesting a reinforced single melodic line. The accompaniment to verse 1 is static, providing just a vestige of harmony. The regular, repeated triplet rhythms of the friend's verse provide life and movement – the five- and six-part chords are much heavier and forceful than the three-part chords of the introduction.

Area of Study: Instrumental music

Concerto in D minor Op. 3 No. 11 (Vivaldi)

a. 'Continuo' is short for 'basso continuo', Italian for 'continuous bass'. It comprises the instrumental (string) bass line, plus an improvised accompaniment on keyboard or lute with full harmony, usually in response to figurings such as '6' and '♯'.

b. See the relevant part of the section on 'Texture' (beginning on page 121).

c. See the section 'Musical context', sub-section 'The concerto' (page 113).

d. Movement 3 is slow and in compound quadruple metre ($\frac{12}{8}$), whereas Movement 4 is fast and in simple quadruple metre (**C**). Movement 3 is in the style of a siciliana (with much use of a characteristic dotted rhythm), while Movement 4 features much continuous semiquaver movement. Further, see section 'Tempo, metre and rhythm' (from page 124).

e. There are some passages for one solo violin only (notably in the Largo), but neither here nor elsewhere does this violin part make exceptional demands.

Question 6

In answering the A Level question, your remarks on the *three* elements should demonstrate the amount of contrast involved.

The three-bar Adagio provides a strong contrast of tempo and texture with the following Allegro section. It is homorhythmic (rather than polyphonic/contrapuntal like the Allegro). The latter opens in fugal style and has three main melodic ideas, which Vivaldi works very hard (thus ensuring a strong sense of unity) but whose varied treatment also provides plenty of contrast. Structurally, the Allegro has block contrasts of texture in a manner typical of many late Baroque concertos.

The Allegro begins and ends in D minor, with some contrast provided by excursions to A minor and G minor – but Vivaldi does not exploit the stronger contrast achievable through extended use of any *major* key. The Adagio is best viewed as in D minor also, but with some striking chromatic chords (which contrast strongly with the diatonic harmony of the Allegro).

Piano Trio in G minor Op. 17: Movement 1 (Clara Schumann)

a. i. for example, bar 137; ii. bars 139–143; iii. for example, bar 147, beat 3 (piano, RH).

b. 'Parallel motion' occurs when two or more parts move in the same direction and the same interval apart. For example: bars 17[4]–20 (violin and cello): minor 10ths descending; bars 85[3]–89: octaves in piano LH to strengthen bass line; bar 93: melody doubled in octaves for prominence, with piano RH parallel six-three chords over C minor dominant pedal.

c. See section on 'Texture' (from 'The pianist is busy...' on page 129).

d. The cello sometimes provides the bass part (alone or doubling piano, LH). Elsewhere it has a melodic role, jointly with the violin or occasionally on its own, notably when it is involved in imitation (as at bar 125).

e. See section on 'Structure and Tonality' (beginning page 129).

Question 6

In answering the A Level question, your remarks on the *three* elements should demonstrate how typical their treatment is of 'highly expressive Romantic writing'.

The opening melody in particular is lyrical and expansive – almost songlike – in the manner of many melodies in Romantic instrumental music, and with the intensity of much minor-key writing. Later motivic developments provide additional emotional intensity. There is some striking chromaticism both melodically (as in bars 18–19) and harmonically (particularly with diminished seventh chords). Dissonance often suggests pathos, as for example at bars 45[4], 46[4], and with the appoggiatura at 47[1].

Dynamics are varied (from ***ff*** to ***p***) with a wide use of crescendo and diminuendo (as in the expressive melodic surges in violin and cello at bars 61 and 65) and powerful sforzandi to build tension in the coda.

Symphonie Fantastique, Movement 1 (Berlioz)

a. See section on 'Structure and Tonality', under the sub-heading 'The slow introduction' (page 141).

b. Chiefly the move to much shorter note values together with the direction 'plus vite' ('faster'); difficulties of ensemble, partly because of triplet quavers against sextuplet semiquavers – all requiring practice of parts separately.

c. If comparing bars 72 and 410, you might refer to use of the same key but different register (octave higher at 410); light scoring at 72 but much fuller and louder orchestration at 410; differences of rhythm (more syncopation at 410), and so on.

d. Berlioz's approach is free in terms of 'textbook' definitions of sonata form. For details, see section on 'Structure and Tonality', under the sub-heading 'The Allegro' (beginning on page 141).

e. The many changes of musical mood, scoring and dynamics directly reflect the demands of the programme. Examples include the minor key, chromaticism and slow tempo of the opening – reflecting 'dreamy melancholy' – and the extremely quiet and slow chordal ending representing the consolations of religion.

Question 6

There is much variety in the handling of all three elements, always with the intention of illustrating the programme, and creating a strong dramatic impact.

Scoring varies from the minimal (notably violin and flute at the start of the idée fixe) to the full use of large orchestra for moments of exceptional passion, rage, jealousy, and so on. There are varied groupings of intermediate size, as in bar 3 and onwards, where a state of dreamy melancholy is portrayed with strings only, minus double basses, or at the end where the 'consolations of religion' are suggested by sustained writing for woodwind and horns with strings (possibly meant to be reminiscent of the organ).

In early 19th-century terms, dynamics are sometimes extreme and strongly contrasting (e.g. p-ff-p in bars 28–29).

Rhythms are various, and occasionally difficult or complex (as Berlioz himself realised with the triplets and sextuplets at bar 17). Simple devices, such as chains of repeated notes, are also found – notably at bar 198, in an energetic section based on rising and falling chromatic movement with rapid dynamic change.

Area of Study: Music for film

Cues from *Batman Returns* (Danny Elfman)

a. See score.

b. Batman motif ('Birth of a Penguin Part 1', bars 1–2). Penguin motif ('Birth of a Penguin Part 1', bar 3).

c. Musical devices include: rapid quaver movement; rapid exchange of short motifs between various instruments; unusual instruments and effects, e.g. whistle, fairground steam organ, violin glissandi, horn glissandi, extreme lip trill, oboe extreme vibrato, brass cluster chord.

d. Refer to table on page 161.

e. High sustained violin line, broken-chord figures in cellos and violins, pedal notes (bars 1–4); detached, heavily accented accompanying parts in homophony (bar 25 onwards); violin melody in octaves (bars 69–72); tremolando chords (bar 81).

Question 6

In answering the A Level question, you should try to refer to the dramatic significance of the *three* elements named in the question.

Take care, however, to avoid simply retelling the story of the film. You need only make passing references to the plot.

In your answer you should refer to the size of the orchestra and the presence of instruments you do not usually find in an orchestra, e.g. pipe organ, synthesiser, vocalising choir (refer to the section on Sonority, texture and dynamics (page 154) for further information).

There is little point in listing all the instruments you can see in the score as you can normally take it for granted that an orchestra will include strings, woodwind, brass and percussion. It is more helpful to highlight unusual additions, such as a particularly large woodwind or brass section and instruments you would not normally expect to find, e.g. the fairground organ.

You should also comment on the way the instruments are used, e.g. tremolando strings, tam-tam roll, harp glissandi, and the ways the forces are contrasted, whether in terms of timbre or extreme dynamics.

In addition, you should remark not just on the fact that most of the textures are homophonic or a type of melody-dominated homophony, but the various ways textures are constructed or contrast in density (see the section on Texture).

You should refer to the two main motifs which appear in these cues. You should locate clearly the Batman motif and show how it is presented in different forms to demonstrate its dramatic significance at various points of the narrative, e.g. 'portentous' at the opening to 'heroic' in Part II (see Organisation of Pitch – Melody (page 157)).

Again, you should locate clearly the Penguin motif at its first appearance, the way it is presented in different forms and keys, and its fading away at the close of Part 1 reflecting the unfortunate circumstances of the birth of the character (see Organisation of Pitch – Melody).

Cues from *The Duchess* (Rachel Portman)

a. Mixolydian elements can be heard in the melody (i.e. C naturals), and in both 'Opening' and 'Mistake of Your Life' use is made of modal dominant chords with unraised leading-notes.

b. At the beginning, the single line becomes a pedal note (sometimes inner). The first part is melody-dominated homophony with melody in violins and quaver figures in accompanying parts. At bar 22 there is a sustained chord with timpani figure, and from bar 26, sustained thirds in upper parts with quaver figures on harp, combined with pedal in bass and timpani figures.

c. 'Opening' draws only on D major and A minor chords, whereas 'End Titles' also includes chords of F major, G major (first inversion) and Em^7. A suspension is added at bar 43.

d. The cue opens with pizz. strings and harp; from bar 3 there is a melody in violin (arco) with interjections on strings and horn. Tutti from bar 16; arco strings from bar 24.

e. The melody from bar 19, rising from tonic to dominant by step relates in general shape to bars 17–18 of the 'Opening'. The theme at bar 35, with auxiliary-note pattern, relates to bar 2 of 'Opening'.

Question 6

In the A Level question, you will relate the three elements given in the question to the catastrophic change of circumstances in which the Duchess finds herself.

'Six Years Later' falls into two separate sections, so you must always make it quite clear to which section you are referring.

Concerning the first part, you will need to characterise the style of the music, possibly as a waltz (though the score is notated in $\frac{6}{8}$ rather than simple triple time). The rhythmic scheme is comparatively simple, the main theme consisting of three quavers followed by a longer note. Subsidiary motifs use semiquavers.

The melody is composed of an ascending broken chord of D and descending broken chord of A minor – a reference to the underlying modal harmonic structure of the first cue – while the subsidiary motives contain chromatic auxiliary notes.

The second part of 'Six Years Later' takes up the melodic and rhythmic content of the first cue, so you will need to locate the return to quadruple time, and the use of quavers, syncopation and triplets.

When describing the melody of this section, you should refer to conjunct movement, modality and appoggiaturas.

In connection with harmony in 'Six Years Later', you will refer to its limited chord choice and use of augmented triad.

The prevailing mood of this cue is obviously much more light-hearted than that of 'Never see your children again', in which the heroine's catastrophic situation is reflected in the slow triple time, the ominous timpani rhythm, and the repeated slurred, often dissonant quaver patterns.

Further factors contributing to the oppressive atmosphere are the melody line, so stretched out in long notes that it is difficult to discern, the pedal D which lasts throughout and the closing G diminished chord.

Cues from *Psycho* (Bernard Herrmann)

a. Dissonant, involving major sevenths and diminished octaves. From bar 17 there are two alternating chords. The bass part moves by semitones (F–E; B♭–A), before closing on a tritone chord (F♯–C).

b. Octaves at start lead to the main part of the movement which is polyphonic, imitative and reminiscent of a fugue. Later, octaves in upper parts are supported by sustained bass (bar 47); sustained chords at close.

c. Fast (very agitated), in duple time, with almost constant quaver movement, energetic triplet figures, dotted rhythms and suddenly broken rhythms. The rhythm of the opening chords frequently recurs.

d. Wistful, sequentially descending three-note figure featuring a falling perfect fifth. The melody is cast in diatonic C major.

e. Strings only, muted throughout except for 'The Murder' (Shower Scene). For notable performing techniques throughout the work, see comments on 'musical elements' for each section (from page 175).

Question 6

This could prove to be a difficult essay to organise as you are asked to comment on three aspects of the music and three contrasting cues. It may prove best to discuss a single aspect at a time across all three cues.

Regarding dynamics, Herrmann requires muted strings throughout his score, with the exception of 'The Murder' where, to emphasise the horror of the scene, microphones were placed close to the instruments to emphasise the screaming string sound. In addition, each chord was heavily accentuated with repeated down bows.

In 'The Murder', there is a marked absence of melody. In contrast, the 'Prelude' is built from a series of short motifs, subject to variation, and one longer, more lyrical line. Marion's vulnerability in the remaining cue is hinted at in the sweet, diatonic C major melody with descending sequences.

Herrmann's harmonic language is advanced and frequently highly dissonant. The dissonances of 'The Murder' arise from major 7ths and diminished octaves. The opening dissonance of the 'Prelude' becomes something of a leitmotif, and is often heard in other cues (notice the ominous conclusion of 'Marion'). You will need to refer to other characteristic harmonic devices, notably false relations, 13th chords ('Prelude'), pedals ('Prelude'), 'tritonal' dominants in 'Prelude' (see section on Organisation of Pitch , page 176) and suspensions ('Marion').

Area of Study: Popular music and jazz

Tracks from *Back in the Day* (Courtney Pine)

a. 'Lady Day and (John Coltrane)' in particular contains a number of examples of extended technique: e.g. note-bending (bar 45); fall-offs (bar 50); sliding up to pitch (bar 52); glissandos (bar 55); unpitched notes (bar 60); multiphonics (bar 127); key clicks (bar 130).

b. Gershwin's song 'Summertime' in 'Inner State (of Mind)'; cover versions of Gil Scott-Heron's *Lady Day and (John Coltrane)* and Joan Armatrading's *Love and Affection*.

c. Notice in the introduction the two alternating seventh chords on C and D, with Dorian inflections; the chord selection broadens to include C minor and F; false relation at 'Knowledge is power'; later a ninth chord on E♭, a half-diminished chord on D and a seventh chord on D♭; broadly parallel quartal chords (bars 70–71).

d. Blues influence is evident in the many examples of blue notes and the use of an underlying blues progression in 'Lady Day and (John Coltrane)'.

e. Extra sounds seem to refer to the existence of the world outside the bounds of the song. See comments on individual numbers (beginning on page 195) for further details.

Question 6

Wherever possible, with this A Level question stress the presence of blues elements. In this case, list the resources used in each song, and refer to the occasional use of extended performance techniques, e.g. multiphonics and key clicks. You should also comment on the way the drum-kit is used in 'Lady Day and (John Coltrane)', whether faint, prominent or entirely absent, giving locations wherever possible.

Although the texture of 'Lady Day and (John Coltrane)' is essentially melody-dominated homophony, you should comment on various aspects such as use of riff, the way the vocal part is woven into the texture, the use of fills, close harmony horns and the bvox parts.

In contrast, you should show how the texture of 'Love and Affection' moves from melody-dominated homophony at the opening to the polyphony of the final stages of the number.

In your remarks on harmony, you will be able to comment on a number of blues-related aspects, e.g. the underlying progressions of 'Lady Day and (John Coltrane)'. Other noteworthy features in this number include the false relations and the extended chords involving 7ths, 9ths and 13ths; you should remember to include examples of all these.

Other interesting devices used in 'Lady Day and (John Coltrane)' are substitution chords, chromatic movement of chords (see bars 53–55 and bar 65) and the fourths harmony at bar 75. In the coda, there is a side-shift of chords from B♭^{13} to B^{11} and a final slowing of the harmonic rhythm, making prominent use of an augmented chord.

In 'Love and Affection', the harmony is more direct, with minor chords dominating the opening section. Latterly, the number is propelled by a riff with primary major chords.

Chromaticism also occurs in 'Love and Affection', e.g. at bar 62, along with false relations (bar 68) and blue notes (bar 68 and bar 72).

Tracks from *Hounds of Love* (Kate Bush)

a. 'Cloudbusting': string sextet, drums, balalaika, Fairlight CMI (Computer Musical Instrument) and whistles.

'And dream of sheep': piano, bouzouki, whistles and dubbed voices and effects

'Under Ice': synthesised string sounds and effects, dubbed voices

b. 'Cloudbusting': G♯ below middle C to B a 10th higher

'And dream of sheep': B to C♯ (major 9th)

'Under Ice': A below middle C to C a 10th higher.

c. In all three songs, the word setting is mainly syllabic with slurred pairs. 'And dream of sheep' contains some melismas.

d. The texture of 'Under ice' is lean with the vocal line supported only by a bass line and short, two-part string figurations. 'And dream of sheep' is melody-dominated homophony, with broken-chord accompaniment and bouzouki figurations.

e. Steady moderate mainly quadruple pulse with occasional $\frac{2}{4}$ and $\frac{6}{4}$ bars. For other notable features, see section on rhythm on page 210.

Question 6

In this case, keep your remarks about the narrative content to the minimum, perhaps outlining briefly the 'plot' in an opening sentence or two.

In 'And Dream of Sheep', the melody is to be found entirely in the vocal part. There are prominent instrumental parts in 'Under Ice', but the main melodic content here is also in the vocal line. You should make some general comments about the range of the parts and the tendency for the lines to keep to the lower parts of the range in both numbers.

The melody of 'And Dream of Sheep' is sometimes rather fragmentary and declamatory to underline the textual content, and aspects of the word-setting clearly contribute to the song's narrative, e.g. the slurred pairs of notes and brief melismas contrasting with the predominantly syllabic word-setting. You should also mention the distinctive leaps at the start, the repeated notes and the reiterated thirds ('If they find me racing…').

'Under Ice' is markedly more fragmentary, often using a step-wise two-note figure, with only the occasional more extended line ('The river has frozen over'), involving wider intervals. The word-setting is mainly syllabic with some slurred pairs, and there is a dramatic chromatic portamento at the close to emphasise the desperate cry for help.

'And Dream of Sheep' is in a functional E major throughout with a verse-chorus structure (remember to give bar numbers to show this). The structure of 'Under Ice' is through-composed with alternations of fragmentary melodic motifs. The tonality of the song is A minor, though the electronic sounds towards the close weaken the sense of key.

Tracks from *Revolver* (The Beatles)

a. 'Double' string quartet, i.e. 4 violins, 2 violas, 2 cellos.

b. Refer to the table on Page 221.

c. Melody is in mixolydian mode. Flattened thirds can be heard on the tape loops. The song is underpinned by a drone, and chords of B♭ and C can also be heard.

d. Brisk quadruple time with jazz quavers and triplet crotchets. See section on rhythm on page 225 for further details.

e. Electronic content is virtually impossible to recreate outside a studio.

Question 6

In your response to this question, it would be useful at the outset to summarise the general content of each number, i.e. the depiction of loneliness in 'Eleanor Rigby' and the straightforward expression of love in 'Here, there and everywhere'.

As the question refers to 'different experiences', you may find it helpful to discuss each element (rhythm, harmony and tonality) in turn, enabling you to make comparisons where appropriate.

It would be appropriate to refer to the brutal, hard-driven rhythms of 'Eleanor Rigby', describing such features as the repeated crotchets and syncopated lines. In contrast, there are some irregularities in the metrical scheme of 'Here, there and everywhere', and a rubato approach to its performance.

There is a corresponding rigidity in the harmony of 'Eleanor Rigby', restricted in the main to just two chords. There is considerably more variety in the harmonies of 'Here, there and everywhere'. You would do well to comment on the parallelism at the opening, and other features such as appoggiaturas, false relations, sequence, and also to the fact that this number uses functional progressions which are impossible in the case of 'Eleanor Rigby'.

'Here, there and everywhere' is in the key of G major and its tonal scheme is fluid enough to embrace B♭ major. 'Eleanor Rigby' never escapes the key of E minor, though variety is assured by the use of modal inflections (see the section on Melody).

Area of Study: Fusions

Estampes: Nos. 1 and 2 (Debussy)

a. Pentatonic.

b. Any three of the features listed on page 242.

c. Tempo and dotted rhythm.

d. The harmonic rhythm is slow because of the pentatonicism. For further features see section beginning on page 237.

e. Bar 3: melody with chordal accompaniment. Bar 23: brief two-part imitative figure and pedal notes.

Question 6

You could start your response to the A Level question with remarks concerning the extent to which Impressionism played a part in the composition of this piece. This would lead you naturally to a description of characteristic aspects of pianistic Impressionism. You could comment on the wide range of the piano Debussy used, and also on the way the pedals are applied, perhaps referring to the composer's wish to make the piano sound as though it had no hammers.

You should also refer to the way sonorities and textures are varied through contrast of ranges. You may not be able to write about the entire piece in the time you have at your disposal, but take care to show how Debussy produces very different sounds at various points, e.g. bars 1–2, 7–10, 19–20, 23–26, 31–36 and 78–98 (See Table in the section on Sonority, texture and dynamics on pages 234–235).

The melodic material is largely based on the pentatonic scale. The opening melody (bar 3) is presented in different rhythms: notice the triplets at bar 11. At bar 15 a different range of notes is introduced, and at bar 19 the note order of the original pitch-range is varied.

In contrast, a more stringent sound arises at bar 33 with the chromatic note, E♯, though the melody line itself consists of just five notes. A final, contrasting pentatonic motif appears at bar 37.

Tracks from *Caña Quema* (Familia Valera Miranda)

a. Refer to the list of points on the 'son' on page 246.

b. Moderate duple time and lyrical qualities associated with romantic subject matter.

c. Four double-course guitar-like instrument.

d. Vocal range of 'Allá va candela' spans a 12th (B–F♯); that of 'Se quema la chumbambá', lead vocal, is a minor 6th (G to E♭), while backing vocals span a minor 9th (D to E♭).

e. This refers to the two-bar 'son clave' rhythm in the configuration where the first bar has three notes and the second, two. See page 247 for more details.

Question 6

In answering the A Level question, you will need to refer to the contrasting vocal ranges, that of 'Alla vá candela' being wider. There is also a very marked contrast to be made between the minor mode of *Se quema* and the major mode of 'Allá va candela'.

Reference should be made to the various melodic features of each number (see pages 248 and 251), and here there could be mention of the more lyrical (bolero) qualities of 'Allá va candela', and the fact that in Cuba the bolero was in duple time as opposed to the triple-time European version (see e.g. Ravel's *Bolero*). The rhythmic features of the son (3:2 clave rhythm, syncopation, etc) should also be described.

You should also comment on the rhythmic differences between the extended instrumental sections of each song (see sections starting on pages 247 and 250).

Regarding structure, you should refer to the use of repetition (verse-chorus) in 'Se quema la chumbambá', as opposed to the more freely evolving scheme of 'Allá va candela' in which the opening section is not subsequently repeated.

In both songs, an extended instrumental section plays a prominent role.

Tracks from *Breathing Under Water* (Anoushka Shankar)

a. The melody uses predominantly long notes without syncopation (except in bars 14 and 16) in contrast to the sitar melody. See also section 'Organisation of pitch: Melody', sub-section: 'String melodies' (page 262).

b. N.C. = no chord; C♯m = C sharp minor chord; C♯m$^{(add4)}$/G♯ = chord of C sharp minor with added 4th (F sharp) and G sharp in bass; A$^{maj7(♯4)}$ = A major chord with major 7th (G sharp) and sharpened 4th (D sharp).

c. See sub-section 'Breathing under water' under 'Tonality' (page 260). This includes several references to harmony.

d. Main points include the following. The sitarist is soloist in 'Breathing under water' and plays almost without a break, while in 'Easy', after a very florid part in the introduction the sitarist is often limited to vamping (bar 9) or to providing fills between vocal phrases. Further, see sub-section 'Sitar melodies' under 'Organisation of pitch: Melody' (page 262).

e. See the sub-section 'Easy' under 'Structure' (page 259).

Question 6

Your answer can identify Indian and Western styles separately in discussion of each element, but 'fusion' refers to how they co-exist (whether side-by-side or simultaneously). The music is remarkable and innovative by virtue of its frequently simultaneous use of aspects of both styles.

For sonority, the Indian classical tradition is chiefly apparent in Shankar's sitar playing, but note also sarangi ('Burn') and tabla ('Breathing Under Water'). The Indian 'Bollywood' tradition is represented by the Bombay Cinematic Orchestra Strings (there is a degree of fusion even within this tradition, and do not forget the use of cello, flute, etc.). Electric guitar, synthesiser and programmed drums are characteristic of Western popular and rock music, but we hear (Indian) manjira together with Western percussion in 'Burn'.

In 'Burn' the Eastern-style narrowness and repetitiveness of the melodic lines co-exists with some apparent use of the Western harmonic minor scale. In 'Breathing Under Water' some chromatic notes may be comparable to 'blue' notes from the jazz tradition. In both songs Indian styles are the source of microtonal intervals and ornamentation.

The structure of 'Burn' is basically Western (verse-chorus), but the improvisatory style of the opening may suggest the *alap* section of a raga. 'Breathing Under Water' takes the form of a 'gradual unfolding' that does not strongly suggest either Indian or Western models.

Area of Study: New directions

Three Dances for Two Prepared Pianos: Dance No. 1 (John Cage)

a. See section 'Musical Context', sub-section 'Composer', paragraph beginning 'Providing...' (page 269).

b. Piano 1, RH is given prominence by being marked f, while there are two levels of accompaniment (p in Piano 2 and pp in Piano 1, LH).

c. See the sub-section 'Numbers' under 'Structure' (page 271).

d. The principal point is that repetition is not used in the manner of traditional forms such as sonata form or rondo, although conceivably there are vestiges of ternary form. For detail, see the sub-section 'Repetition' under 'Structure' (from page 272).

e. It is entirely appropriate because the music has been successfully choreographed and performed. However it may not seem dance-like to those expecting the regular rhythms and beat of more conventional classical or popular dance types.

Question 6

In answering the A Level question, your remarks on the *three* elements should show how novel their treatment was in the mid 1940s.

The prepared piano was Cage's creation (first used in *Bacchanale,* c.1940), but there had been partial precedents, notably with Cowell's 'string piano' in which the pianist plucked or hit strings manually. As early as 1912–1914, Maurice Delage's *Ragamalika* required one note on a piano to be muted to simulate an Indian drum.

Some aspects of texture are not novel, notably the (occasional) use of homorhythm, a device used for centuries. On the other hand there is very limited precedent for the two piano parts being entirely independent in content, and altogether avoiding devices such as imitation and canon within a contrapuntal texture. Such consistent use of two-part writing in both pianos is also unusual but not necessarily 'novel' in character.

Because precise pitches are avoided, the emphasis on rhythm is exceptionally strong. However Edgard Varèse (1883–1965) had written works before the 1940s whose principal elements are timbre and rhythm (including *Ionisation* for percussion instruments (1929–1931). It is doubtful that any aspects of rhythm in the Three Dances are entirely original, but the extent of Cage's use of rhythm to obscure rather than clarify metre is remarkable for any time.

Petals (Kaija Saariaho)

a. See the section on 'Structure', including the table (from page 281).

b. 'Double-stopping': bowing (or plucking) two strings simultaneously to produce two pitches; 'glissando': produced by sliding the finger up or down a string to produce a continuous rise or fall in pitch; 'artificial harmonics': the player stops a string with one finger while with another finger lightly touching a different point on the string, thereby producing one of the harmonics of the stopped note.

c. There are successive 'bursts' of sound, which tend to become longer as the passage continues. All begin with bottom C (and most continue with B and A sharp) and end with trills, glissandi and harmonics. There is much dynamic contrast, especially between staves 19 and 20–21.

d. The second section is more clearly melodic than the first – for detailed information see section on 'Organisation of pitch: Melody' (page 286).

e. By making electronics 'optional' Saariaho is content for the cello to stand alone. However she gives very precise instructions for the use of the harmoniser and reverb unit, and without these devices the music as heard (for example) on the Anthology recording lacks much of its distinctive character.

Question 6

In answering the A Level question, you should show how the *three* elements are used to exploit the expressive and technical potential of the cello.

Saariaho exploits various playing techniques not available to cellists until well into the 20th century – or not to the extent that she uses them. These include extensive use of *sul ponticello*, harmonics, glissandi and microintervals. Most striking is the increasing of bow pressure to produce a scratching sound that results in noise instead of precise pitch. In addition, optional use of electronics (harmoniser and reverb) extends the range of available sonorities.

Dynamics are sometimes outside the 'normal' limits and involve extreme contrasts – notably the use of *ppp* and *ffff* in staves 25–26.

The wide use of a very slow tempo (Lento) challenges the player's technical control (e.g. with extended trills), as does the use of very short note values in the more energetic sections (notably from stave 4).

In terms of expressive potential, changes of tempo and the contrasts of material that go with them contribute to 'forc[ing] the interpreter to stretch his sensibility' in Saariaho's own words.

Movements from *Le Sacre du Printemps* (Stravinsky)

a. Bassoon; tenor clef.

b. Refer to the section on Organisation of pitch – melody on page 295.

c. Because of the relatively pure pedigree with regard to pagan music.

d. 'Les augures printaniers'; refer to section on Tempo, metre and rhythm on page 295.

e. Bitonal chord; for further details see the section on harmony on page 298.

Question 6

Notice that the question asks about how the various elements can be contrasted.

You may wish to refer to the contrast between rubato and *giusto* approaches to rhythm in the two sections.

The first section is characterised by many changes of time signature, whereas 'Les augures printaniers' is almost entirely in duple time (but draw attention to the few variations which occur).

There is a remarkably flexible approach to rhythmic patterns in the Introduction but a stricter, less varied approach to groupings in parts of 'Les augures printaniers'. In this section of the work, however, there is a striking use of asymmetric stresses.

There is a relatively florid application of ornamentation in the Introduction, and many melodic lines are angular, with prominent use of 4ths and 7ths.

Acknowledgements

Batman Returns: Music by Daniel Elfman,
© Copyright 1992 Warner-Barham Music LLC.,
Universal/MCA Music Limited. All Rights Reserved.
International Copyright Secured.

Breathing Under Water: Words & Music by
Anoushka Shankar, Utkarsha Kale & Gaurav Raina,
© Copyright 2007 Anourag Music Publishing/
Mighty Junn Music/GR Music Publishing, Chester Music/
Bucks Music Group. All Rights Reserved.
International Copyright Secured.

Caña Quema: Words & Music by Lorenzo Hierrezuelo,
© Copyright Peer International Corp, Peermusic (UK)
Ltd. All Rights Reserved. International Copyright
Secured.

The Duchess: Music by Rachel Portman,
© Copyright 2008 Berkeley Music Publishing Co.,
Bucks Music Group Ltd. All Rights Reserved.
International Copyright Secured.

'Eleanor Rigby': Words & Music by John Lennon &
Paul McCartney, © Copyright 1966 Sony/ATV Music
Publishing. All Rights Reserved. International Copyright
Secured.

'Here, There And Everywhere': Words & Music by
John Lennon & Paul McCartney, © Copyright 1966
Sony/ATV Music Publishing. All Rights Reserved.
International Copyright Secured.

Hounds Of Love: Words & Music by Kate Bush,
© Copyright 1985 Noble and Brite Ltd., EMI Music
Publishing Limited. All Rights Reserved. International
Copyright Secured.

'Inner State (Of Mind)': Music by Courtney Pine,
© Copyright 2000 Songs Of Polygram International Inc.,
Universal Music Publishing Limited. All Rights Reserved.
International Copyright Secured.

'I Want To Tell You': Words & Music by George Harrison,
© Copyright 1966 Northern Songs Ltd., Sony/ATV Music
Publishing. All Rights Reserved. International Copyright
Secured.

'Lady Day And (John Coltrane)': Words & Music by
Gil Scott-Heron, © Copyright 1971 Bienstock Publishing
Co., Carlin Music Corporation. All Rights Reserved.
International Copyright Secured.

'Love And Affection': Words & Music by Joan
Armatrading, © Copyright 1976 Imagem Songs Limited.
All Rights Reserved. International Copyright Secured.

On Wenlock Edge: Words by A.E. Housman, Music by Ralph Vaughan Williams, © Copyright 1923 Boosey & Hawkes Music Publishing Limited. All Rights Reserved. International Copyright Secured.

Petals: Music by Kaija Saariaho, © Copyright 1990 Ed Wilhelm Hansen Helsinki Oy., Chester Music Limited. All Rights Reserved. International Copyright Secured.

Psycho: Music by Bernard Herrmann, © Copyright 1960 Sony/ATV Melody, Famous Music Corporation. All Rights Reserved. International Copyright Secured

The Rite Of Spring: Music by Igor Stravinsky, © Copyright 1913 Boosey & Hawkes Music Publishers Limited. All Rights Reserved. International Copyright Secured.

Three Dances For Two Prepared Pianos: Music by John Cage, © Copyright 1945 Peters Editions Ltd. All Rights Reserved. International Copyright Secured

Picture credits:
Pages 7 and 8: photographs courtesy of Ruth Keating, assisted by Lisa Cox and James Welland. Special thanks to the pupils at St Benedict's School, Ealing and their Director of Music Christopher Eastwood for taking part in the photo shoot; page 15: Areebarbar/Shutterstock.com; page 18: Nikolaenko Viacheslav/Alamy; page 46: dpa picture alliance/Alamy; page 65: PrinceOfLove/Shutterstock.com; page 75: Claudio Divizia/Shutterstock.com; page 98: Music-Images/Alamy; page 104: Colin Underhill/Alamy; page 112: Stokkete/Shutterstock.com; page 123: gvictoria/Shutterstock.com; page 126: Paul Fearn/Alamy; Page 136: Everett Historical/Shutterstock.com; page 145: Pictoral Press Ltd/Alamy; page 150: AF archive/Alamy; page 160: Everett Collection, Inc./Alamy; page 164: Giles Keyte; page 167: AF archive/Alamy; page 174: Everett Collection Inc/Alamy; page 189: Phil Rees/Alamy; page 192: Pictorial Press Ltd/Alamy; page 193: Pictorial Press Ltd/Alamy; Page 194: Tyzhnenko Dmitry/Shutterstock.com; page 207: Christopher Jones/Alamy; page 208: Pictorial Press Ltd/Alamy; Page 216: Pictorial Press Ltd/Alamy; lucky vectorstudio/Shutterstock.com; page 248: robertharding/Alamy; page 253: simonyc; page 277: Jack Mitchell/Getty Images; p279: Priska Ketterer; page 288: Muriel von Braun. Images on pages 74, 86, 114, 120, 153, 232, 256, 267, 268, 289 and 291 are licensed under Wikimedia commons.